Project Management Institute

FUNDAMENTALS OF PROGRAM MANAGEMENT: STRATEGIC PROGRAM BOOTSTRAPPING FOR BUSINESS INNOVATION AND CHANGE

Motoh Shimizu, DR.Eng, PMP

Library of Congress Cataloging-in-Publication Data

Shimizu, Motoh.
  Fundamentals of program management : strategic program bootstrapping for
business innovation and change / Motoh Shimizu.
      p. cm.
  ISBN 978-1-935589-63-1 (alk. paper)
1. Project management. 2. Strategic planning. I. Title.
  HD69.P75S534 2012
  658.4'012—dc23

                                                                    2012035398

ISBN: 978-1-935589-63-1

Published by: Project Management Institute, Inc.
                           14 Campus Boulevard
                           Newtown Square, Pennsylvania 19073-3299 USA
                           Phone: +610-356-4600
                           Fax: +610-356-4647
                           Email: customercare@pmi.org
                           Internet: www.PMI.org

PMI Publications welcomes corrections and comments on its books. Please feel free to send
comments on typographical, formatting, or other errors. Simply make a copy of the relevant
page of the book, mark the error, and send it to: Book Editor, PMI Publications, 14 Campus
Boulevard, Newtown Square, PA 19073-3299 USA.

To inquire about discounts for resale or educational purposes, please contact the PMI Book
Service Center.
                           PMI Book Service Center
                           P.O. Box 932683, Atlanta, GA 31193-2683 USA
                           Phone: 1-866-276-4764 (within the U.S. or Canada)
                           or +1-770-280-4129 (globally)
                           Fax: +1-770-280-4113
                           Email: info@bookorders.pmi.org

Table of Contents

Preface

In today's volatile economic environment, organizations everywhere are concerned with efficient achievement of their strategic objectives. This requires developing better strategies than competitors have, or than the organization had in the past, and then implementing them in a realistic manner. This requirement is common to all kinds of organizations, including business entities, government agencies, and nonprofit organizations. In many cases, strategic objectives are achieved through project execution. To realize its strategy in the current complicated business environment, a business entity needs an effective combination of multiple projects, called a *strategic program*. In my previous work *Jissen Purojekuto & Puroguramu Manejimento* (*Project & Program Management in Practice*), which was published in Japan by JMA Management Center (Nihon Noritsu-kyokai Manejimento-senta), I focused on the relationships among strategies, projects and programs in order to present an integrated perspective covering the continuum from strategy to project execution, with practical project management methods given throughout. An English translation of the core part of that book, dealing specifically with strategy and programs, I present here as *Fundamentals of Program Management: Strategic Program Bootstrapping for Business Innovation and Change.* In this book, some amendments to the previous work have been made for the purposes of translation, and to minimize topics unfamiliar to readers outside Japan.

There are three conditions vital for successful realization of a strategy: appropriate planning, sufficient and appropriate capability in the execution, organization, and motivation among executing staff members. Failure to meet any one of these conditions can jeopardize strategic success. The world is full of enterprises in decline due to lack of appropriate strategic plans. There are too many cases to number where strategies planned by top management ended in failure in the course of execution. For successful implementation of strategy, this book is devoted to describing *Strategic Program Bootstrapping.*

Bootstrapping is used to describe such process by which an entrepreneur successfully launches a business through his/her own power. The word expresses the core concept in which a program manager makes effort to implement a strategy through a program in bootstrapping manner.

Strategic success is diverse. The success itself can take various forms and so can the paths to it. For finding such paths to strategic success, Strategic Program Bootstrapping is distinctive in that it defines a program as a refined expression of a strategy itself, and expects program management to be deeply involved in concrete strategy planning and its implementation, in contrast to the top-down approach. In Strategic Program Bootstrapping, a *strategy* and a *program* are seen as one and inseparable. Program managers are presented with a strategic objective in the form of an initial program mission concept that has the potential for various forms of success. The program manager analyzes and interprets what the success of the strategy presented to him/her should be, and redefines it as a group of goals, the achievement of which is most effective for arriving at the desired success. In many cases, each of the goals is realized through execution of one or more projects. Program management is a set of techniques to mold the various measures aimed at goals into bundles of projects, plan an effective combination of such project bundles, and execute them.

What makes Strategic Program Bootstrapping a unique approach is that it raises the probability of strategic success by having program managers take the initiative in refining the strategy into an executable form, based on his/her detailed knowledge of the relevant market, organizations, human resources, and technological trends. Throughout the process, proper communication between the program manager and top management is essential, as a matter of course. Another important characteristic of Strategic Program Bootstrapping is that it may increase execution members' motivation significantly. Involvement in the early stages of program planning develops among the members a sense of commitment to the program that they have planned themselves, rather than obligation to tasks placed upon them. Program members who understand the essential aspects of the program are considered likely to participate earnestly during deliberations in preparation for the execution phases. With the diffusion of *A Guide to the Project Management Body of Knowledge's* process methodology, the assessment of organizational maturity, establishment of information infrastructure and organizing of project management offices (PMOs), a surfacing significant issue today is the question of how to address the psychological aspects of organization, including leadership and motivation. Although not directly aimed at improving motivation, the Bootstrapping method is considerably effective at supporting the morale of program participants.

In Japan, Prof. Shigenobu Ohara spearheaded the compilation of "Project & Program Management for Enterprise Innovation (P2M)," which is a new body of knowledge for integral solution and value creation in the 21st century. In 2001, a guidebook on P2M was published by the Engineering Advancement Association of Japan (ENAA), exclusively for the plant engineering industry and people concerned with project management. General publication of the guidebook was done by PHP Institute in 2003. P2M defines a program as something that executes practical strategy to create new value under "the holistic mission" assigned by top management, and that its basic attributes are ambiguity (multiplicity of context), complexity, scalability, and uncertainty. Ambiguity is specific to the initial stages of a program originating in strategy and is clarified through program integration's *profiling* process. Thus, the primary role of program management is to examine the initial ambiguous concept of a program mission from the viewpoints of effectiveness and feasibility, in pursuit of total optimization and concrete definition of strategic objectives and goals.

This book shares the same perspective on program management as P2M, with a closer look at the relationship between strategy and program. What is often referred to as "Japanese project management" is not an idea exclusive to Japan, but is, I maintain, universal. It may be true that there is a historical tendency for Japanese organizations to involve internal members' wisdom in their strategy development phase, rather than accepting external objective decisions on strategy. Japanese corporate strategies are inconspicuous, as they occur within corporate organizations. This may have led some people to believe that Japanese companies indulge in their operational efficiency and are lacking in strategy. This belief, however, is incorrect. Without strategy, how could Japanese companies have ever survived the past four decades, during which the dollar-yen exchange rate rose nearly 500%, for instance? Today's Japanese economy is characterized by the existence of many enterprises with annual sales ranging between several hundred million and several billion dollars. These large but not gigantic entities specialize in industrial products and have a worldwide market share in their respective areas. They do not intend to dominate in the huge end-product markets, but focus on smaller areas, taking advantage of their technology, product characteristics, and thorough knowledge of relevant market trends. These enterprises, as well as their strategies, do not attract much attention from outsiders. Bootstrapping-type program management has developed as part of the backdrop of the industrial environment of Japan.

In reality, it is common in all countries that the Bootstrapping method, leveraging internal senior manager competencies, is effective for small and medium-sized businesses, company divisions and entrepreneurs. Such organizations cannot spare sufficient human resources for jobs dedicated entirely to business environment research/assessment, market trend analysis, and meticulous development of objectives and strategy. Additionally, there is another reason why Bootstrapping is effective for these organizations: A smaller organization can take advantage of its population's ease in sharing knowledge, grasping strategic tasks, and taking rapid action.

Large-scale projects and programs date back at least to the era of the ancient Egyptian pyramids (26th century BC). In Japan, for instance, there is a construction firm called Kongo-gumi in Osaka that traces its history back to AD 578, when a Korean architect named Kongo Shigemitsu was invited by Prince Shotoku to build Shitennoji Temple in Osaka. Since then, the temple/shrine building organization founded by Kongo has survived for over 1,400 years on its expertise and management. In Japan, in the 16th century, it became common that major castle building projects (e.g., Osaka Castle) would be managed via the *Waribushin* system, which divided construction into a number of areas contracted out to *Daimyo* (feudal lords) across the country. The entire construction project was controlled by a management organization led by a general manager called *So-bugyo*, under whom managers called *Bugyo* were in charge of such functional organizations as engineering, architecture, accounting, recording, and so forth. So it is obvious that project-type management of this sort has been carried out since ancient times the world over.

Strategy, too, has a long pedigree. Sun-tzu's *The Art of War* was written around the 5th century BC. The book is a comprehensive description of war strategies and tactics. It is thought to have timeless value because it places importance on national management strategies, including prevention of war. In China, *The Art of War* has been highly appreciated and remained influential among national leaders from the emperor of Wei (or Cao Cao of the 3rd century, a famous figure in "The Romance of the Three Kingdoms"), who compiled a commentary on *The Art of War*, to Mao Zedong in the 20th century. Japan and other neighboring countries have shown similar appreciation for *The Art of War,* now considered among the world's classics on strategy.

So we can see that both *project* and *strategy* are many centuries old. However, it was in the middle of the 20th century that *strategy* became a major subject of academic study, with analysis of *business management strategies* to help industries and business management. Systematization of *project management* started a little later.

In the increasingly complicated society of the 21st century, every manager concerned with program/project execution should be aware of the relationships between his/her tasks and the organization's strategy. Organizational strategies have generally been a matter for top management, while project management has been for those engaging in practical tasks. Strategic studies have been interested in analyzing the commonalities among various sample cases, to find effective strategic elements. Project management has concerned itself with the methodological importance of applying a certain technique to real project planning. Because of this wide difference, *strategy* and *projects* have been discussed separately, without integration of the two. In the practical world, efforts to do so have usually been left to the personal knowledge and expertise of managers engaging in actual working tasks, aiming to realize organizational strategy.

This book's primary mission is to provide a linkage between *strategy* and *project management* through *program,* and to offer a framework for integrating strategy, program, and project. I hope it will help those practitioners who engage with strategies and program management practices.

Acknowledgment

I am deeply grateful to Dr. Edwin J. Andrews (PMI Director, Academic and Educational Programs & Services) and Dr. Hiroshi Tanaka (former Chair of the Board of Directors, Project Management Association of Japan). Dr. Andrews, upon learning of the publication of my previous work in Japanese (*Project & Program Management in Practice*), strongly recommended that I issue an English version through PMI, which helped me to decide to publish this book. Dr. Tanaka, who helped in many ways to publish the previous work, again gave me strong support.

The systematization of project/program management knowledge is the fruit of efforts made by Prof. Ohara, and many other practical experts and researchers, and the field continues to progress. Although I have not enough space to capture the details, I would like to extend my deepest gratitude to these people for their efforts. I have been, and remain, a fortunate beneficiary of many others' hard work, allowing me to make my own small contributions to the field.

Hiromi Nemoto, Director of the Publishing Division, JMA Management Center, gave me his willing agreement to publish through PMI, for which I am truly grateful. I would like to give special thanks to Donn Greenburg of PMI for his strong support for this publication project and to Barbara Walsh of PMI for her kind communication with me and timely support. Without the cooperation of these people, the publication of this book would have never been realized.

I have been very fortunate to have an excellent team for translating this book. Translation of Japanese into English is more difficult than generally thought. Translation of English into Japanese is relatively easy because there are many Japanese translators who are familiar with the literature in their respective fields. In contrast, books like this one impose considerable burdens on those involved. The book's Japanese text was translated into English by Fumio Yokoi (Chapters 1, 2 & 5) and me (Chapters 3 & 4). The English translation was then reviewed by Shigekatsu Yamauchi, who examined the accuracy of the translated text with the original. Lastly, John Von Pischke, who is well versed in both U.S. and Japanese cultures, reviewed the English document to improve its friendliness to English-speaking readers. I truly appreciate their great efforts. Despite their involvement in the above process, final responsibility for the material in this book rests with me.

Motoh Shimizu

Chapter 1

Programs and Business Management

Chapter Overview

1. Business Strategy and Programs
    1.1 The Growing Importance of Projects in Business
    1.2 Project Management and Improvement of Project Productivity
    1.3 Business Strategy and Program Management
    1.4 Hierarchical Structures in Business Management
    1.5 Program Environment

2. Definition and Essential Nature of Programs
    2.1 Definitions of Program
    2.2 The Typology of Programs
    2.3 The Essential Nature of Programs
    2.4 Concept of Strategic Programs
    2.5 Large-Scale System Programs

3. Strategic Program Bootstrapping
    3.1 Strategy Implementation and Programs
    3.2 Bootstrapping Program Management
    3.3 The Background of Program Bootstrapping

4. Business Value Creation and Management Behavior
    4.1 Business Value Creation
        4.1.1 Business Value and Projects
        4.1.2 Types of Values
        4.1.3 Value, Assets and resources
        4.1.4 Value Creation in Programs
    4.2 Fundamentals of Management Behavior
        4.2.1 The Management Cycle
        4.2.2 Decision Making
        4.2.3 Difficulty in Project Management
        4.2.4 Project Management Activities and Knowledge Areas

Chapter 1

Programs and Business Management

Chapter Overview

In most businesses, it is daily operations that earn the profits. Projects and strategic programs, which themselves are integrated projects, are implemented to build or reform operational systems for capturing new profits or securing sustainable profits. The increasing complexity of today's industrial society only enhances the importance of programs and projects. In this first chapter, the relationship between strategy and programs is discussed first, followed by definition and the essential nature of programs. The third section introduces program management bootstrapping, which is this book's main theme. The next section addresses management difficulties that arise during programs and projects in relation to management behavior vis-à-vis value creation, which is the program's main objective. While projects/programs aim to build systems most of the time, the project itself can be viewed as a process-type system. The fifth section incorporates this perspective and outlines the complexities of systems and how to cope with them. The sixth section summarizes the composition of the program management knowledge areas relating to the contents of this book.

1. Business Strategy and Programs

1.1 The Growing Importance of Projects in Business

The first two decades of the 21st century have been a period of intensive globalization and the growth of networks with close political and economic ties among countries, rapid expansion of affluent consumer markets, a borderless commonality in youth culture, the expansion of higher education, the advancement of science and technology, and heightened global population mobility. These phenomena originated in the late 20th century, leading to quite a different world. We have now a "mega society" where overall homogeneity dominates locally derived heterogeneity. This, coupled with the increase in global population, expands homogeneous needs and therefore homogeneous markets around the world. The mobility of technological knowledge has increased the complexity of industrial society, initiating fierce competition and drastic change.

However, a little closer look reveals that the supremacy of homogeneity is linked especially to phases of production and the distribution of goods, while heterogeneity is a feature of utilization and consumption. This requires that every enterprise create a policy for each of its businesses. The question becomes whether to focus on the homogeneity or the potential found in heterogeneity when seeking continued customer growth and the maintenance of sustainable profits.

Most business profits are generated from day-to-day operations, such as producing and selling goods, or offering services. However, in today's homogeneous and highly competitive global market environment, a company's survival depends on constant efforts to create new customer value. Projects that pursue new value creation launch new businesses, develop new technologies or new products, create factories or stores, or innovate production lines or sales organizations. Government agency efforts, such as the construction of public facilities or social infrastructure, and the introduction of new social programs, are also carried out as projects. In today's organizations, all members of management have to be competent project managers.

Projects themselves are no longer a special domain peripheral to business operation. Instead they are integrated, working in tandem with routine operations, which supports business efficiency. During the late 19th century and through the turn of the 20th, business growth meant scaled expansion of routine operations for both manufacturers and service providers. The major factor that contributed to business efficiency was the specialization of each function and people working for it, whether production, sales, production management, and so on. In some cases, it was best to build a system in which specialization by individual employees was not necessary, by making each job as simple as the mere assembly of small parts. Business strategy and planning were in the hands of head office management, while worksite management focused on controlling deviations from plans and rules.

In contrast, project management today determines, as its initial responsibility, what to plan, before engaging in operational control. This often includes development of ideas that precede plans. Project management is focused on an integrated whole, via cross-functional integration, not just the management of individual elements. This is because, in today's world, enterprises cannot remain competitive by operational excellence alone. The times require total management that ranges from individual functional reinforcement to development of strategic plans and ideas.

Even government agencies and non-profit organizations, with constituents living in an ever-changing business environment, are expected to execute projects that create new value for citizens.

Increasingly, programs comprised of multiple projects are typical in business. It is crucial for commercial enterprises or government agencies to cope with growing scale and business complexity, while implementing holistic or individual business strategies. An organization's strategy aims for sustainable success and growth by innovating its scope of business and organizational structure. Strategy provides the organization with a guiding framework for its desires and energies so that its resources can be harnessed for success. Programs deploy strategic ideas via a bundle of projects embodying realistic and concrete approaches.

In her *Economic Policy and Projects*, Joan Thirsk (1978, p. 3) wrote, "(in England) in the seventeenth century two of the keywords that characterized the new era were 'project' and 'projector'. Everyone with a scheme, whether to make money, to employ the poor, or to explore the far corners of the earth had a 'project.'" *Project* here meant a new business enterprise. England was then a society comprised of small self-sufficient farming communities. Enterprises arose, some growing into large businesses, employing hundreds of women and children. Thirsk gave a detailed account of the woad (a dye-yielding plant) business that prospered in southern England from the late 16th through the 17th centuries. According to Thirsk, other business enterprises (projects) at the time included manufacturing businesses for knit socks, buttons, pins, cutlery and smoking pipes, as well as agricultural businesses for oil-bearing plants, hemp, flax, tobacco, and the like. While some of these were launched as fresh business enterprises, others had existed in different villages, though they produced low-quality products. These smaller operations were in turn organized into larger businesses with secured raw materials supplies and resources, unified product quality, and well-organized sales channels.

Project was, therefore, a historical term for *business enterprise.* Modern business management procedures have become increasingly dependent on the segmentation or specialization of functions and processes, which is remarkably effective at achieving higher efficiency. However, the root sense of the word *project* may have been forgotten in the course of long industrial growth. Discussion in this book uses *project(s)* with the modern definition as a matter of course, although Thirsk's research is a helpful reminder of the importance of broader aspects of study.

Meanwhile, some industries find increasing opportunities in making contracted execution of projects itself as their business. Some operations are making businesses of undertaking projects in the early stages of a value chain, making use of their technological expertise. Historical examples of these businesses are various types of construction and heavy machinery supplying physical capital systems, as well as resource and space development. IT solutions have entered this business segment and are now leading players in terms of industrial scale and the size of their workforces.

Driven by these trends, the period between the late 1990s and 2000 was a turning point in the understanding of project management, which spread rapidly into all levels of businesses around the world (see note below). Project management knowledge has been theorized and systematized into *PMBOK®* *Guide* (worldwide), *PRINCE2®* (European), *P2M®* (Japanese), and other knowledge systems. Universities are also making rapid progress in this field.

One feature characterizing the new generation of project management theory is program management, which integrates multiple projects. The theories and knowledge of project management that have been presented to date are based on the experience of project-based companies in such industries as IT solutions, plant construction, and space development focusing on building systems. These theories, therefore, cannot be regarded as paying sufficient attention to the concerns of business administration or strategic management, as these have the tacit premise of continuously ongoing routine operations for capturing values. An important goal of today's program management theories is the integration of these two perspectives. This book addresses this very point.

Note

According to MIT Professor Brynjolfsson (2004, p. 53), important technical inventions and discoveries need about 30 years before they materially affect industrial innovation. Assuming the publication of the *PMBOK® Guide's* first edition in 1987 as the starting point in a change towards modern project management, its effects may become obvious in the 2010s. (For Brynjolfsson's observation, see Chapter 4, 4.6 Value of Intangible Assets.)

1.2 Project Management and Improvement of Project Productivity

Building construction, satellite development, and new product development – these are all projects with specific and obvious goals to achieve. Project management is intended to improve project productivity while leading the project to reliable and efficient achievement of the goal. The problem with projects is that the risk of failure is very high, due to a lack of relevant repetitive experience, because requirements differ from one to another. Tacit knowledge about job content is difficult to be accumulated and passed from one generation to another inside the organization. This contrasts with routine operations, where experience has been accumulated through repetition.

Fundamental to project management is the definition of generic processes for carrying out project jobs, instead of merely defining specific job contents. In reality, organizations customize generic processes as explicit knowledge related to their respective business and environment. The purposes are (i) to furnish an organization with common explicit knowledge about project execution processes, (ii) to establish a scheme for smooth execution of project management elements such as project planning, project monitoring, and so forth, and (iii) to integrate measures taken to address past failures into standard procedures to avoid recurrences. In many cases, an organization can deal with each individual project by partially altering standard procedures. It is essential for improving a project's productivity that knowledge about project management not reside in a project manager alone, but be shared within the organization.

In the information and communication technology (ICT) industry, such products as computer software, once completed, can be reproduced at essentially zero cost. Cost in these industries is, therefore, subject to the quality of the outcome of non-recurring work, that is, the outcome of software development projects. The system integration (SI) industry is characterized by individual development projects contracted on a customer-order basis and is thus another business endeavor that depends entirely on project outcome. In that sense, these industries fall into the category of project-based businesses, which include the traditional space development and plant engineering industries. The ICT industry in particular faces difficulty in the product development process because the attributes that define a product's function and performance cannot be as clear as those for mechanical or hardware products. With virtually no physical size restrictions, there are few perceived limits to higher functionality or sophistication. This is another reason that more steadfast project management is important in this field.

1.3 Business Strategy and Program Management

A program is an undertaking that coordinates multiple projects in order to achieve significant organizational objectives. Though the term *program* has been defined in many ways, we discuss programs following the above definition in this book.

(1) Systems and Complexity

Our life is filled with various instruments and products. Pick up any Japanese brand electronic product and you are likely to find the words "Made in China," "Made in Thailand," or "Made in Malaysia." Inside that product are parts and materials made in Japan, Korea, or Taiwan, perhaps with software developed in the U.S. or Europe. To survive global competition, companies work to improve productivity by mobilizing competitive suppliers around the world. Companies no longer manufacture only their own products. If a company receives an order for a personal computer through the Internet from a customer in Tokyo, it may gather a Korean-made LCD panel and module parts from Taiwan, have them assembled in China, and then use a home delivery service to send the product to the customer. This whole process may happen within four or five days after order placement. Needless to say, this cannot work without reliable setups, such as ordering systems, payment methods and after-sales services, the creation of which is another important task of modern business operations.

Whatever the product, it reaches a customer after various types of work are done. This process is called the *value chain*, which includes things like product design, part and material production/procurement, assembly, packaging, shipping, and sales. In addition, the process relies on business planning, accounting, human resource administration, research, and other support work. All these activities together make a value chain, which may be further subdivided and become complex depending on the product or company. In the past, most notably in Japan and Korea, large companies honored efficiency by operating the entire value chain within the vertical integration offered by their group companies. In today's global competition, dealing with this complexity through in-house efforts alone incurs substantial inefficiency. For an organization to become competitive, its most important task is to identify which parts of the value chain should remain in-house. In other words, an organization should focus its strategy on its area of specialization. Based on this, the organization should coordinate external suppliers of materials, parts, services, and so forth, to build an optimum combination to achieve its objectives and competitive advantages.

What to coordinate to achieve objectives, and how? What are the specific objectives in the first place? Programs are created to answer these questions.

Organizations that make changes swiftly, companies that create innovative products in a short period of time, or entities capable of building plants and sales channels worldwide – these are excellent modern enterprises with strategic superiority. Apple, Google, Toyota, and Samsung, for example, are distinguished for their project/program management. Today, a company cannot keep up with the competition if it depends only on excellence in routine operations. It is ability in project and program management that now constitutes the foundation of superior business management and growth.

(2) Strategy, Program and Project

When a corporate or business strategy is implemented, detailed tasks are each executed as projects. Each project, however, is not generated directly from the overall strategy of the organization. The strategy and the project are bridged by a program. The program takes the strategy, which in itself is a conceptual idea, and provides shape or structure for its application in the real world. Suppose that a company has a strategy to obtain a competitive edge via *economies of scale*. The first thing that must be done is to question what the strategy essentially means to the company. That is, "What does 'economies of scale' exactly mean to the company? Is it the quantity of sales of individual products, or of the entire product line?" Or "What should be done to increase the quantity of sales? Remodel the products? Increase sales channels? Develop a new production line?" Answers to these questions must then be formulated in the form of various strategic goals, which should specify what is to be done to best serve the strategy given limited resources. Determination of strategic goals is, therefore, determination of "what to make" or "what to build." The next step is to develop a scenario that leads to achieving the goal. This scenario is then deployed across multiple projects. In strategy implementation, program management's role is to design and execute a strategy as a group of specific activities, or an aggregation of projects. Therefore, the details of individual projects are designed within the context of the program. In project management, on the other hand, the center of attention is how to execute the individual projects steadfastly and efficiently; in other words, focus is on "how to make" or "how to build."

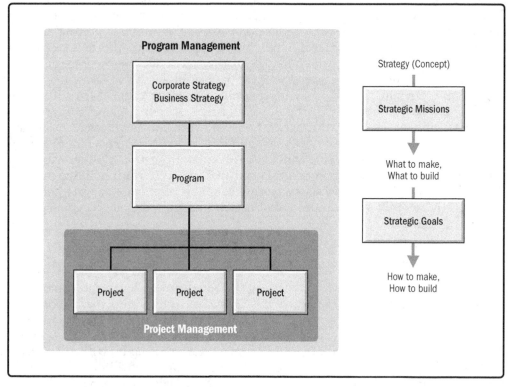

Exhibit 1.1.1: Strategy, Program and Project

1.4 Hierarchical Structures in Business Management

(1) Hierarchical Structure in Business Management

Business management is increasingly complex, keeping pace with the complexity of society. Enterprises deal with a wide variety of products, relying on complex supply chains. Business management complexity, however, is segmented into manageable portions handled by management or during day-to-day operations. This is what is known as the hierarchy of management and the division of labor.

In general, an enterprise is separated into several business divisions, with each further divided into a number of functional organizations (departments). These functional organizations each have their own subgroups (sections, subsections, etc.) responsible for daily operations. This organizational structure for regular operations is not unique to commercial enterprises but is also the case with government agencies and administrative corporations.

In contrast, a project, or a program as an aggregation of projects, deals with non-routine or ad hoc matters. Apart from the regular functional structure, project management is implemented by creating organizations dedicated to each project. Such special-purpose activities are broken down into levels of enterprise, business unit, program, and project in a hierarchical structure. It is not unusual for a project to have plural levels of subprojects to assign parts of the work. Mini-projects, however, are often implemented by small temporary groups created within a regular functional organization.

(2) Hierarchical Structures of Missions and Strategies

The activities of an organization are the way that it realizes its missions and visions. An organization's strategy is the set of principles prepared for guiding such activity.

Mission, vision, and strategy are hierarchical in parallel to the structure of business management. For example, there are corporate-level missions, division-level missions, program missions, and project missions. Similarly, there are corporate strategies, business strategies, program-level strategies, and project-level strategies. Although often omitted where evident from the context, in this book they will be specified where necessary.

1.5 Program Environment

Organizations conduct business in a changing environment. This environment includes society, the market and the organization's internal structure. Changes such as market expansion/shrinkage, new scientific discoveries and new technologies, new products from competitors, market entry by low-price suppliers and changes in customer purchasing power or values have a powerful impact on execution of an organization's strategy. While the competitive situation is obvious to commercial organizations, it also exists among government agencies and public organizations in that they are service providers whose customers are the national and municipal citizenry. They are subject to changes in their customers' needs that challenge their *raison d'être*, and to competition with other organizations, both domestic and overseas. Typical examples of economic-level competition that public organizations can face domestically or internationally are competition for hub status among harbors or airports; competition to lure manufacturing plants via infrastructure provision or subsidy (competition over location advantage); and, competition with rival countries' trade controls or corporate tax laws.

What is unique to the contemporary market environment is that the personal sense of values supporting end-user demand is changing most rapidly. This trend is largely attributable to digitalization, in which information is distributed with drastically increasing volume and speed at drastically decreasing cost. During the past two decades, formerly socialist countries (China, Russia, Eastern European countries, and Vietnam), as well as India and Brazil, have surged onto the world economic scene as new gigantic markets and/or powerful low-price suppliers. In addition, the nature of new product development has been shifting from hardware (manufactured goods), to software such as information and services. Another cause for drastic market changes is that it has become difficult for enterprises to keep their technologies and know-how to themselves, as purchasing these things has become easier.

Globalization has an effect on the nature of competition faced by enterprise. Traditional competition by a product itself has been gradually replaced by competition between product development processes, production processes, supply processes and business systems for recovering investment from the market. Moreover, the systems themselves have also become complex through the expansion of a geographic division of labor. At the same time, the transportation and telecommunication infrastructure necessary to run these processes have developed globally, greatly reducing geographic barriers to accessing low-cost labor, consequently globalizing competition in the supply market. Contemporary enterprises in both developed and emerging economies are now required to develop various strategies and to build various processes. Programs are the practical action to achieve such goals.

2. Definition and Essential Nature of Programs

2.1 Definitions of Program

A program is defined as "an undertaking in which a group of projects are organically combined for achieving a holistic mission" (ENAA, 2001, p. 65) (see note below). Another definition is "a group of related projects managed in a coordinated way to obtain benefits and control not available from managing them individually" (PMI, 2006a, p. 4).

Note

Organic is used to express that many different projects contribute to the operation of the whole structure, in a coordinated fashion.

A program is not limited merely to building or developing a huge, complex system. What is really required in a program is to achieve its true value through a wide spectrum of planning and execution management, including using and operating the system. A program consists of multiple projects and, where necessary, some ongoing operational elements as well. For a plant-building program, for example, operational production activities at the completed plant bring forth business profit. The primary purpose of IT system development is to create value through use of the system in regular operations. Organizational reform programs, such as corporate restructuring or mergers and acquisitions (M&A), are an effort to improve business outcomes through operation of the reformed organization.

P2M explains that an integrated group of projects constitutes a program by introducing a concept called the *service-type project,* which is a project form equivalent to the system operation phase. In *The Standard for Program Management,* PMI (2006) stated that "programs may include elements of related work outside of the scope of the discrete projects in the program." The *elements of related work* here include continuous operations. A program includes operations as its elements. These operational elements play an important role for programs, as they allow creation and capture of value. P2M's explanation reflects the situation of business management today, where operations cannot remain with their missions unchanged but may need major alterations after a certain period of time.

The idea of defining a *service-type project* implies to examine operational work across the business as a part of the program, while in the program mission profiling phase. This indicates the potential for the program to create new value by total optimization or reform of the business (see note below).

Note

Harold Kerzner (1979, p. 22) pointed out that U.S. government agencies like USAF and NASA are historically based on a three-level concept, with *system* at the top, *program* in the middle, and *project* at the bottom. At the system level are the Intercontinental Ballistic Missile System, Manned Space Flight Systems, and others, whose infinite lifetime and constant upgrading are implied. The program level represents subsystems that are time-phased activities for upgrading these permanent systems. The project level consists of the program's time-phased subsystems, with clearly defined objectives and a scheduled time period with a start and an end.

2.2 The Typology of Programs

Programs can be classified into two types: large-scale system programs and strategic programs. Plants, railways, airports, and the like are built through large-scale system programs. Such programs start with their execution concept more or less known among the stakeholders. In contrast, strategic programs tend to start without any specific execution concept, for many of these programs are virtually new to stakeholders in both knowledge and experience, as summarized in Exhibit 1.2.1. P2M calls the former *operational-type* or *conventional-type,* and the latter *creation-type* or *innovation-type* (see Exhibit 1.2.2). In recent years, the world has experienced

Type	Characteristics
Large-Scale System Programs (Operational)	• Realization of complex hardware/software systems • Stakeholders usually have experience with similar programs • Execution concept is more or less shared among stakeholders from the outset
Strategic Programs(creation, innovation type?	• Clarification and execution of organizational strategies (corporate/business strategies) • Stakeholders usually have no experience with similar programs • Execution concept is not clear at the outset in many cases

Exhibit 1.2.1: Program Types

	Program Categories	Program Type	Examples
1	Organizational reform	Innovation	Corporate M&A, business alliance, restructuring, transfer of business divisions, factory/branch closure, government restructuring or privatization
2	Mineral resources business	Operational	Metal and mineral exploration, oil rig drilling, LNG chain, pipeline building, mine development and operation
3	Construction	Mainly Operational	Social infrastructure construction (airports, railways, etc.), large commercial area construction, urban redevelopment
4	Plant and factory building	Mainly Operational	Plant (petrochemical, steel, semiconductor, LCD, etc.), construction, nuclear & thermal power plants
5	ICT system	Mainly Operational	Bank and/or accounting, production, and supercomputer systems, communication and broadcasting systems
6	Product development	Innovation at the outset; Operational later	High-tech industrial products (hybrid cars, high performance game machines, 3rd generation mobile phones, nanotech materials, etc.), pharmaceutical development, plant seed development, packaged software
7	Launching of new business system	Mainly Creation and Innovation	Takkyu-bin (delivery service launched in 1976), I-mode (mobile internet service launched in 1999), ebookstores, Internet search services, free Internet services
8	Sales and service system (network building included)	Mainly Innovation; shifting later mainly to Operational	New brand car dealership systems, sales franchise networks (coffee shops, convenience stores, fast food chains, etc.), broadband network services, theme parks
9	Events	Mainly Creation	Olympic Games, World Cup Soccer, World Expo
10	High-tech and large-scale scientific R&D	Starts as Creation; shifts later to Operational	Space development (space station, Mars exploration), nuclear fusion study, human genome study, high-tech military equipment development, global environmental studies (e.g., IPCC)
11	Human resource proficiency development	Starts as Creation; shifts later to Operational	Official development assistance (international cooperation), university establishment, employee training systems
12	Creative activity	Mainly Creation	Movie production, TV drama production

Exhibit 1.2.2: Program Categories and Examples

Source: PMAJ (2007), *Shinpan P2M purojekuto & puroguramu manejimento hyoujun gaidobukku* [New P2M standard guidebook for project & program management], Tokyo, JMA Management Center, p. 77.

many technological innovations, along with radical changes in economic and social environments, such as the advance of digital technology and the Internet, rapid growth in emerging economies, violent fluctuations in crude oil prices, economic bubbles, and global environmental problems. The impact of these changes is unavoidable, and every organization, regardless of whether public or private, needs to cope by developing an entirely new business or by executing organizational reformation through strategic (i.e., creation/innovation type) programs.

2.3 The Essential Nature of Programs

Programs start from business concepts posed by higher management levels of organization and have such basic characteristics as multiplicity of contexts, scalability, complexity, and uncertainty (Ohara, 2003, p. 73).

Multiplicity of contexts means that the initial concept of a program's mission is a complex of multiple ideas and requirements, reflecting the complicated social environment surrounding the organization. With combinations of these ideas and requirements, programs usually have the characteristic of *scalability* in their size, range, and architecture. A program at its early stages represents an abstract concept of the program mission, which gradually becomes specific in the course of the program's life cycle. With relevant projects combined during that process, the program develops detailed *complexity* within itself. Since it is intended to be an innovation to the status quo, *uncertainty* is an essential characteristic of a program. During its long-term execution process, a program is exposed to changes in external environments such as the market and through competition, as well as to the impact of dynamic complexity in interactions between external changes and the program. The uncertainty of a program is amplified by long-term exposure to these changes.

One of the basic approaches for dealing with complexity is hierarchical structuring, which places projects under a program. In the case of a highly complex program, more projects are created, forming a multi-level hierarchy. In addition to hierarchical structuring, uncertainty can be dealt with effectively by (i) progressive elaboration of program mission definition and design, (ii) making changes in lower-level structure with projects as the relevant unit, or (iii) setting up, during the planning stage, options reserved for future eventualities.

2.4 Concept of Strategic Programs

Exhibit 1.2.3 illustrates the relationship between strategy and program by referring to the strategy game tree model (Mishina, 2006). In the game tree, an organization has a strategy, with candidate programs A and B to implement as specific measures. Only one can be chosen. The programs each comprise their own combination of projects with the probability of program success represented by a percentage.

(a) If probabilities are unknown beforehand, there is nothing to do except submit to consequences. Comparative evaluation of any decision regarding program execution and the consequences has no significance in terms of management. Since the other program is left unexecuted, there is no telling which program should have been chosen.

(b) If probabilities of success can be presumed at the point of decision-making, we have another situation altogether. The program manager will choose program A and, at the same time, will try to identify the program's risk factors and seek the best ways to lower the probability of failure to below 20%. Whatever program management means at this stage, whether development of new products, further cost reductions, enhancement of sales channels, or any other outcome, optimization of program structure to most effectively serve the strategic intention is the goal. In short, program management's role at this stage is to plan program design. With an optimized structure, program A comprises multiple projects, each of which is defined with a specific goal. The projects are placed under project management, to execute the plan for each project so as to achieve its specific goal steadfastly and efficiently.

(c) Program B's probability of success is obviously small. But what would the program manager do if benefits from its success were judged to be far higher than that of program A? The program manager would react the same way as to program A, trying to identify program B's risk factors and working on every possible way to drastically reduce the 80% failure probability. (If the

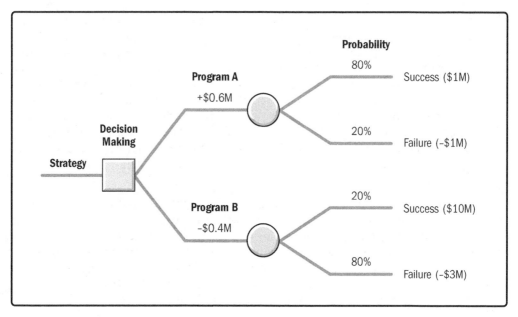

Exhibit 1.2.3: Strategy Game Tree

success probability is improved only to 50%, for example, expectations change to +$3.5M from -$0.4M.) The consequent decision on whether to execute project B depends on the organization's situation, resources, and the program manager's value judgment.

Program managers should question whether their program execution is mere pursuit of some kind of result as referred to in case (a) above. Usually, there are a variety of possible programs. Program managers are required to judge the best one among them; this is the mission profiling of programs discussed in Chapter 2.

2.5 Large-Scale System Programs

Although some strategic programs are extensive, it is not the scale that characterizes them. What characterizes a strategic program is that it is related to the strategy-level innovation in an organization or the change in its scope of business and, above all, that it involves high uncertainty. Program managers are expected to have in-depth insight into this uncertainty and complexity.

Large-scale system programs, however, generally have major stakeholders with relevant experience, allowing them to share some understanding of the current program. This means the primary requirement for program management is not innovation, but efficient and reliable control of the organization and program-related information, which grow in parallel with program size.

Large-scale system programs are contract-based businesses of the type frequently found in construction, space systems, plant engineering, and the ICT industry. In contract-based business, a competitive edge is generally unobtainable through technical skill alone. This is because, with limited exceptions, most jobs involved in program execution are widely understood within the relevant industry. In construction, for example, any one of design planning, materials procurement, construction, or process control is not unique to a specific contractor. The source of a competitive edge in this kind of program-oriented business lies primarily in the technical and management skill of organizing a great number of complex elements completely into a system without omissions. Secondarily, a competitive edge lies in the capabilities of information management and planning in a broader sense, which organize the vast knowledge and information regarding requirements, performance, prices, procurement methods, and so forth, to create an optimum system solution. The important point is the ability to handle the complexity of a great number of segmented technical elements, human resource matters for design, production, and construction, and the physical resources associated with materials and subsystems. Ever-changing information today is another reason why this type of program is difficult. In addition, the growing scale of need for technology, human resources, and funds further pressures business programs to seriously improve ability in building schemes for execution and financing corresponding to program scale.

Strategic programs and large-scale system programs are different from each other in their purposes and management focuses. In many cases, however, management processes are almost the same, with a few exceptions for operational elements included in a strategic program implemented through its management. In this book, discussions hereafter focus mainly on strategic programs, which include large-scale system program management within their scope.

3. Strategic Program Bootstrapping

3.1 Strategy Implementation and Programs

Practical schemes for strategy implementation are classified roughly into three types (PMAJ, 2007, p. 72). Type 1 enhances the organization's members' awareness and behavior through establishing policies or frameworks for day-to-day operations and decision making. This scheme often aims at *developing a sturdy human organization* (see note below).

Note

Developing a sturdy human organization means not merely building an appropriate organizational structure, but creating an organizational culture where people are highly motivated to work and produce effective results. A typical example is Toyota's "lean production system" (LPS). The biggest reason for its success lies in the fact that the company established an organizational culture for production improvement described as "squeezing a dry cloth" in the course of executing the LPS (meaning to squeeze waterdrops from an apparently dry cloth). Other examples are the Daimler/Chrysler merger at the end of the 1990s and the Renault/Nissan partnership around the same time. Both of these merged companies built cross-functional cooperative organizations and pursued synergistic effects in their own way. However, the merger of one group collapsed, while the other had great success. The success was not because the partner was a Japanese company, but is directly attributable to the top leader, Carlos Ghosn. The strategy of building a sturdy organization has universal value irrespective of, and across, culture.

Type	Outline	Examples
1. Establishment of policies and frameworks	A scheme to enhance the organization members' awareness and behavior through establishing certain policies or frameworks for day-to-day operations and decision making	Developing a sturdy human organization that ensures: • high-quality production • high-efficiency customer service • high-capability R&D
2. Creating new systems	A scheme to create and have in place various *new systems* to help the organization's activities	Physical systems: Facilities, equipment, machines, mechanical systems, etc. Soft systems: Organization establishment and reorganization, institutions, operating processes, business models, etc.
3. Creating new value	A scheme to create *new value* that an organization will provide externally in the form of products and/or services, thereby enhancing the raison d'être of the organization itself	• Developing new products • Starting new services

Exhibit 1.3.1: Schemes for Strategy Implementation (PMAJ, 2007, p. 72)

Type 2 is to create and have in place various *new systems* to help the organization's activities. The systems are diverse, ranging from hardware to software, the former represented by facilities, equipment, and machines, while the latter includes organizations (e.g., organization establishment and/or reorganization), systems, operating processes, and business models.

Type 3 is to create *new value* that an organization provides externally in the form of products and/or services. This scheme can influence the raison d'être of the organization itself.

Types 2 and 3 are a kind that cannot be achieved within regular operations. In practice they must be implemented as programs and often require a great quantity of resources to accomplish.

An organization's strategy is a rather abstract concept, which can be expressed in form of strategic missions, each of which is scheduled to be implemented by programs or other measures. A program mission is such a strategic mission, or a part of it. Each of these programs is carried out as an aggregation of projects, which are themselves individual and more specific processes of implementation. Depending on the size, capacity, or necessity of an organization, programs may be carried out either one at a time or simultaneously.

Programs and *tactics* are different things. Programs are parts of strategy that are detailed to prepare for strategy execution while tactics is a set of techniques that are used during execution of strategy.

3.2 Bootstrapping Program Management

The term *bootstrapping* means to accomplish something without external help. For example, it may mean that a complex operating system for a personal computer is triggered to launch by one single input signal; in the business community, the word may mean that an entrepreneur launches a company without any external funding. For the purposes of this book, bootstrapping means that an abstract strategic concept from above is the trigger or input initiating a self-propelled program implementation.

There are several approaches to systematizing program management. Bootstrapping program management, which this book discusses, is an approach by which the program manager and the program organization take the initiative to specify and detail the business strategy to be implemented. Top-down program management, in contrast, is a reductionist approach where business strategy is subjected to systematic detailed design by top management before entering the execution phase.

PMI (2006b, p9) explained the process from strategy design to detailed execution using a four-level management hierarchy: executive management – portfolio management – program management – project management. Executive management designs strategic plans and goals while portfolio management prioritizes programs and projects to be executed. In such a top-down approach, programs are authorized with concrete policies and plans specified by top management, and start with clear-cut objectives, goals, and structures. In other words, strategy from above is mutely accepted, free from concern over its complexities.

In P2M, which underlies the bootstrapping approach to program management, a corporate or business strategy is presented as an initial program mission concept, while still comprised of a good deal of ambiguity and complexity. The program manager and the program organization analyze the initial concept of the program mission to elucidate the essential meaning of a strategy and what the strategy should be. In this approach, the program or execution-level organization accepts the complexity of the original high-level strategy and then efficiently reduces complexity through mission profiling, reflecting the implementing organization's viewpoint where necessary (PMAJ, 2007, p. 79).

Strategic program bootstrapping focuses on who should be responsible for molding strategic concepts into a concrete program architecture. Obviously, this is the responsibility and authority of top management. Meanwhile, the market complexity has become significant and the business management has become more complicated. It has significantly increased the necessity and frequency of strategic activities. And it also keeps top management away from the worksite. While this may provide opportunities for top management to gain an objective view of their business, more probably they run the risk of being alienated from the complexities of day-to-day business, including being involved in every strategic decision-making process in a corporation.

Small- to medium-sized companies and startup businesses, where human resources are limited, have little room to spare for specialists in systematic strategy development grounded in a comprehensive environmental analysis. This is much the same in the divisions and subsidiaries of large companies. In the strategic program bootstrapping approach, the program manager and program organization elucidate and detail essential strategic requirements in order to gain a concrete understanding of the relevant *program mission*. This effort is part of deploying top management's initial concept.Both the top-down approach and the bootstrapping approach have pros and cons. Exhibit 1.3.2 summarizes the characteristics of the bootstrapping approach.

Outlines	
Clarification of Strategy	• Top management presents initial strategy concept.
	• Program manager and organization define concrete details of the strategy.
Advantages	• Program manager's practical expertise in market and/or technology ensures reliability of strategy clarification.
	• Applicable to strategy implementation by small to medium-sized organizations or startup companies, which have limited human resources with high competence in strategy development.
Challenges	• Difficult to apply to discontinuous reformation of the status quo or to a strategy that negates the existing organization.
	• High-level ability is required of program manager and program organization.

Exhibit 1.3.2: Characteristics of Bootstrapping Program Management

3.3 The Background of Program Bootstrapping

(1) P2M

Chaired by S. Ohara, the Project Management Development and Introduction Committee of the Engineering Advancement Association of Japan (ENAA) developed a project management system called "Project and Program Management for Enterprise Innovation" (P2M) in 2001.

P2M focuses particularly on two perspectives. One is value creation, beyond just discussing processes of efficient project execution. The other is the proactive leadership role played by the program manager to profile program details. Business concepts or requirements presented by the business owner or top management are defined as a *program mission* or *holistic mission*. This program mission incorporates the ambiguity of a multiplicity of contents and complexity. During the subsequent *mission profiling* process, the program missions' essential meaning is defined by the program organization (ENAA, 2001; Ohara, 2003, p. 73; PMAJ, 2007, p. 78). This is where P2M is decisively different from the top-down approach. In P2M, the program organization, a practical-work level group, is involved in business strategy development.

The top-down approach is a normative idea derived from organizational governance's view on what a strategy should be. It is, in a way, an *idealized* method in that executive management exercises its authority to provide an ample supply of highly competent human resources for strategy development. In contrast, P2M is executed under the initiative of senior managers. This approach is a realistic and efficient method that fits small-scale organizations with their limited available resources for strategy development (see note below).

Note

As stated in its title (specifically: "for enterprise innovation"), P2M aims principally at innovation of business organizations in general, not at small- and medium-sized organizations alone. It does not intend to encourage developing the complex hierarchy of strategy. It focuses, instead, on providing program-level activities, allowing emergence of value where "the whole is more than the sum of its parts."

---

(2) Space Program Management

The basic concept for strategic program bootstrapping in this book further clarifies the relationship between the program integration management process and business management strategy, in the following chapters. The processes of mission profiling and program design in this book refer broadly to the techniques found in space mission analysis and design (see, e.g., Larson & Wertz, 1992, p. 19). NASA stated also that "terms such as mission analysis and engineering are often used to describe all study and design efforts that relate to determination of what the project's mission should be and how it should be carried out" (NASA, 1995).

However, in the space development context, *project mission* is always a flight mission. The environment of management strategies and general businesses is far more complicated, covering a broad swathe of concepts. To be consistent with real management strategies, our discussion refers also to complex system theory, and separates scenario development concepts into environmental scenarios and execution scenarios.

(3) Business Practices Among Cultures

The difference between the two types can be explained as reflecting a different mindset about management strategy in the U.S. and Japan. From the Japanese point of view, having a program manager who knows much about practical worksite management is an advantage in that the program can be designed well and rooted in realities. At the same time, however, there is a risk that the program is too close to the reality, which requires special attention be paid to the program manager's competence.

Business administration studies were developed in the U.S. in the early 20th century in an effort to standardize scientific business management principles. The basic idea of management strategy is that a strategy is planned based on objective judgment of the environment, which binds all plans and business activity execution. "Structure follows strategy" is a straightforward expression of the idea. It means that organizational matters are a management resource subordinate to strategic management. It also implies that being "scientific" means that every event allows reductionist analysis.

Advanced scientific management theories have been deeply appreciated in Japan, too. In Japan however, despite the increase in top-down strategy-led M&A and scrap-and-build practices, these strategic theories are not widely accepted. For example, Nidec Corporation, Japan's most active M&A practitioner, makes it a rule not to dissolve the employees and organizations of companies they have acquired through M&A. Instead, Nidec buys out loss-incurring companies and leads them toward growth by improving their business process efficiency, while retaining their original employees and keeping organizations intact. The perspective on organizational structure in Japan is not as clear-cut as in America; while Japanese people agree that "organization follows strategy," many of them also believe that "organization influences strategy." This obviously means that another value standard, for instance "organizational retention and growth," in addition to "making profit," can be introduced to strategy. It may be the case that applying different value standards from "making profit" is a deviation from the scientific viewpoint that a strategy can be determined by external objective judgment. For instance, Numayama emphasizes the importance of establishing a new strategic management theory that agrees with Japanese social values (Numayama, 2000).

"Structure (organization) follows strategy" is absolutely right as far as project organization is concerned, because project organization is supposed to be formed in keeping with the objectives of a project. However, Japanese companies planning to execute a certain project or program need to make effective use of the human resources available within their existing organization, because it does not match Japanese business custom to hire external specialists for projects and then dismiss them when it is over. Accordingly, even strategy, which is an extremely senior-level activity, cannot be smoothly executed through programs or projects without proper respect for organizational concerns.

Even with such a cultural background, Japanese enterprises also conduct top-down management, depending on the situation. On the other hand, every country has small or startup companies lacking in human resources. And the bootstrapping approach, where a strategy becomes concrete under the initiative of program management, should be highly effective for these organizations, regardless of their cultural background.

4. Business Value Creation and Management Behavior

Both projects and programs are forms of organizational business implementation, the management of which is basically consistent with ordinary management that is tacitly premised on routine operations. In this section, basic notions of management and project management activities are summarized in a general sense to provide a basis for the subsequent discussion of program management.

4.1 Business Value Creation
4.1.1 Business Value and Projects

Growth is essential for economic structures such as businesses enterprises. In capitalist economies, return on investment is the driving force. A business will decline if it does not see any growth. If sales and profits, or free cash flow, do not increase continuously, the company will have difficulty securing financial and human resources, face shrinkage, and decline. An increase in sales without profit is meaningless unless only temporary. An increase in profits without an increase in sales is questionable in terms of growth when viewed from the standpoint of the strength of products or demand. When growth is not on the horizon, a company will downsize and restructure itself, leaving only portions likely to grow – that is, the company has to attempt growth in its new structure after incurring huge costs through sales reductions and temporary losses.

For growth, a company needs to get as many customers as possible by providing them with higher value. Whether selling expensive products (Lexus and Louis Vuitton), mass-market items (Suzuki and Uniqlo (see note below), parts and materials (Intel and Bridgestone), or free information services driven by advertising and shopping (Yahoo! and Google), businesses need to provide value desired by customers to drive corporate growth.

Note

Suzuki makes affordable compact cars and motorcycles. UNIQLO is a Japanese brand of low-priced casual wear.

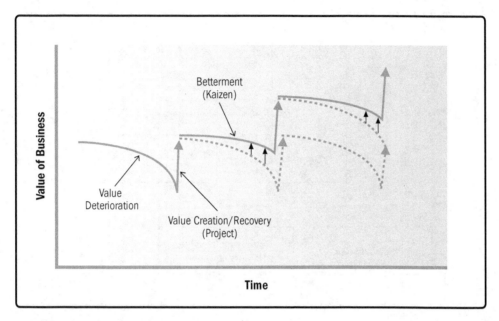

Exhibit 1.4.1: Business Value and Projects

Customers are not limitless, nor is their buying power, and both domestic and foreign companies compete for them. As long as there is competition, prices of equivalent goods tend to decrease. A company will lose market share if competitors introduce more appealing products. Product value deteriorates with time, decreasing a company's value. To retain and boost its organization, companies are in constant need of new customers, or customers willing to pay more. To achieve this, continuous efforts to create new customer value are required.

Among efforts to recover value lost over time, those made continuously in daily operations are a betterment, or *kaizen*, activity. Those made discontinuously to create new value (e.g., the launch of a new product) are project activities. With today's harsh competition, strong competitiveness requires a combination of (i) constant value recovery efforts by continuous *kaizen*, and (ii) strong value creation efforts through powerful projects. This is the case in industry and other business fields.

4.1.2 Types of Values

The goal of business strategy is to create new value, thereby creating customers.

While the word *value* has a broad definition, here we discuss economic and non-economic value, as shown in Exhibit 1.4.2. Economic value usually means what is commercially gained from products or services in the market, as well as what is directly connected to that gain. The main element of economic value is financial value, typically represented by money itself. Land, plant, equipment, and other financially measurable assets also have financial value. Economic value also includes the non-financial value of production technology and management capacity incorporated into an organization, which is generally difficult to measure financially. Non-financial value consists of many other intangible properties.

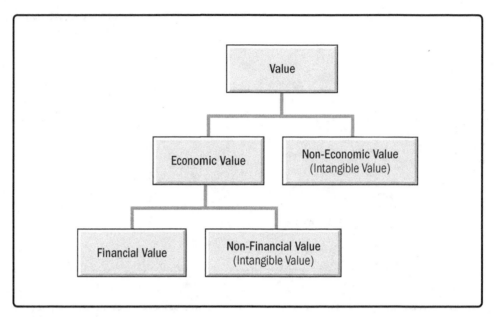

Exhibit 1.4.2: Types of Values

Non-economic value, on the other hand, is based on personal or group-specific values, such as health, sense of security, literacy, knowledge, aesthetics, ethics, and contentment. It is not true, however, that non-economic value has nothing to do with economic value. Basic research in a certain area of physical science may attract attention one day and be used for commercial purposes. Personal values such as health or security are the target of commercial medical products or other relevant services. Many more such cases can be found throughout society.

In this book, our study focuses mainly on economic value, touching briefly on intangible value.

4.1.3 Value, Assets and Resources

First, let us look at value in programs in relation to assets and resources. Value is often associated with the evaluation of financial, physical, or intellectual assets. Value and assets, however, are not always equal.

The purpose of an enterprise is sustainable development of its organization through securing profit – that is, increasing its financial value. Contemporary projects, even though independent of regular business operations, are managed within the scope of their principal organization's purpose. For an organization, the value of its assets is realized only when they are used as business resources. Cash and other liquid financial assets are always ready and are almighty. They have virtually no need to be viewed separately from assets, resources, and value, as long as they are discussed in money terms. Other physical or intellectual assets, however, cannot necessarily be used as resources in all situations, and time and cost must be taken into account when converting them into value.

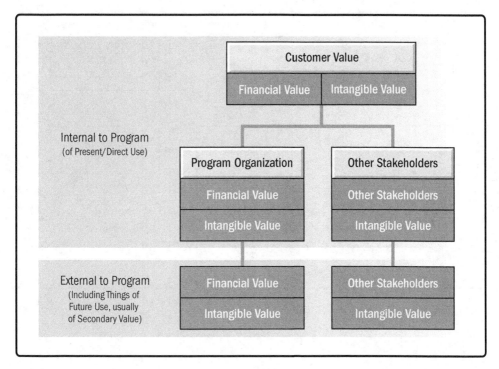

Exhibit 1.4.3: Value Creation in Program

A program aims to create *new systems* or *new values,* as shown in Exhibit 1.3.1. This is not to merely create assets; it is rather to create new capital resources for business operation.

As for non-economic value, it is obvious that it is irrelevant to the concepts of assets or resources directly.

4.1.4 Value Creation in Programs
Programs create and provide customer value, and the program organization (the principal organization) and other stakeholders gain program value in return. Both customer value and program value consist of financial value and intangible value. Further, the program organization and stakeholders may find, within program value, secondary values that work as resources for future programs or new business development.

4.2 Fundamentals of Management Behavior
4.2.1 The Management Cycles
Organizational management behavior is fundamentally of two types: PDCA (Plan-Do-Check-Act) and SDCA (Standardize-Do-Check-Act). Whatever they may be called, the ideas are found in every modern organization.

Exhibit 1.4.4 illustrates a PDCA cycle in the operations of typical retailers or mass production manufacturers. Information such as sales results from the previous week or the market outlook for the coming year is used as a basis for production or

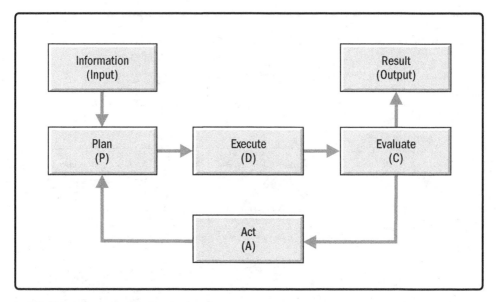

Exhibit 1.4.4: Basic PDCA Cycle

sales planning. Based on the plan, material procurement, manufacturing, or stock purchasing is conducted. Experience from repeated operations makes things like labor hours and costs known, and these are accurately reflected in the plan. Unexpected events are managed by amendments or reflected in subsequent work plans. The PDCA cycle provides greater accuracy when the operation is small in scale and the market not volatile; it becomes difficult to make good use of PDCA as business grows complicated or markets become volatile.

In an SDCA cycle, plans are not made afresh. Instead, work is executed in accordance with certain standard procedures and default values, which are fixed or defined on an event-by-event basis. The SDCA cycle, often emphasized in Total Quality Management (TQM), is a basic method for manufacturers as well as service providers to maintain high quality implementation. Management behavior in the SDCA cycle focuses on preparation and maintenance of an environment that enables smooth progress of the cycle.

4.2.2 Decision Making
The daily work of individual managers includes communication, coordination, negotiation, surveys, analysis, planning, and so forth. Some of these require highly intellectual judgment (information processing), while others require skills in human relations and personnel management. The most essential behavior of managers is decision-making for the organization, which managers do either as part of their daily work, or as the most important duty in it.

In today's business world, organizational structures and business management are extremely complicated, with intricate hierarchies for people and organizations. Organizational decision-making is also complicated by intertwined decisions.

Anzof (1988, p. 4) described this as comprising three classes of decision-making: strategic, administrative, and daily operational.

The task of strategic decision-making is to select the best product/market mix to optimize potential return on investment by deciding to allocate resources to products and market opportunities. Administrative decision-making is for developing an optimum resource structure by selecting outsourcing or in-house development as appropriate. Daily operational decision-making is for realizing potential return on investment by allocating resources in the form of budgets, planning time schedules, supervising, and controlling.

While these classes basically correspond to the hierarchical structure of the organization, most managers' work includes elements of all three classes. Obviously, there should be inter-class harmony when decisions are made. Appropriate delegation of authority is important. Excessive top-down processing, total surrender of authority, and absence of respect for higher authorities must be avoided, because they obstruct proper management. It is also important that strategic decisions not get forgotten amid the flood of daily operational decisions.

4.2.3 Difficulty in Project Management

The PDCA cycle is also fundamental to project management, although the cycle's "Plan" and "Do (Execute)" phases are more difficult to apply, compared to ordinary operations. This is due to the following three features:

The first is that, due to its individuality, a project is always a new experience. This inevitably lowers planning accuracy. In its execution phase, where operators (workers and managers) are inexperienced, delays and additional costs can occur. For organizations and workers, experience in one project may not directly contribute to other projects' planning and execution. Difficulty arising from a project's uniqueness can be quite costly.

Another feature making PDCA difficult to apply to projects is that their management tends to be both large and complex, with this tendency increasing. Scale and complexity make it difficult to comprehend the overall project. Increases in the number of subsystems and their details require more stakeholders (e.g., contractors), and increases risk. Increases in scale can intensify the impact of risks. For example, after the success of the Apollo Program, NASA steadily increased the complexity of subsequent space programs. Skylab, the Space Shuttle, and the International Space Station encountered serious cost and schedule problems. NASA also pushed its earth observation and space exploration projects toward larger scale and greater complexity, resulting in overruns and failures. NASA made a major shift around 1990 to the "Faster, Better, Cheaper" (FBC) policy with smaller spacecraft, lower costs, and shorter schedules.

Increasing scale also leads to complexity in the system's hierarchical design. The PDCA cycle inevitably becomes elongated and complicated. The long PDCA cycle for execution makes it nearly impossible to make use of feedback from outcome evaluation in the plan and design phases. If market conditions and other expectations used for planning change, execution of the plan may succeed but the project itself may fail. Also, the prolonged cycle reduces opportunities for project managers to gain experience.

In short, these are important reasons why project management, a complex system of knowledge and competence, is called for, in addition to conventional management. A company will gain a competitive edge if it learns how to accumulate and reuse experiential knowledge and competence while minimizing project duration.

Dealing with these issues, a project manager begins with dividing a complex system into appropriate layered functional units, and then allocates them to autonomous organizations. These *stratification steps* are executed sequentially along the program timeline, which is an important part of project lifecycle management. The entire system is thus divided into functional units now ready to be managed unit by unit, based on lifecycle phase. It is important to shorten the span of the PDCA management cycle in this way, while also shortening the overall project time span.

4.2.4 Project Management Activities and Knowledge Areas

As conceptualized in Exhibit 1.4.5, project management is executed via three types of management activity with three corresponding types of knowledge and skills. Deliverable Systems Management is a process to conceptualize, design and build the systems that the project aims to achieve. Project Implementation Management is the activity that plans efficient execution of Deliverable Systems Management, which involves a great amount of labor, and that monitors and controls planned progress.

These management activities are closely related. Especially Deliverable Systems Management and Project Implementation Management are executed as an inseparable whole. Deliverable Systems Management deals mainly with systems and their component elements, which will result and remain as tangible deliverables of hardware and/or software. In contrast, Project Implementation Management represents the "work" of supporting and controlling the realization of the system. It does not leave any tangible results after closing the project. Still, experience is accumulated within the organization as an intellectual asset of crucial importance.

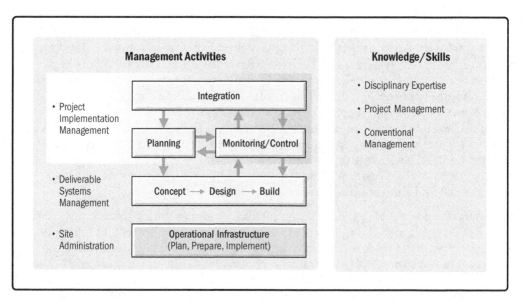

Exhibit 1.4.5: Three Types of Management and Three Types of Knowledge/Skills

Planning basically breaks up the project mission, dividing systems into appropriate units of work, and allocating the work to the appropriate organizational entity, along with resources and time. Planning also specifies individual goals that the organizational entities execute subject to their own Deliverable Systems Management. Another function found in Project Implementation Management is monitoring both the execution process and its resultant system, exercising control where necessary.

In pursuit of achieving the project mission, it is divided into units of appropriate scale (work packages) in the planning process. It is not self-evident, however, that the work packages are relevant and suited to the project's environment and available resources, or that work package results will be integrated to achieve the mission as expected. *Integration* of projects is a management process that validates and verifies that the division of the work packages is appropriate and that their integration will successfully achieve mission goals.

For a large construction program, for example, site administration (or field administration) prepares and supports business execution infrastructure, which comprises basic resources and functions for operations. These include: financial/accounting, personnel (employment, work, and payroll management), supply and maintenance of the work environment (office, accommodations, and communication networks), procurement/outsourcing management, transportation, contracting, legal affairs, public relations, worksite security and health, environmental management, and community affairs, among others. Site administration is a crucial element of large-scale construction projects, especially those implemented overseas. In manufacturing, or IT projects implemented in-house, these functions are already in place and in most cases outside of users' awareness (see note below).

Books on project management typically do not discuss Site Administration, except in direct relation to Project Implementation Management (also the case in this book). In some companies, Site Administration is simply called *administration*. In other cases, activities made on behalf of the project owner are called *project administration*. This book uses *Site Administration* to avoid confusion.

Note
This may be one reason why manufacturers or IT organizations with inadequate site experience often confuse system projects, which comprise large or distant worksite operations, with installations or test runs. Sufficient attention should be paid to preparation for Site Administration.

Implementation of project management requires knowledge and skills in three different areas:

- Disciplinary technological knowledge and skills unique to a certain field of projects such as plant construction, mechanical products development, or IT solution systems
- Knowledge and skills unique to project management required for project execution, regardless of the field
- Knowledge and skills related to conventional management that are widely needed for business management in general, including Site Administration, because projects are part of business operations

The importance of knowledge and skills in (b) and (c) above are greater in the higher levels of project organization.

5. Systems and Complexity

Almost everything is complex today – society, economy, markets, enterprises, products, etc. Simple "industrial products" on shelves in convenience stores are no exception. Consider snack noodles or potato chips, for example: The packaging lists a dozen ingredients and their manufacturing plants are subject to strict quality control systems. Bananas, lettuce or beef sold in supermarkets do not list ingredients, but their processes of production and transportation are never simple. Understanding such complexity, as well as understanding the methodology of systems to deal with it, is crucial for implementation by management.

5.1 The Concept of Systems

System has a broad range of applications with a diversity of definitions. Its definition in engineering and industry is multiple elements coordinated in a group for certain functions. *Coordinated* means that all of the multiple elements are appropriately correlated to form an integrated whole. In the course of the progress of science, technology, and industry, both products and production facilities have become more and more sophisticated with complex systems comprising multiple elements. To respond to such sophistication and complexity, the systems engineering approach has become widely applied.

Products like machinery and equipment for sale are physical objects. For a manager, they are not objects in the real world but systems to be dealt with, as a succinct description of the objects' essences (model). When taking the factor of time into account, a substance can be viewed as two types of system. One is the system as a snapshot of a subject taken at a certain point in time. This is called the *product system.* Industrial products such as automobiles and electrical appliances, as well as software, plants, equipment, buildings, and even human organizations in a company are systems snapshots called *products.* Pharmaceuticals and chemicals consisting of a complex of ingredients can also be regarded as a system. However, a *process* of change occurring from one point in time to another is also consistent with the general definition of *system* (Myers & Kaposi, 2004, p. 29). Manufacturing activities in a factory, and various project activities, achieve their objectives through a coordinated combination of a variety of elements, including planning, procurement, assembly, testing, cost management, and so on. These can all be considered to be a system composed of dynamic elements called human labor, and can be called a *process system.* In many cases, a project realizes a product system, although the project itself can be viewed as a process system. Frequently, systems engineering is used to explain project management, partly because a project itself is a system.

Exhibit 1.5.1 compares product system and process system from a systems point of view. Here, *target system* means a product system that is the goal of a project or normal operations. Process systems are either *projects* or *normal operations.* Each has the key elements necessary for their execution, that is, *project management* and *production management* (process control), respectively. The right column of the table shows primary tasks and concerns for each system.

System Category		Key Approach	Primary Tasks and Concerns
Product System	Target System	Systems Engineering	• Divide into elements • Realize system performance via integration of elements • Design, quality and performance
Process System	Project	Project Management	• Divide into work elements • Accomplish mission via integration of work-element outcomes • Plan and efficiency
	Normal Operations	Production Management (Process Control)	• Plan and efficiency (Scope of work and deliverables are well-known)

Exhibit 1.5.1: Product System and Process System

5.2 Complexity of systems

Most modern products are systems. This, of course, also includes industrial products. Products such as fresh food, raw materials, energy sources, and clothing are not systems, but their production and distribution processes are highly systematic, accelerating in complexity. Every service provider today is a system itself, using very sophisticated ICT systems. High-speed rail, airlines, ATMs, home delivery services, convenience store chains, and mail-order services are only a few examples of such services.

There are two types of system complexity. Modern electronic devices and mechanical products are composed of a great number of elements, with elaborate structures and complex interrelations between elements. This type of complexity is called *detailed complexity*. The other type of complexity is intricacy – as in "intricacies of the situation" – which means that various elements are intertwined too intricately to understand the cause-effect relations between them. Some systems or events demonstrate this type of complexity, which is called *dynamic complexity* (Senge, 1990, p. 68). This complexity is often seen in social systems.

An arid region had a sudden increase in agricultural production after deep wells were drilled for irrigation. However, when the wells eventually dried up, the region suffered a fatal blow. This is an example of one action resulting in completely different outcomes between short-term and long-term time factors. The steep rise in crude oil prices in the summer of 2008 was an event inexplicable by supply-and-demand theory. It was said to be partly due to the U.S. economic depression triggered by the subprime mortgage crisis. When it developed into a global financial crisis, crude oil prices showed a sudden fall in the autumn of the same year. These are examples of complicated events, whose cause-effect relations are incomprehensible to those involved. Dynamic complexity means that an event or action has unexpected influences on other events or actions. The causes and effects of such influences are so distant from each other in terms of time and/or space that the relationship is clouded beyond recognition.

Since dynamic complexity so obviously affects not just project management but any modern management effort, its constituent factors are the subject of a variety of research efforts. Among them, dynamic modeling research emphasizes such factors as feedback (positive/negative), time delays, stock and flow (effects of accumulation), and nonlinearity (Sterman, 2001). When research subjects include human behavior in a system, the scope of studies should extend as far as "complexity for actors" and "complexity derived from recognition." The former relates to how correctly an actor (a human) inside a system can judge the external environment, while the latter relates to how well a manager can recognize the complexity of that system from the outside (Shiozawa, 1997, p. 187).

5.3 Integration and Decomposition of Systems
5.3.1 Hierarchical Analysis and Decomposability
Basic education today is a perfectly hierarchical and classified process. It starts from the elementary school curriculum, which is segmented into parent language, arithmetic, science, and civics. Through this education process, people obtain tacit confidence that "the whole is decomposable into parts." In contrast, complex systems research, which has a history of more than 30 years, maintains that "the whole is greater than the sum of its parts," acknowledging that the whole cannot be understood just by decomposition.

Putting 100 bolts together in a bag does not make a system. Neither does gathering ten such bags together. In these cases, the whole is strictly equal to the sum of its parts, never creating any additional value, no matter how big the sum may be. In the case of a system, the sum of its parts creates new value when the parts are combined with each other in a coordinated manner. Following these examples, we can see that physics, chemistry, and biology can be described as reductionist sciences that study the structure of a system by detailing it into smaller units with the help of mathematics. Engineering, however, is a science with an integration vector for the realization of system value.

Take the automobile, for example. It is a system in itself, which can be divided into subsystems such as the power train with engine, body, and controls. The body can be further divided into body shell, doors, interiors, and so forth, each of which is nested in further functional subsets. The systems can be divided into multiple subsystems, each of which can in turn be regarded as a system for further decomposition into component subsystems. This decomposition can be repeated to the most minute elements or parts. This indicates that a system is necessarily understood – or designed – as a hierarchy that integrates plural levels of subsets, each of which is nested with its own subsets. In many systems, the functional subsets in lower levels are more detailed and require higher specialization and sophistication of expertise. In general, therefore, each subsystem is provided with a special organization that is fitted to its function.

Simon (1962) compared two watch craftsmen, each assembling a watch with 1,000 parts. One craftsman decomposes the watch system into a hierarchical structure with ten large subsystems, each of which has ten smaller subsystems each comprising ten parts. The other craftsman starts with the 1,000 parts directly without arranging them in a hierarchical structure. With this comparison, Simon explained the great contribution to efficiency that a hierarchical approach makes. Simon said, "A simple system develops into a complex system much faster with a stable intermediary than without," pointing out that "with a stable intermediary, the generated complexity will be hierarchical." A hierarchical structure in which a system is decomposed into plural subsystems brings higher efficiency by virtue of concurrent and specialized execution of the plural subsystems. This demonstrates the great significance of the hierarchical approach, which has been widely experienced in the development of artificial systems or in production management.

In a system composed of subsystems, interactions among subsystems are usually less strong than interactions among parts within a subsystem. Simon called systems with this characteristic "nearly decomposable systems." He demonstrated the case where subsystem interactions are not important in a short span of time by referring to a house with well-insulated outer walls and a number of rooms divided by less well-insulated panels. As for near decomposability, the theory on the Design Structure Matrix (DSM) for modularized systems was developed in the 1990s (see note below).

As long as "a system has a certain function created by multiple elements integrated into a coordinated whole," the elements (i.e., subsystems) necessarily interact with each other. In the modern artificial systems that projects aim to create, the significance of near decomposability is not that the subsystems' interactions may be disregarded in a short span of time, but that direct interdependence among subsystems is minimized, thus improving system development's efficiency and stability for efficient execution.

Note
A module is a semi-autonomous subsystem, whose combination with other subsystems (e.g., other modules) under certain interface rules creates a higher-level system with more complex functions. Because of this, modules can be developed simply by following the interface specifications without any concerns about other subsystems. Advantages of modularized design are that a system creator using modularized subsystems can find good cost/performance subsystems around the world, and that a supplier of excellent modules can pursue higher quality and lower costs by expanding its market worldwide.

5.3.2 System Composition, Decomposition, and Integration
Suppose a project manager receives a project mission such as (i) build a 25-story building in the business area of central Tokyo; (ii) develop an information network for a company; or, (iii) run a marketing campaign for release of a new car. What should the project manager do first?

The first important step for a project is to clearly identify the customers and their needs in light of the purpose of the deliverable or outcome. A project usually has two customers: a project owner who orders it, and an end user of the project's outcome who purchases or uses the outcome. The project manager's basic responsibility is to maximize the project owner's profit, which requires end-customer satisfaction. In the first mission, the building must be completed to maximize the profit of the project owner, who is also the building owner. But, for that mission to succeed, the end users of the building (the tenants) must also be satisfied with the building. In the second mission, the user is generally the company's internal users or managers of the information network, although external end users' satisfaction could be more important, depending on the nature of the system. In the third mission, the deliverable is

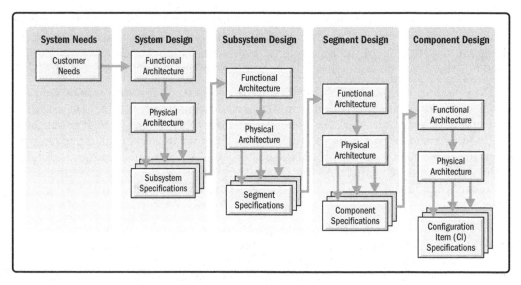

Exhibit 1.5.2: Hierarchical Design Process of a System

expected to be a "soft" system to organize and manage the promotion campaign. The end user in this case can be those who buy the car. But, depending on the campaign's nature, it is also probable that car dealers are the most important customer.

Starting from the clarification of customer needs, the project's deliverable outcome system should translate the customer's needs into system functions, determine a feasible system structure, and then detail that structure through serial decomposition. The hierarchical design process of a system is illustrated in Exhibit 1.5.2. This diagram implies two things: One is the design process, which breaks down the system to be realized into its multilayered details; the other is that the program is also concurrently broken down into its details, as programs and projects are themselves process systems. Here, the program mission corresponding to the customer needs in the diagram is detailed into program objectives and program goals, which correspond to the system functional architecture and subsystem specifications. Program goals, in many cases, also correspond to the missions of individual projects.

The exhibit indicates the process in which upper-level specifications lead to lower-level ones. At first, the system's functional architecture is determined in accordance with customer needs, and then the corresponding physical architecture is specified. Based on the physical architecture, the system is divided into feasible subsystems with defined specifications. Based on subsystem specifications, lower-level specifications are determined serially from the segment level down to the component and the configuration item (CI) levels.

In realizing a system in practice, system requirements are "decomposed" into the simplest feasible level of elements, which are created and then assembled to produce the upper levels. This means that making a system real is an upward-flowing serial process of assembly. Exhibit 1.5.3 provides the entire picture of the process of system design and production (or construction, in the case of a building, for example). In the diagram, the upper half of the entire process is the modeling stage consisting of decomposition

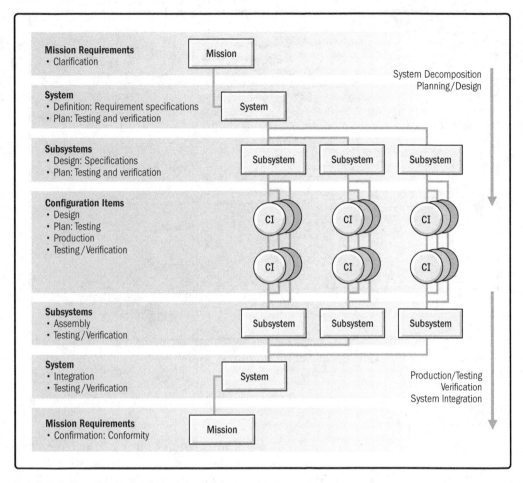

Exhibit 1.5.3: System Decomposition and Integration

and planning and design. The lower half is the stage of assembling hardware/software in the real world into target items serially by a process of system integration, production, testing, and verification. There are usually some additional levels between subsystems and configuration items, depending on the nature of the system.

5.4 Complex Systems Involving Managers

In the process of managing, a manager is inevitably involved in at least three types of complex systems, as shown in Exhibit 1.5.4. The first is artificial systems, which include mechanical and other products for consumers, equipment for production, buildings to construct, and information networks. All these are *target systems* for the purpose of our discussion. The second type of system is the organization of people to realize a target system. The third is the environment that surrounds the first and second systems, which can be referred to as competitive markets, industry, and society.

Modern target systems are highly complex, as are the organizations that deal with them. Both target systems and organizations are hierarchically structured to cope with complexity. Though not expressed in this simple conceptualization, in

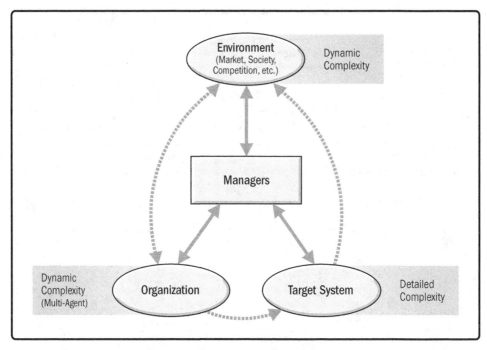

Exhibit 1.5.4: Three Complex Systems Involving Managers

the real world there are managers interdependently functioning in vertical and/or horizontal directions.

Exhibit 1.5.5 indicates management tasks and primary measures to cope with task complexity. Target systems are artificial and complex, but basically comprehensible in their details. Systems of this type are product systems. Their structure, whether hardware or software or some mix, can be decomposed by a systems engineering approach. Product systems can be achieved using project management approaches. Environmental complexity, which surrounds all organizations, is classified in multiple dimensions ranging from complex but stable environments familiar to managers, to dynamic complexity that reveals unexpected volatility attributable to factors far removed from the manager's organization, such as dramatic growth in emerging economies or a collapse in demand caused by sudden global economic unrest. There may be virtually no organization that can evade all effects of the dynamic complexity arising from developments in globalization. A target system (or product system), which is a snapshot taken at a certain point in time, is not capable of responding to long-term changes caused by such environmental complexity. Sustainable measures to combat changes in the market environment are obtained only by an organizational or business strategy and the programs derived therefrom.

Business organizations are composed of humans, every one of whom is a system element capable of independent judgment and action. In this sense, an organization is a multi-agent system with dynamic complexity controllable to some extent by management. To deal with business as it grows increasingly complex, it is highly

Management Subjects	Complexity	Primary Measures to Reduce Complexity
Target System	Detailed Complexity	• Systems Engineering • Project Management
Environment (market, society, customers, etc.)	Dynamic Complexity (nonlinear, multi-agent, etc.)	• Business Strategy • Program Management
Organization	Dynamic Complexity (mainly multi-agent)	• Organization Management, Leadership, Community of Practice

Exhibit 1.5.5: Management Subjects and Primary Measures against Complexity

inefficient, and effectively impossible, for a manager to give detailed instructions to every member of the organization. What is needed in the organization is leadership, or a community of practice, which makes it possible for the organization to perform with fewer instructions relative to workload.

This analysis should lead to an understanding of the growing importance of program/project-based management in the complex modern business environment. For a company whose business is project execution by contract, no matter how complex the target system may be, it is basically detailed complexity. Once the contract is concluded, this complexity can be handled through a systems engineering approach and project management. To sustain business over a long period of time, however, it is important to respond to the dynamic complexities of market, society, and customers.

For manufacturing or service companies based on repetitive operations, the dynamic complexity of market and customer is of a greater significance. An important challenge for these companies is to properly develop the target systems required to respond to such complexity.

6. Knowledge Areas of Program Management

Program management is implemented by integrating a wide range of knowledge areas. As shown in Exhibit 1.6.1, this book discusses in chapters 2 through 5 the knowledge areas that are important from the strategic bootstrapping point of view. Since a program contains projects within itself, the discussion is obviously based on knowledge areas related to project management as typically included in the *PMBOK® Guide*.

Knowledge Areas	Outline	
Program integration management		
Implementation management processes	Mission profiling, Program design, Integration management of program execution	Chapter 2
Strategy management and risk management	Program strategy management, Relation between strategy and risk in program, Program risk management	Chapter 3
Value assessment	Program value and its assessment, Assessment methodology, Assessment of non-commercial programs	Chapter 4
Project organization and project management competency	Project organization and the community of practice, Project management competency	Chapter 5

Exhibit 1.6.1: Knowledge Areas of Program Management

Besides the areas mentioned here, program management covers other important knowledge areas, such as finance management and information management, but these are outside the scope of this book.

References

Anzof, I. (1988). *The new corporate strategy.* New York, NY: John Wiley & Sons.

Brynjolfsson, E. (2004). Intanjiburu asetto [Intangible asset]. Tokyo, Japan: DIAMOND [based on several theses presented by Brynjolfsson, the book is written in Japanese and published in Japan].

ENAA (Engineering Advancement Association). (2001). Committee for Introduction Development, and Research on Project Management, P2M Purojekuto & puroguramu manejimento hyoujun gaidobukku [Project & Program Management for Enterprise Innovation: P2M]. [Limited publication in Japanese. The book's general readership version by Ohara was published in 2003.]

Kerzner, H. (1979). *Project management: A systems approach to planning, scheduling and controlling.* New York, NY: Van Nostrand Reinhold.

Larson, W., & Wertz J. (Eds.) (1992). *Space mission analysis and design.* Torrance, CA: Microcosm.

Mishina, K. (2006). Miezaru rieki [Invisible profit]. *Hitotsubashi Business Review, 56*(1), 2008, 6.

Myers, M., & Kaposi, A. (2004). *A first systems book, technology and management* (2nd ed.). London, UK: Imperial College Press.

NASA. (June 1995). SP-610S, Systems engineering handbook, Section 2.4.

Numayama, T. (2000). 20 Seiki no keieigaku: Kagaku karano dakkyaku [Business management of the 20th century: Freeing from science]. *Hitotsubashi Business Review,* Winter 2000, 22.

Ohara, S. (Ed.). (2003). P2M purojekuto & puroguramu manejimento hyoujun gaidobukku [Project & program management for enterprise innovation: P2M]. Tokyo, Japan: PHP Institute.

PMAJ (Project Management Association of Japan). (2007). Shinpan P2M purojekuto & puroguramu gaidobukku [New edition P2M project & program management standard guidebook]. Tokyo, Japan: JMAM (JMA Management Center.

PMI. (2006a). *The standard for program management.* Newtown Square, PA: Project Management Institute

PMI. (2006b). *The standard for portfolio management.* Newtown Square, PA: Project Management Institute.

Senge, P. (1990) *The fifth discipline.* New York, NY: Currency.

Simon, H. (1962). The architecture of complexity. *Proceedings of the American Philosophical Society, 106*(6), 467.

Shiozawa, Y. (1997). Fukuzatsukei keizaigaku *nyūmon* [An introduction to economics of complex systems]. Tokyo, Japan: Japan Productivity Center.

Sterman, J. (2001). Systems dynamics modeling: Tools for learning in a complex world. *California Management Review, 43*(4).

Thirsk, J. (1978). *Economic policy and projects.* Oxford University Press.

Chapter 2

Program Implementation Management Processes

Chapter Overview

Chapter 2

Program Implementation Management Processes

Chapter Overview

This chapter starts with an outline of the essential characteristics of program management. The subsequent discussion of program integration management is the core of program implementation. The discussion focuses on implementation management processes, classified as concept formation, design, and execution of programs, describing them along an implementation timeline. This corresponds with the area within the dotted line in Exhibit 2.0, which gives the entire picture of program integration management.

The enclosed area consists roughly of three phases:

- The mission profiling phase, when program execution scenarios are made based on strategy
- The program design phase, when the program and its projects are designed in detail
- The execution phase, during which autonomous, distributed project plans are implemented

Mission profiling is a phase where a mission's essential objectives are clarified through mission definition, with mission execution scenarios developed in light of resource and environmental restrictions. The program design phase, based on an execution scenario, designs a program architecture composed of multiple projects. Each project has specifications, resources and an implementation schedule.

Projects are executed independently of each other in the execution phase. Program integration management is responsible for controlling the projects as a whole, to achieve the program's mission of *value creation*.

1. Program Management

1.1 What is Program Management?

The purpose of program management is to achieve program missions that arise from business strategy. Multiple projects are defined with optimized combination structures and correlations for this purpose and are executed to create the value the mission requires. A program mission in its early stages is ambiguous, with a multiplicity of contexts, and the relationship with the program environment is

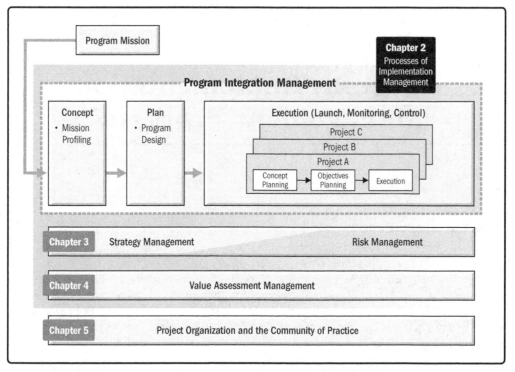

Exhibit 2.0: The Knowledge Base of Program Management

often vague. Program management begins here, and conceptualizes a program's autonomous distributed activities and the framework for their integration, so that each project is defined as its specific units of activity. Program management then plans and executes each project comprising the program. There are two core functions of program management: (i) program integration management, through which the program architecture is designed and executed, and (ii) management of organization and the community of practice, i.e., managing the human resources for program implementation.

Program integration management consists of (i) implementation management processes that are directly involved in program planning and execution, and (ii) basic management knowledge that provides policies and criteria for planning and execution. Processes for implementation management are further divided into mission profiling, program design and integration management during program execution. Basic knowledge for management includes strategy as well as risk management and value assessment management, which will be discussed in Chapters 3 and 4, respectively. This chapter focuses on processes for implementation management.

1.2 The Role of Program Integration Management

Program integration coordinates the designs and execution plans of multiple projects that share the program mission and, in the mission execution phase, controls these projects' activities with a view toward mission accomplishment.

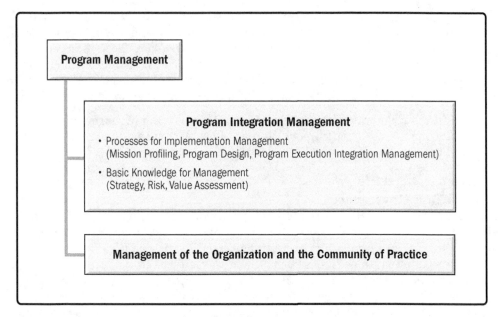

Exhibit 2.1.1: The Main Elements of Program Management

The role of integration management processes is (PMAJ, 2007, p. 86):

Defining of Organizational Course of Action: The initial concept of program mission is defined more specifically and the program's organizational course of action is clarified through a program scenario. This is part of mission profiling.

Program Structuring: This is part of program design, including (i) program architecture with projects as components, (ii) fund and budget preparation, and (iii) scheduling. Architecture design includes preparation of (i) project configuration charts defining program structure, (ii) project mission descriptions for each project, and (iii) documents describing inter-project relations. Also included in program design are budget allocation plans for each project, as well as basic schedule plans.

Control of Organizational Action: This is a role that integration management assumes in the program execution phase. At its core are (i) control of each project's execution from the holistic program point of view, and (ii) coordination of stakeholder action.

To ensure effective program integration, important management activities include program strategy management, which determines strategic policies from a proper understanding of the program's nature; risk management in response to uncertainty; and value assessment, which makes up the basis for decision-making at each phase. More specifically:

Program Strategy Management: Program strategy has two different perspectives. One is program effectiveness from the point of view of the organization's principal business strategy (the primary strategy), and the other is from the point of view of the strategy for program execution, with an eye toward sound and efficient concrete achievement of program goals.

Risk Management: Uncertainty is unavoidable, and risk management deals with it from a broad perspective. Risks are identified and assessed during mission profiling within the scope of strategy management. These efforts to avoid risk are inconspicuous at this stage, as they are incorporated into strategy management activities. At the execution stage, however, risk management is an important independent function for both the entire program and each project.

Value Assessment: Every stage of program integration management relies on the value assessed compared with the value creation that the program is aiming for. This applies over the entire life of the program.

1.3 Governance and Lifecycle

1.3.1 Program Governance

Program governance is to ensure that the quality of program management is maintained at the level required for the overall purposes of the enterprise or organization, and that its mission is properly implemented in the end (Garland. 2009, p.1). The purpose of program governance is almost the same as that of program integration management, except that the former places importance on establishing and maintaining organizational systems and procedures that facilitate strategy-level decision-making and implementation, while the latter regards the program implementation processes as important.

A program needs to ensure that every one of its diverse and multiple project organizations properly achieves its mission and maintains its management quality. Program governance aims for continuity of the organization's upper-level policies in lower-level organizational activities. The specific requirements of governance are strategic decisions properly made as the program progresses. This needs an appropriate organizational system including an authority structure, schemes for interactive communication, and a program lifecycle design that facilitates decision-making at the appropriate time.

1.3.2 Design of Program Lifecycle

For reasons of program governance, it is important that the "who, what, and how" of decision-making is defined in advance for each stage of the program lifecycle. Up to the program design stage, it is naturally program management that makes decisions about the program lifecycle as well as any assessments to perform at each phase. After the program execution stage starts, the program lifecycle becomes an aggregation of individual project lifecycles. For accomplishment of the program mission, however, it is important that the program lifecycle not be designed in a bottom-up manner. Instead, it should be designed in a manner that enables the program as a whole to make necessary assessments, decisions, and adjustments at appropriate times. The individual project's lifecycle must be defined in accordance with the program lifecycle, as a matter of course.

2. Program Integration Management (1): Concept Formation

2.1 Processes of Concept Formation and Design

The first half of implementation management processes in program integration management is dedicated to breaking down programs into individual projects by mission profiling, program design, and the arranging of individual projects into a system of autonomous distributed activities. Through this process, the ambiguously conceptualized initial program mission is boiled down to its essence, which is specified and detailed into a set of concrete projects. A program is designed as a group of projects that work in deliberate combination. However, it is usually impossible to create such a program design immediately out of the initial program mission concept. It is important here to start with a step-by-step clarification of the mission concept before breaking it down to fine detail.

Exhibit 2.2.1 displays the outline of mission profiling and program design. What comes first is the initial concept of the program mission, which contains requirements that are abstract and ambiguous but of the real world. The initial concept is detailed and developed into a scenario through mission description before it is advanced to the stage of specific project design. In this way, the essence of the program is extracted and modeled (see note below). The outputs are a mission description, a program execution scenario, and a program concept planning document. All of these are modeled expression of programs, which have been detailed as to their respective needs. The program concept planning document includes (i) program architecture that is systematized as a group of projects, and (ii) a mission description and the requirements/specifications for each project.

Note

A model is an expression of one or more noteworthy essences extracted from the limitlessly complex details of a real world matter. Modeling facilitates simplification of a complex reality (e.g., machinery, systems, etc.). Personal thoughts and notions about the real world are also difficult to define due to their ambiguity or foundation in personal tacit knowledge. By modeling, ambiguous thoughts and notions can be approximated to explicit knowledge to share among the people concerned.

Projects defined as the result of program design are based in models. An outcome that a program (the aggregation of the models) would achieve is compared with that of the initially conceived mission. Based on this, with some revisions where necessary, program design proceeds. If program design is identified as relevant to the program mission, the process advances to the next stage – program execution. (Though local feedback between initial mission and mission description, mission description and scenario, and scenario and projects exists as a matter of course, it is excluded from Exhibit 2.2.1.)

Major problems in this program design process are (i) the modeling work requires high-level skills to begin with, (ii) comparative assessment between the consequently designed program (i.e., integrated projects) and the initial mission idea is no easy task, and (iii) the criteria for assessment are difficult to define. "Programs are difficult," as is often heard, is not simply a comment on handling size and complexity. What really makes a program difficult is appropriate definition of its mission and the comparison between it and the set of projects comprising the mission model. A program manager needs deep understanding and weathered mission profiling skills to perform reliable mission definition.

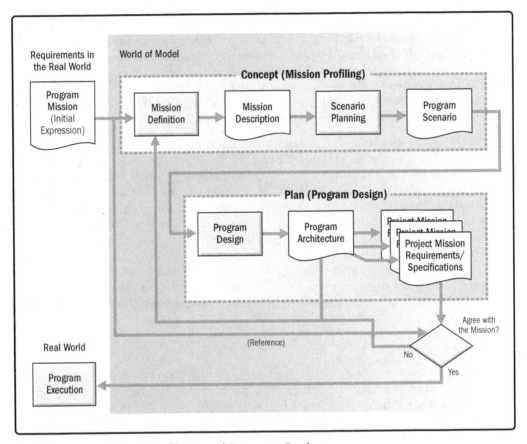

Exhibit 2.2.1: Mission Profiling and Program Design

2.2 Mission Profiling

What is *value creation* in a program? The objective of project management is maximization of results (profit or other value) from within the defined scope of a project. "How" is the main theme here for project management. In contrast, "why" or "what" is the concern for an enterprise's strategy, whose task is development of projects to be executed for creation of value (Ohara, 2004, p. 33). A program's value creation is, by its nature, what is achieved through integration of projects, not by each individual project. At the core of this value creation process is mission profiling consisting of mission definition and scenario development.

2.3 Mission Definition

The core proposition of scope management in project management is to break down the given project into properly defined tasks, known as a work breakdown structure (WBS). However, the mission definition process in mission profiling is not the same as in the case of project management. The value concept in the initial program mission includes a number of possibilities, while the surrounding environment is also too complicated to be broken down simply. Therefore, the mission definition in strategic program bootstrapping first places its essential importance on developing the mission concept into a number of more specific possibilities. Then the possibilities are studied to find an optimum combination of goals to replace the initial program mission with, taking into account the organization's strategic requirements and restrictions. The aggregation of the goals should be the one that accomplishes the initial project mission most effectively. This requires the ability to deal with a proposition that is not only broad in range but also highly complex. In many cases, the essential part of profiling is performed by a small number of senior managers, or even just one, whose personal knowledge, ability, sense of values, experience, and insight are reliable. As profiling often relates to the organization's strategy, the process is rarely open to the "public" or larger organization.

2.3.1 What is Mission Definition?

The initial program missions have various possible interpretations as the cases illustrated below. *Mission definition* is the process to determine the best option, taking into account elements such as value capture, competition, organizational capacity, resources, and risks.

(a) Company A, a manufacturer, developed a mission (initial expression) to "improve the profitability of a particular business segment." The initial expression of the mission included extremely diverse choices of solutions such as reducing existing product costs, modifying existing products and increasing their sales volume, developing new products, reinforcing sales channels, rearranging or shifting sales channels, and acquiring new customers.

(b) Company B, a computing services company, is working on how to "launch a new consumer business," based on its newly developed content management software technology. The company is now making a comparative study of several possible business models, such as directly charging content end users jointly with content rights holders, earning web advertising fees in cooperation with other companies, building a content supply platform for other companies to use, and so on.

(c) Company C, a large retailer, intends to merge with Company D, which is suffering a slump in business. Company C wants to gain a competitive advantage over its major rivals by "optimization through business upsizing." The company is wondering whether to integrate D's main shop nearby into C's main shop operation as an annex or to retain D's brand to use in a separate operation.

After examining market trends, the organizational ability of the segment in question, and many other conditions, the companies defined a concrete program mission. In Case (a) above, the mission read as "to increase sales volume through major modification of existing products combined with reinforcement of sales channels."

Defining the mission requires comprehending the true meaning or essence implied in the vague and ambiguous initial expression of a program mission, and restating it more precisely. Mission definition is supposed to clarify what a business or an organization, or its action, does best.

In the following case Van der Heijden (1996) illustrated, as an example, how a vague wish (mission), "to become a successful entrepreneur," is defined through a combination of three essential and concrete objectives:

Essential success results from a combination of three ideas:

- Discovering a new way of creating value for customers
- Bringing together a combination of competencies, which creates this value
- Creating uniqueness in this formula in order to appropriate part of the value created (Van der Heijden, 1996, p. 60)

As shown in Exhibit 2.2.2, this stage defines the program mission derived from the business strategy, in a specific mission description. Mission description breaks the defined program mission down into specific objectives, and into sub-objectives where necessary. The objectives are then further detailed in the form of program goals, including numerical targets. Through this procedure, the program mission moves beyond its abstract initial state to a more concrete mission expression of the organization or enterprise.

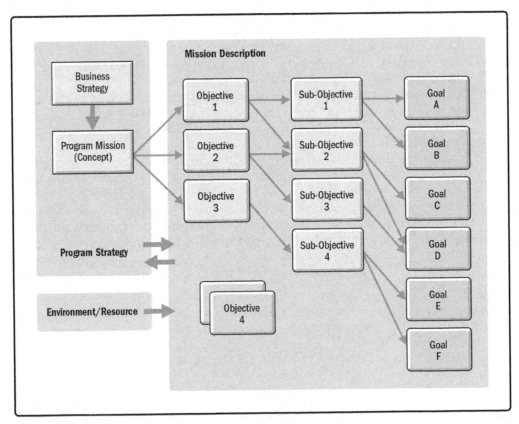

Exhibit 2.2.2: Mission Description (Objectives and Goals)

2.3.2 Example of Mission Definition – JAXA Asteroid Exploration Program

The mission profiling process in a commercial program, where mission-specific conditions are entwined in a complex manner, is difficult for outsiders to understand. To gain a clearer notion about mission profiling, a space program is a helpful example as such a scientific program doesn't have many speculative risk elements in market.

In May 2003, the Japan Aerospace Exploration Agency (JAXA) launched, from a domestic launch site, a spacecraft named Hayabusa (MUSES-C), with a mission to return from an asteroid with a material sample. After collecting samples from the asteroid Itokawa, the spacecraft returned to Earth orbit in June 2010. The capsule containing the samples was released from Hayabusa and landed in the Australian desert. About four decades before Hayabusa, NASA's Apollo program completed sequential missions with a great quantity of Moon rocks brought back to Earth. Those rocks had experienced metamorphoses in the formative period of the moon, during the era of large planet formation. Meanwhile, the asteroid samples brought back by Hayabusa are very small in amount but may clarify what space was like before planets were formed. The success of the Hayabusa program has motivated JAXA to launch the Hayabusa II program.

Based on this example, Exhibit 2.2.3 describes the mission definition process. The supreme purpose (i.e., JAXA's primary strategy) has been "study of the origins of the solar system." The initial mission concept "collection of extraterrestrial samples," was selected from among various missions applicable to the strategy. To achieve this mission, there are a number of possible approaches, including moon landings like those of the Apollo program. Rocks on Mars and other planets, or comet dust, are also candidates for collection. In addition, financial and technological constraints are major influences on strategy selection and execution. Japan's space science programs are particularly constrained by budgets and launch vehicle capacity. Asteroids orbit on the far side of Mars, and extremely long flight is required to reach any of them. However, their gravity is much lower than that of the moon or Mars, providing easy takeoff after sample collection. The great distances involved, which even radio waves take tens of minutes to traverse, cause various technical issues. For example, spacecraft not capable of instantaneous control from the earth need autonomous navigation. After all the various constraints and requirements were analyzed, returning an asteroid sample was selected as the most viable and scientifically valuable program mission.

The subsequent mission definition process determines the program's objectives and goals. The program objectives determined here are (i) round-trip flight to the target body, (ii) sample collection on the target body, (iii) the spacecraft's atmospheric reentry with landing/recovery of the sample capsule, and (iv) sample analysis and subsequent space science studies. The program mission is accomplished only when these four objectives are achieved. As shown in this example, objectives for scientific and technological missions tend to be relatively clear compared with commercial programs. Even so, the program must become more specific by further breaking down these objectives into concrete goals, examples of which are in the boxes at the far right of the exhibit. In many cases, these goals are each adopted as a mission of a relevant individual project. In this diagram, the five goals in the box at the top are the project missions relating mainly to a

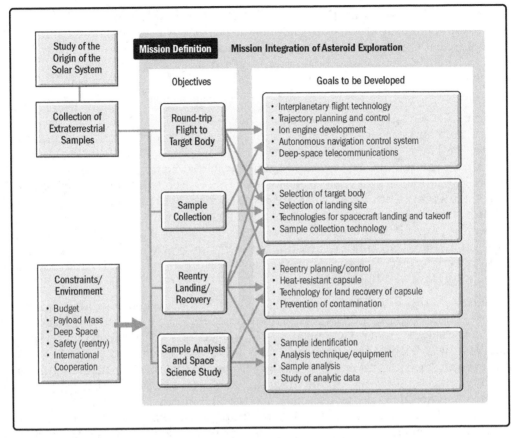

Exhibit 2.2.3: Example of Mission Definition (Hayabusa Program)

round-trip flight to the target body; the four goals in the 2nd box are primarily for sample collection; the next four goals in the 3rd box are relevant to reentry, landing and recovery; and the rest are goals associated with sample analysis and space science studies. However, as indicated by arrows, the goals relating to the flight are also related with sample collection and reentry at the same time. Therefore, each goal must be designed to meet all relevant requirements for the different program objectives.

As previously described, mission definition is the process to define objectives and goals in accordance with the program mission, and mission description is the output of the process.

2.3.3 Value Creation by Mission Definition

Mission definition determines the essence of future value. *Value* here essentially means something of value to the customer, or any relevant feature. Many missions, such as those to improve production efficiency or financial strength, and to develop human resources, may not be directly connected to customers, but they must be related to customer value in the end because the goal of an organization is to increase its customers.

(1) Converting Knowledge into Customer Value

Knowledge is an important value in itself. However, this value cannot become tangible economic value without turning the knowledge into customer value. A powerful historical example is the transistor radio, which triggered the buildup of the enormous consumer electronics industry. The transistor was invented by William Shockley at AT&T's Bell Laboratories, but it was Tokyo Tsushin Kogyo that converted it into general customer value. Later, the company adopted the transistor radio's brand name as its new corporate name, Sony, winning an enormous customer following, as well as a huge amount of economic value.

Similar cases are found in almost every field. The Internet was developed as part of U.S. national defense policy, but it was firms such as Amazon.com, Yahoo!, and Google that started the effective use of it in a way that created broad customer usage value. In a different fashion, when embodied in the Toyota Prius, hybrid car technology gathered environmentally conscious customer value. High-temperature superconductivity is an example of technological knowledge with high potential value, yet no current customer value. The human genome is in a similar situation. The worldwide spread of mobile phones has created customer value featuring communication "anytime, anywhere, with anybody," low prices, and easy portability. It is the companies that have brought customer values to the marketplace that have survived. In this market, competition in creating new customers is quite important, because the less the technological differentiation, the more intense the competition.

Generally, customers are unaware of what kind of value they want. They realize it when businesses present it to them. Examples include Apple's iPod with iTunes, UNIQLO's fleece jackets (see Note 1), and Nintendo's Wii (see Note 2). In short, enterprises need to create new value.

In addition to new product development, enterprises make efforts to lower prices, increase efficiency, improve quality, shorten production periods, create new sales methods, and so forth. In pursuit of an advantageous position in the market, they try to translate their knowledge and capacity into customer value. Reorganization of an enterprise or corporate integration or separation may complement such efforts.

(2) Types of Innovation

Value creation for a private firm may be described as customer-driven new products or their supply methods that are developed through the following types of innovation:

(a) Expanding and enhancing the status quo: Expand or enhance present value, assuming that the future is an extension of the past. This is typical in common practices for steady accumulation of improvements, addition of functions, and increases in product lines. This includes downsizing, transferring, or sale of an unprofitable business segment to reduce losses.

(b) Alternative technologies: Replace the current value supply framework with a technological alternative for expanded or enhanced value. New value can be added by engineering technologies and in many other ways, including changing chemical processes, oil to natural gas conversion for thermal power generation, switching from dedicated software systems to use of packaged software, changing suppliers, and changing methods of funding. These types of changes take place while current products and services are left unchanged for customers.

(c) Qualitative breakthrough: Make drastic changes to products and services. A typical example is digitalization of telecommunication and electronic technologies. Digitalization of telecommunication systems resulted in a rapid increase in information and traffic volume, the spread of communication and data-processing integration with interactive network applications, mobile phone networks, and various other services. There have also been major changes in quality. The bullet train and the expressway network were examples of "hard" infrastructure innovation many decades ago. Deregulation gave opportunities for convenient door-to-door delivery services and 24-hour shops. Privatization of Japan's national telegraph-telephone service and national railways produced a service quality improvement. University hospitals in Japan have made remarkable progress in their service quality, partially owing to their use of digital technology. Innovation in animal display made the Asahiyama Zoo in Asahikawa, Hokkaido (see Note 3) a must-visit site, attracting tourists from all over Japan, even in winter.

(d) Creating unprecedented types of value: Provide entirely new types of products or services, which may partly relate to type (c) innovation above. Typical examples are the Internet and its associated services (e.g., information retrieval, online shopping, online stock trading, etc.). Car navigation systems, ETC (electronic toll collection) systems, hybrid cars, and future electric cars are also examples of this type of innovation

Notes

Note 1. **UNIQLO** is Japan's largest chain of clothing stores. The name is also the brand of the basic goods that the company develops, manufactures in China, and sells from its stores. The company took a great leap forward in 1998 when it popularized its fleece jackets. UNIQLO made its fleece jackets in many colors and sold them at about $20 a jacket, at a time when such jackets were thought as special items with the price of around $100.

Note 2. **The Wii** is a video game console released by Nintendo in 2006. It features a wireless remote control with a motion sensor and the Internet link. A substantial software lineup has attracted even those traditionally unfamiliar with video games, such as women and seniors. Sales amounted to 20,000,000 units 60 weeks after launch.

Note 3. **Asahiyama Zoo** is a municipal zoological garden in Asahikawa City, Hokkaido. Located in the northernmost part of Japan, the zoo suffers a critical disadvantage of - 20°C temperatures in winter. Although there are no pandas or koalas, Asahiyama Zoo's innovation is the animal behavior exhibit system. Visitors see animals engage in natural behavior, not performance: penguins and seals demonstrating their remarkable underwater activities, polar bears diving vigorously into water, orangutans moving from rope to rope far above the ground, and so forth. In 2006 the zoo recorded 3.04 million visitors, ranking next to the 3.5 million visitors to Tokyo's Ueno Zoo, which is Japan's largest.

Modern businesses cannot sustain themselves by merely producing and selling goods. For instance, in Japan even agricultural products require distinctive quality to be competitive. Industrial commodities made in Japan are severely handicapped by both intense price competition with emerging industrial economies and by domestic market prospects that are unpromising due to an aging society with fewer children. An industrial product, whether it is a unit or a system, cannot appeal unless it is combined with some "soft" value.

Given a product's lifecycle, every market stage – introduction, growth, maturity, and decline – must be combined with relevant innovations such as commercialization of technology, response to customer needs or revamping of production process to create and gain value (Moore, 2005, p. 61).

(3) Where to Substantiate Value

The first priority for a company is to determine a focus area in which to create value. This is a matter of how the company defines the market or selects customer needs on which to focus. It also concerns the part of the value chain to focus on among the products offered in the market. There are a variety of strategies, depending on the company's situation and future vision. Exhibit 2.2.4 gives examples classified by primary focus area. Determining the areas for value substantiation depends on how the company can apply its competence in these areas of focus. The task here includes technological capacity, production facilities, brand, sales channels, and other abilities characterizing the company. The company needs to assess its current business model, its system of value delivery to customers, and its profit. It must assess whether these are applicable to the focus areas, or if a new business model is called for. In essence, the company must ask itself how it views its future strategy.

2.4 Scenario Development

The results of mission definition provide the basis for a concrete definition of program mission. It gives an overall picture of the program and how to proceed. However, there are many uncertain factors to be clarified and plans to be framed before turning to action. Scenario development is a necessary process. Several

Focus Areas		Examples
Market	Industry Areas	Automobile, Electronics, Construction, Financing
	Customer Areas	Consumers, Enterprises, Public Agencies
	Customer Attributes	Gender, Age, Standard Products/Commodities, Tailored Products
	Regions	Local, Domestic, Overseas
Value Chain	End-Products Production	Products Design and Assembly, Construction, IT Systems, Medical Products, Household Utensils, Entertainment & Hobby Software (music, games, etc.)
	Parts and Materials Supply	Modules/Parts/Materials Production; Standard products, Tailored products
	Distribution	Wholesale, Retail, Export & Import; Brick and mortar stores, Mail order/e-commerce
	Services	Consumer Services, Medical/Nursing Services, System Operation/Maintenance, Commissioned Production, etc.
	Complementary Products	Expendable/Maintenance Supplies (electric cells, tires, etc.), Individualization

Exhibit 2.2.4: Where to Substantiate Value (Examples)

detailed scenarios must be examined and compared to determine a decisive scenario for execution. Mission definition and scenario development may, in some cases, be done as one process, as both are for devising a concrete and detailed program mission concept. The scenario, the final output of this process or these two processes, forms a framework for program design, which is another step discussed later.

2.4.1 Execution Scenario and Environment Scenario

The product of mission definition is a mission description, which reveals the program finish line. Scenario development is the process for planning the sequence of events for executing the program to its finish.

The scenario is divided in two. One category projects the organization's future actions and their consequences like a play's script, and the other predicts changes in the business environment that the organization could face. In this book, the former is referred to as the *execution scenario* and the latter as the *environment scenario*. As a program usually progresses in a changing environment, it is crucial to understand the environment scenario when determining an execution scenario at the mission profiling stage. An environment scenario may include changes or fluctuations related to population, exchange rates, crude oil prices, the environmental policies of a country, customer preferences in major markets, and competitor behavior.

2.4.2 Environment Scenario and Strategic Thought Paradigm

Because programs are implemented in a business environment subject to the dynamic complexity of the real world, scenario development is not a process for making a plan based on one's own favorite story line. During mission profiling, it is important to clarify environment scenarios through scrutinizing whether the program environment is predictable as an extension of the past and whether, or to what extent, the predicted environment or its projected impact on the program can be controlled or managed within the program.

Van der Heijden, a researcher with advanced experience in strategic scenario planning at Royal Dutch/Shell, studied strategic decisions that organizations make in response to scenarios involving external business environmental change. He proposed three paradigms for strategic decisions: the rationalistic paradigm, the evolutionary paradigm, and the process-oriented paradigm (Van der Heijden, 1996, p. 23).

Strategic decision-making in the rationalistic paradigm selects the most effective among several scenarios predicting future events, based on the assumption that there is one correct answer, and that the strategy is an accurate response to that correct answer. The rationalistic paradigm works only when the environment is relatively stable. In this approach, all predictions are extensions of past experience. Typified by a simple extrapolation of a 10% annual market growth rate, for example, the rationalistic paradigm includes scenario building methods, selecting the most effective one from multiple predictions, using sensitivity analysis or sales estimates with upper/lower limits and maximum likelihood estimates. Prediction of the future as an extension of the past may turn out vastly wrong if unexamined environmental variables change.

In his book, Van der Heijden (1996, p. 27) referred to an effort at crude oil price prediction made by Royal Dutch/Shell experts in 1971. In the Delphi study, no one in the expert group was able to predict future prices to rise above $2 a barrel (see note below). Van der Heijden pointed out that, in a world of extreme volatility, scenarios should describe multiple future visions that are equally probable but different from each other in structure, adding that rationalistic prediction can contribute to corporate performance in a gradually changing environment, but is insufficient to cope with the structural changes we are now facing.

Note
The fourth Arab-Israeli War, which broke out in October 1973, caused crude oil prices to rocket as high as $11.70 per barrel by January 1974, under the influence of the Organization of Petroleum Exporting Countries (OPEC), most members of which are oil-producing countries in the Middle East. This "1973 Oil Crisis" seriously affected the global economy.

Opposed to the rationalistic paradigm is the evolutionary paradigm, which denies the possibility of permanent strategic success in a competitive environment. It acknowledges, instead, that predicting the future is difficult in a world of complexity. Management may respond to every event differently on a best-efforts basis, only to discover over time a certain pattern to successful responses and come to regard this as a strategy. In other words, the evolutionary paradigm views *strategy* as an emergent successful behavioral pattern. Managers whose responsibility is *strategy planning* may not like to think of this as a method of strategy formulation, but it is a truth of industrial history that certain cases should be understood this way.

Between the above two paradigms is the process-oriented paradigm. It presumes that there are no fixed rules for business success, and that success, therefore, depends on original ideas that people have when they are actively engaged in the business. At the core of this paradigm is the following personal process: reflecting on experience; hypothesizing a new worldview based on current reality and the products of reflection; carrying out new action based on the hypothesis; and attaining new experience through the new action. Learning from this loop, which is repetition of the "experience – reflection – hypothesis – action – new experience" cycle, is applied in strategy development. Depending on neither a one-and-only answer, nor on foresight, this process-oriented paradigm pursues outputs through flexibility in step-by-step forward efforts, and responds to structural changes in the environment as well. An example of the process-oriented paradigm is the "emergent learning process" idea of Mintzberg (1987), who advocated that strategies are not outputs of well-organized strategy planning, but formed through a trial-and-error procedure he called "strategy crafting." This "crafting" reflects wisdom and feel gained through past experience.

2.4.3 Framework for Scenario Development
(1) Impact of Environment Scenario
Scenario development is for formulating the program's execution scenarios, which map the course for the organization to follow from present to future. In many cases, a predicted future has two aspects. One is reactive, emphasizing response to external changes predicted in the environment scenario. The

other is proactive, where the organization positively changes itself to effect preferred environmental changes. Many firms appeal to consumers with slogans like "Turn dream into reality," "Changing impossible to possible," or "Grab the future." Inside the firm, managers discuss "What should our organization be like?" or "It's time we broke the status quo." Behind these words is a proactive view of the future, hoping to harness or to change a predicted future in environment scenarios. Programs maintain a balance between such reactive and proactive factors.

It is important to consider how accurately a manager can actually predict the future. Except demographics, Moore's Law, and some other phenomena that allow a long-term (up to 10-year) prediction, most variables are difficult or impossible to predict. These include exchange rates, crude oil prices, and other like fluctuations; unexpected socio-economic changes like economic bubbles and the subprime mortgage financial crisis; as well as changes in the market environment such as technology or service innovation by others, alternative lower-cost technology, and new overseas competition. Difficulty with predictions is obvious. Even government agencies and experts often fail to forecast sudden economic changes. Excessive efforts at prediction are not advisable, even if deemed necessary.

For environmental scenario assessments, both PEST (or PESTEL) analysis and SWOT analysis frameworks are widely used. PEST/PESTEL is used for macro environmental analysis on the societal or state level. PEST stands for Political, Economic, Social, and Technological factors. Adding Environmental and Legal factors makes PESTEL. Here, *environmental* is used in the context of global warming, environmental pollution, and the like, while SWOT is a framework for analyzing the micro-environment that individual companies have to face, such as relevant industries.

For some programs, changes in the external environment may be highly predictable, may have little impact, or may even need to be ignored. However, this is frequently not the case. Larger programs in particular have exposure to various external changes due to their complicated interaction with the environment and their long execution period.

The first thing to do in execution scenario development is to determine whether external environmental changes are material. If they are, the program must be structured with measures responsive to external change. The following are principles for considering such measures:

- Design the program with an external-impact-proof structure.
- Provide a method to alter program structure in response to external changes.
- Reduce the length of the program execution period, or reduce response times in cases of change.

(2) Scenario Elements and Analysis of Their Interrelations

Key elements of an execution scenario must be clarified and detailed enough for individual projects and inter-project relations to be designed at the subsequent stage – the program design stage. The elements of the execution scenario can be divided roughly into target elements, constraint elements, and stakeholder elements.

Categories	Outlines
Target elements	Program targets specified for achievement as program mission values. Numerical targets to be included.
Constraint elements	Internal/external environment, necessary resources & available resources, time, etc.
Stakeholder elements	Clients (direct customers and end-customers) and other stakeholders

Exhibit 2.2.5: Scenario Elements

Target elements: Targets to achieve through organizational action. These targets are designed to realize the mission, which has been detailed and specified at the mission defining stage. The conceptual program mission at the initial stage is redefined in the form of multiple objectives. In general, each objective is further specified with target elements. As already described in section 3.1 of Chapter 1, a program's mission, in many cases, is to create new value through establishing a strong human resource capacity, providing new systems, or launching new products and services. Target elements proposed in a draft scenario must be examined to see if they really ensure mission achievement. In other words, the feasibility of value creation must be confirmed.

Constraint elements: These include the internal/external environment (market, competition, legal restrictions, internal projects competing for the same resources, etc.), necessary resources (human, material, funding, technological, informational, etc.), and time. Environmental elements are mostly clarified in the environment scenario. Some resource-related elements can be translated into money or time elements by outsourcing, for instance.

Stakeholder elements: Stakeholders can be divided into two groups, program customers and others. *Stakeholders* here means those who benefit from the program and its value creation. In this regard, it is important that the scenario clarify what kind of benefit shall be distributed, who among the stakeholders shall receive that benefit, and in what ways the distribution shall take place. In addition, it is necessary to review to which customers the program is really intended to provide the created value. In many cases, there are direct customers with end customers beyond them, forming a hierarchical structure. Take a contract for IT system development, for instance. The system provider's direct customer is the IT division of the ordering company. Those who use or maintain the IT system at the ordering company are indirect customers, and end customers are the consumers who use the IT system. Anticipating and creating end user satisfaction is an important task of the program, not to mention providing satisfaction to direct customers. Stakeholders taking part in the program include the relevant divisions within the organization, consortium partners, and major external suppliers of resources. Each such stakeholder should be allocated an appropriate role in target achievement and constraint satisfaction.

The next step is to examine the interrelationship of scenario elements. The inter-element relationship of stakeholder elements is easier to understand. But the inter-relationship between target elements varies; for example, elements can be cooperative or competitive with each other. They can compete or share business infrastructure, or one element may be dependent on another in terms of time.

The relationship among constraint elements is the same in terms of variety, and execution scenarios should take these interrelations into account.

(3) Coping with Discontinuity
The future of an organization is often considered to be an extension of a series of decisions and actions made in the past that continue into the present and beyond. However, the path to the future may conceal major discontinuities. The organization itself may require some intentional discontinuous change as to its structure, marketing, or technology. When facing such a discontinuity, the program needs a leap within itself, incorporating into its scenarios measures for the organization before and after the leap. Examples of such measures include incorporation of technology or expertise relevant to the change (technology introduction, M&A, consultants, etc.); transitional parallel operation of old and new systems (related to physical resources, human resources, operational infrastructure, and cost); and stocking up on supplies and inventory, financial buffers, and backup systems.

(4) Notes on Examining Scenario Elements
Program managers should keep the following in mind when examining the matters above:

- Constraint elements must be classified as predictions, hypotheses, or wishes. Prediction is to expect that something will occur with high probability, based on careful reasoning. A hypothesis is a prospect as a reasonable inference on the assumption that certain conditions will be met. Confusion between hypotheses, wishes, and predictions can develop into a major obstacle to program execution. Similarly, attention should be paid to expectations about stakeholders' abilities.
- A target element has to be distinguished into two parts: one where prediction is applicable, and the other where countermeasures accounting for prediction errors should be prepared.
- Examination must proceed from future to present, not from present to future. Scenario development must start from what the future is likely to be, coming back to what the present is. This is because when a program is supposed to be completed in three years, for instance, the program's outputs and environment also need to be considered first, as to what they are likely to be in three years.
- In scenario development, especially the process to create scenario alternatives, discussions must capture the essence of the subject at hand. One mission description may lead to widely varying future visions and execution scenarios. Scenario elements (i.e., targets, constraints and stakeholders) should not be too complex. Managers should be oriented not toward minuteness, but toward diversity in modeling that allows wide and varying views of conditions and outlook.

2.4.4 Value Creation in Execution Scenarios
A program is required to be creative enough to realize new value. Of all processes, it is mission profiling (i.e., mission definition and scenario development) that demonstrates creativity in designing new value, and defines at the same time the possible limit to the value to be obtained by the program. It is no exaggeration to say that the task of all subsequent processes is to retain this possibility intact. A program is

a business activity, which has as its essence a goal to unleash creativity, realizing unprecedented value. Although there is no recipe for creativity in mission profiling, presented below are several major areas from which hints can be gathered for program value creation: dominant design, business models and networks, service science, open versus closed knowledge, and M&A and alliances.

(1) Dominant Design

Any product or service is easy to approach in many ways in its introductory phase. A great number of businesses enter the initial market for a product or service by marketing their own version. Designs differ from company to company. At a later stage in the market, gaps widen between individual companies mainly in technological capacity to support quality and costs as well as brand power, standards, regulations, strategic actions such as intellectual property policy and business cooperation, response to customers, and many other factors. Through this process, less competitive firms gradually disappear from the market, which is a move toward oligopoly. At the same time, the basic designs of the product/service converge on a *dominant design* (Utterback, 1994, p. 23). Such phenomena are found in the automotive internal combustion engine and four-wheel structure, which were established about a century ago, as well as in television, semiconductor, computer, personal computer, packaged software, and many other fields.

How to approach the dominant design is a main part of the prerequisite agenda for planning a strategy and program scenarios. In general, the dominant design is an advantageous prerequisite for firms with higher-ranked positions in the market. For those in a lower-ranked position and with insufficient resources, the question is whether to rely on the dominant design in an effort to rise in rank or to attempt a design breakthrough to find a path away from the dominant design. In the automotive and heavy electrical industries, the long lifecycle of dominant technologies helps secure the advantage of leading companies because their capital assets and other resources, accumulated over a long period, create barriers to entry. Even in industrial fields with shorter technology lifecycles, the dominant design is a difficult matter to deal with, even for leading companies. This is called the *innovator's dilemma*, which was revealed through study of the rapid changes in dominant technology for external storage for computers (Christensen, 1997, p. 4). A leading company usually has accumulated technology-, market-, and customer-related assets for its products. These assets can cause dilemmas for such companies when new, promising technology arrives. To replace the current technology with the new one would mean that the company would bear the developing and commercializing costs of the new technology, while simultaneously retaining current products' R&D, production, distribution, and services requirements. It also means reducing the lifecycle of current lucrative products, eventually giving up the huge accumulation of technological assets and production equipment. Adoption of a new technology is, therefore, a difficult decision to make. For example, long-established manufacturers of communication equipment had, in the digitalization of telecommunication, a hard time competing with then-emerging producers such as Cisco Systems. Sharp was the first among the leading television manufacturers to make full-scale technological conversion to liquid crystal displays. What happened between Sharp and other firms is another typical example.

(2) Business Model and Network

To develop a business model is to question what part of business implementation shall earn profit. It is an obvious truth that a traditional industry earns profit by selling products and being paid for it. However, this is not always the case with networking business, where there are usually two types of customers. Typical of the networking business is commercial broadcasting, which is run on commercial message (CM) fees paid by customers, that is, sponsors. The other type of customer is the general audience of the broadcast, who is not the source of income but whose satisfaction raises program ratings, which is the key to sustaining the CM business. Newspapers and magazines earn profit from sales of advertising space and from subscription fees. Credit cards profit from collecting fees paid by distributors of goods and services, as well as from credit card membership fees paid in smaller amounts and from interest on installment sales.

The wide spread of digitalization has caused the recent rapid increase in networking-type markets and products, typical examples of which are PC operating systems (Windows), the Internet's portal sites and search engines (Yahoo!, Google, etc.), and video game devices (Nintendo DS, PlayStation, Xbox, etc.). There are two types of customers (i.e., profit sources) in these markets: consumers, and application software and content suppliers. When looking at these products with their two types of customers from the viewpoint of two-sided platforms, a similar relationship structure is found in such markets as mobile telecommunications (consumers and mobile phone distributors), electricity retailing (consumers and power companies) and DVD players (consumers and content producers). Due to their attribute of externality, networking platforms of this type tend to prefer networks with a larger population. Once the membership reaches a critical mass, the law of increasing returns starts to work, consequently leading the network to a state of oligopoly, where a very small number of firms are dominant. Obtaining the prestige of being the *de facto* standard is an advantage for a firm to reach critical mass or to retain its product/service prices. At the same time, alliances with other firms, or disclosure of the standard, in an effort toward prestige, could result in lower profits. Even so, to be a *de facto* standard is difficult without the participation of other firms. Here lies a dilemma again. In the case of two-sided platforms, scenarios to win advantage in the market should be planned by examining how to charge the two types of customers for their respective purchases and how to solve the dilemma of *de facto* standards, taking into account the platform's characteristics, the market situation (customers, demand and players), and the technological position of the firm (Eisenmann, Parker, & Van Alstyne, 2006; Yamada, 2007).

(3) Service Science

The latter half of the 20th century was the beginning of "affluent society," with no fear of starvation for significant numbers of people. Inhabitants of this society do not seek "what things are to them" (i.e., the thing itself) but "what things do to them" (i.e., the utility). They seek what can be found in services. Up until now, most programs and projects have focused on "hard" objectives, but to create the value that people seek now, services must be one main objective to focus on. Selling services has characteristics distinct from selling goods, as indicated in Exhibit 2.2.6.

Characteristics	Outline
Intangibility	Service product has no tangible form.
Simultaneity	Production and consumption occur simultaneously.
Extinction	Service vanishes the moment it is produced and cannot be held in stock.
Heterogeneity	The value of service varies by provider, place and customer.

Exhibit 2.2.6: Characteristics of Service Business (Kameoka, 2007, p. 18)

Due to their characteristics, service businesses impose various constraints and challenges upon providers. A major problem is that the service business is extremely labor-intensive, which is attributable to the business's simultaneity and extinctive nature. Higher profits cannot be earned without an increase in manpower, which means that a simple business model will soon reach the limit of its growth. What is expected of a program, in this regard, is to create systems for profitability improvement. The program's scenario development is, therefore, required to conceptualize a business model that embodies the essence of the service business, and it must develop hard and soft systems based on that business model.

The intangibility of service businesses also causes a major problem: difficulty in pricing. It is no easy task for both providers and customers to assess the quality of service. Frequently targeted for criticism is the pricing of IT solutions, where prices tend to be calculated on a labor-hour basis, regardless of the engineers' ability or quality of work. In the case of medical services, the problem may become visible in the form of needlessly long hospitalization. In spite of various attempts to resolve these issues, they remain the service business' inherent difficulty.

Simultaneity relates to time. Most provision of services occurs with the provider and the customer sharing both time and space. This is not just a matter of service site staffing, but also implicates the importance of certain criteria for efficiency as well as the quality of the staff working at the service site. However, the progress of information network technology has enabled keeping service staff in regions of lower labor costs. For example, U.S. firms have located call centers in India, and Japanese firms have used Okinawa or China.

Perishability means service cannot be kept in stock. This indicates the importance of allocating a huge amount of human and other resources to service sites in order to keep up with changes in demand.

Heterogeneity is an issue from the standpoint of placing importance on homogenous services. Solutions for this include homogenizing shops and other service sites, and making service staff quality equal at all sites by training, manuals, and uniforms. Depending on the customer category, deliberate individuality and heterogeneity should be prioritized in such service businesses as high-end hotels, classy boutiques, consultants, and advanced medical services.

These characteristics may be constraints on service business, but at the same time, in some cases they can be advantages for the business to expand. Simultaneity and perishability are the reason for no importation of services from elsewhere; consequently, competition is limited and the business is highly driven by cultural factors like language and custom. Intangibility makes it impossible for services to be designed with engineering theories, but it works as a barrier to entry from elsewhere. The quality and efficiency of service products can be improved only by using accumulated patterned information about service demand and supply.

(4) Open Knowledge and Closed Knowledge

The main force that drove industrial growth in the 20th century was manufacturing. Manufacturers at the time were operating primarily with their own knowledge. They would individually develop new knowledge through internal innovation efforts that drove new product development. They kept new knowledge inside to protect it from being copied and to keep their advantage in the market. Recent sophistication in products and production methods has changed this situation; today solo development efforts are not only inefficient but also disadvantageous in the market (Fujimoto et al., 2001, p. 62; Gawer & Cusumano, 2002, p. 51; Aoki & Ando, 2002, p. 165; Chesbrough, 2003, p. 63).

Open knowledge means that a firm's own information is made open to the public in order to use external skills and capabilities for business growth. Major advantages of open knowledge are:

- Disclosure of the interface of a firm's own products stimulates complementary good production by other firms. Typical examples demonstrating this are personal computers and their peripherals or application software, and game consoles and game software. When a firm needs large resource mobilization for developing and marketing an entire system, drawing out contributions from specialist firms improves overall efficiency, expanding the market as a whole, and securing the firm's profitability. Open knowledge is frequently found in markets where network effects are probable. A modularized products business creates an opportunity for open knowledge to be even more advantageous.
- As typified by Linux, keeping information open facilitates innovation where ideas from both inside and outside of firms can be coordinated.

Open knowledge, however, has disadvantages too. Technology developed through open knowledge can be targeted by free riders. Strategic plans are necessary regarding measures to counter this disadvantage and to determine the relationship between what to open and what to close. A system products supplier may open the interface to suppliers of complementary goods, parts, or production equipment, but must secure domains closed to those outside the firm. To gain profit from a modularized business where interface information is open, it is usual to close the module's interior to protect against copying.

(5) Intercompany Integration and Cooperation

Reinforcing business activity by corporate integration (M&A) or business cooperation (alliances) constitutes an important field of program management. The motivation for these strategies varies, case by case. Automotive companies and high-volume retail chains may seek economies of scale. Financial institutions may attempt to reinforce their capital and business footholds. Manufacturers may want to supplement or expand their technologies and product lines. Telecommunication carriers may intend to enlarge service coverage and the membership population by using the network's externalities. In the globalizing economy and market of today, large-scale M&A has become a trend and is common, involving even corporations from countries where business environment and corporate culture differ substantially. The consequences of these strategies have a great positive or negative impact, even on such business giants as automotive companies.

Business expansion by corporate integration does not mean immediate realization of economies of scale. If operated improperly, the integrated organization suffers diseconomies of scale instead. Offering an array of goods ranging from standard to high-end does not always bring a product or market synergy effect. Purchasing a firm with unique technology will be in vain if the experts in the technology leave the firm or a proper environment is not prepared for using that technology. The important thing is to identify the value that the M&A should create and determine the process to achieve it.

With all these possible challenges, achieving economies of scale is one of the most important competition strategies. Japanese firms, however, tend to turn away from M&A, probably due to their special care for their own corporate cultures. In addition, Japanese anti-monopoly policy is not lenient. During the past two decades of economic globalization, overseas enterprises have been actively executing such strategies pursuing concentration in core competence through M&A, while Japanese enterprises have not. As a result, leading Japanese corporations that are domestically regarded as giants are often inferior on the world scene in terms of market share and growth.

Partial sell-offs of a firm's units, or partial closure of a plant or business base, is also a strategic program. Its mission, therefore, should be defined with careful contemplation of goals.

2.4.5 Variation and Selection of Execution Scenarios

Scenario development is the process for determining a scenario that supports the program architecture and project design to be carried out in the subsequent *program design stage.* In scenario development, several scenarios that look promising are planned and compared to select the best one, which becomes the execution scenario. This is because, even if the basic framework through which value will be created has been determined as discussed above, there may be multiple approaches to realizing it. Candidate scenarios have to be detailed to some degree, and examined in terms of progress over time.

Variations in each scenario plan need to be highly feasible from the viewpoints of business strategy and the external environment. Exhibit 2.2.7 shows a variety of viewpoints from which to create such variations.

Comparative evaluation of scenario plans may be approached in various ways, depending on the organization's or program manager's sense of value or the program's situation. Noteworthy viewpoints for evaluation are summarized in Exhibit 2.2.8. Generally speaking, what should take the first priority in evaluation is the effectiveness of program outcomes, followed by efficiency. A program without effect is meaningless and harmful, while an inefficient program diminishes the effect. Feasibility is certainly the vital factor of program implementation. Low-feasibility scenarios must be excluded, but for the purpose of evaluation, the first thing to do is to focus on an effective and efficient project, and then consider how to enhance its feasibility.

Categories	Key Variations	Examples
Market and Product	• Market to focus on • Product line	• Customers, regions, sales channels, price ranges, etc. • Brand, product model configuration/variety, market release interval, etc.
Approach	• Increase in profits • Program executing body • Market penetration • Early release	• Increase in sales, improved profitability, reduced competition through M&A, etc. • In-house unit, consortium, technological partnership/licensing, etc. • Advertisement, test marketing, entry model, free samples, etc. • Use of existing products, use of many standard parts, technology outsourcing, manufacturing outsourcing, etc.
Challenge Hardship and Feasibility	• Price • Feasibility • Distinctive Feature	• High performance/low priced, simple/low priced, high performance/high priced, etc. • Low performance and certain to succeed; high performance with a strict delivery date, etc. • Super-low priced, world's highest performance, *de facto* standard, best in the region, etc.
Response to Environmental Complexity	• Environmental changes • Support from stakeholders	• Easy-to-modify design, swift response to changes, step-by-step expansion, etc. • Consortium, open innovation, licensing, use of specialists, etc.

Exhibit 2.2.7: Viewpoints for Scenario Variations (Examples)

It should be kept in mind that feasibility is subject largely to a scenario's constraint elements, such as resources and response to changes in environment. Speed of program implementation is closely related to feasibility, while having great impact on the effectiveness of outcomes and the efficiency of the program in some cases.

In practice, it is impossible to make scenario plans for all possible variations and evaluate them comparatively. Usual practice is to filter the possibilities in advance to get those that are consistent with the organization's basic strategies, market position, experience, available resources, sales channels, and environmental scenarios, and then to develop several scenario plans for detailed examination. The filtering is usually conducted by the program manager, who makes full use of insight, knowledge, and experience to get candidate scenario plans, with some help from experts.

Evaluation Viewpoints	Outline
Outcome Effectiveness	Viewpoint from target elements: acquisition of market share, unique competitiveness (price, brand, quality, etc.) and technological/sales capacity; reinforcement of specific systems, etc.
Program Efficiency	Viewpoint from target elements: efficiency in system construction phase and operation phase, organizational operation, especially of multiple projects, etc.
Implementation Feasibility and Speed	Viewpoint from constraint elements: technological capability, resources, cost, response to environmental changes, speed at obtaining outcome
Stakeholder Satisfaction	Viewpoint from stakeholder elements: customer satisfaction, other stakeholder satisfaction, win-win relationship building, etc.
Lifecycle	Judging throughout the entire lifecycle of the program (planning, system construction, operation, etc.)

Exhibit 2.2.8: Viewpoints for Scenario Evaluation

3. Program Integration Management (2): Program Design

3.1 Objective

The objective of program design is to design a program architecture that enables achievement of the individual goals of projects and the holistic objectives of the entire program, as have been specified through mission profiling and scenario development. Program design, therefore, includes planning of the systems for execution of the designed program and its subordinate projects.

Program architecture design defines projects that are to share functions required for program execution, and the interfaces among the projects. Important features of the program architecture are that:

- The targets of business strategy are included.
- The execution strategy is designed to ensure efficient and secure execution of the program.
- The program's lifecycle is designed to facilitate appropriate control of program execution.
- The response to uncertainties (risks) is considered, based on the program's environmental scenario.

Although the targets of business strategy have already been set out as individual project goals in the execution scenario, they need to be reconfirmed in this program design process. These features of the program architecture must be incorporated in the program design, taking into consideration the organizations for program execution and the plans for program execution infrastructure.

3.2 Program Architecture

(1) Program Architecture

Program architecture is a formal description or a conceptual model representing the program, which allocates processes to multiple projects for accomplishing the detailed mission goals defined by an execution scenario.

A program is one type of process system. System architecting needs such elements as a systems approach, purpose orientation, and modeling methodology. A systems approach is to "grasp a system as an integrated whole." This is particularly important when making value judgments to determine "what is necessary and what is not" and when making technical decisions to judge "what is feasible." This

---

Objectives of Program Design
(1) To Design Program Architecture
• Definition of projects (assignment of goals/functions) and their interfaces
(a) Achievement of individual goals and general objectives
(b) Inclusion of strategy – i.e., strategic targets and program execution strategy (Chapter 3)
(c) Design of program lifecycle
(d) Response to uncertainty (risks) arising from environmental change (Chapter 3)
(2) To develop a scheme for execution
(a) Organization for program execution and the community of practice (Chapter 5)
(b) Infrastructure for program execution

Exhibit 2.3.1: Objectives of Program Design

is a process to pursue values that can be realized only by an integrated system, not by fragmented elements (Rechtin, 1997, p. 9).

From the systems approach, mission profiling is a process primarily focusing on "what is necessary" although its feasibility is basically assessed in the scenario development process. In contrast, program design is a process to make sure of "what is feasible" by a concrete approach while satisfying the necessity. From the viewpoint of purpose orientation, while the main concerns of the mission profiling process are clarification of program objectives and their breakdown into individual goals, the program design process aims at creation of architecture for achieving these goals and the consequent accomplishment of the holistic objectives of the program.

Modeling may play versatile roles, among which are (i) generating a common understanding of the system among stakeholders, (ii) coordinating individual design activities to ensure the integrity of the entire system, and (iii) supporting the designing process by organizing a systematic record of decisions made. Modeling methodology differs depending on what kind of role is needed (Rechtin, 1997, p. 119). During program design, projects that constitute subsystems are defined as functional models. Mutual relations of these functional models are then systematized and defined as a structural model, which is the program architecture.

(2) Parameters of Architecture Design

Exhibit 2.3.2 indicates the key parameters, which include a variety of requirements, variables, and conditions that require consideration when designing program architecture. The execution scenario assumes that these parameters are mutually consistent, which must be confirmed during the designing process.

Confirmation starts with examining individual goals specific to each project, and then assessing whether those goals will lead to accomplishing the holistic objectives of the program. The program lifecycle must be punctuated by milestones in order that the entire program keeps its integrity along the time phases for accomplishing holistic objectives. Environmental conditions include a competitive environment (demand and competition in the market, technological innovation, the emergence of new markets, etc.), demographic changes (e.g., the customer lifecycle), social and economic changes, regulations, and other things. A competitive market environment, often given top priority among environmental conditions, is actually a matter of the future market environment at the time of program completion, or a matter for its operational/service phase, rather than a present concern. Resources include human, material, financial, infrastructure, information, and knowledge resources. These, with the exception of material and financial resources, do not exist independently, but are part of relevant organizations, so when actually designing a program, the availability of resources is in many cases determined on the basis of the organizations as units. It is therefore important that those designing a program be fully aware of project implementation capacity, as well as of the organization's resource-related attributes. Material resources (raw materials, parts, equipment, etc.) are basically a matter of the individual project using them, except when those resources have a significant impact on the program's holistic objectives. In that situation the physical resources are a matter of program design, which itself requires knowledge about availability and supply in the market.

Key Parameters of Architecture Design
(a) Requirements from holistic objectives and individual goals
(b) Requirements from program lifecycle
(c) Environmental conditions
(d) Resources (including organization and supply market)

Exhibit 2.3.2: Key Parameters of Architecture Design

3.3 Types of Projects

In accordance with their roles to play in a program, projects can be categorized into three types: (i) *scheme-type projects* to plan and consider a program, (ii) *system-type projects* to build systems for value creation, and (iii) *service-type projects* to realize value through using and operating the systems.

(1) Scheme-type Projects

A scheme-type project handles program profiling and basic design processes in a large-scale program. Such projects typically are for business launch programs, where a general framework is conceptualized and a basic plan is developed. In a large-scale program carried out by a governmental agency or by an owner firm, a process preparing program execution, including contractor selection by issuing an RFP, can be regarded as a scheme-type project. In such a case, the contractor firm often carries out a scheme-type project as well, such as by making a feasibility study of the program prior to proposal preparation, as a risky program would also be risky for the contractor.

There are scheme-type projects that lead to stakeholders creating new joint business frameworks very early in the program lifecycle. These arise before the formal launch of a program, and involve coordinating the different interests of relevant stakeholders. For example, it is a scheme-type project that binds resource-owning countries, resource developers, resource users, and institutional investors in the framework of a resource development program. Similar functions of this type of project are also found in various business opportunities, such as industrial complex development, urban redevelopment involving multiple landowners, IC ticket businesses connecting different railway companies, and convenience store franchising, where a network of stores concentrated in a particular area is the key advantage. Such scheme-type projects are also found in gigantic corporations for interdivisional coordination of interests across company-wide programs.

(2) System-type Projects

A system-type project is a project that carries out system creation. Specifically, a system-type project typically constructs, builds, or installs a variety of systems, including plant facilities, production equipment, office buildings, IT solutions or information network systems, and their combinations. In addition, system developments for new products, overseas production systems, new distribution channels, and nationwide delivery are included in a broader sense in the system-type project. In most programs, a system-type project does not work alone, but in combination with other projects to build an integrated system, as depicted in Exhibit 2.3.3(b).

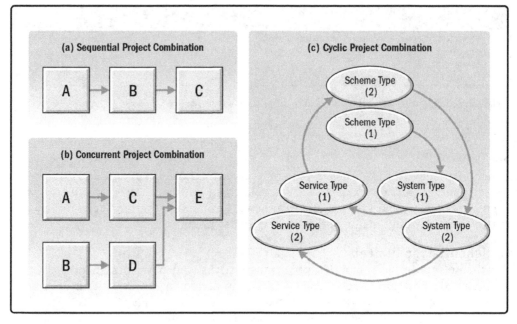

Exhibit 2.3.3: Basic Combinations of Projects

(3) Service-type Projects

Subsequent to system-type project completion is a service-type project, which delivers customer value through day-to-day operation and use of the completed system. This is the process where commercial enterprises earn profits. The duration of continuous use of any one system is ever shorter in current times, and many modern systems have the nature of being fixed-term "projects." This is why P2M defines this process as a service-type project. Nevertheless, some service-type projects are virtually, in nature, permanent operations.

A service-type project is normally explained as being executed upon the delivery of a system-type project's outcome. Use and operation of a system, however, requires a variety of preparations, including staff training, material procurement, license acquisition, and advertisement. In reality, service activities need to start even before delivery of the outcome.

3.4 The Basic Architecture Model

(1) Basic Combinations of Projects

When viewed as combinations of multiple projects, programs can be described as being of three types of sequential, concurrent, and cyclic (or spiral) combinations, as shown in Exhibit 2.3.3. These types frequently combine. For example, a cyclic project combination could include a concurrent project combination as one of its steps (PMAJ, 2007, p. 117).

(2) The Basic Architecture Model

Program architecture is the structure of an entire program. Exhibit 2.3.4 shows the basic model of program architecture. In many cases, program architecture consists

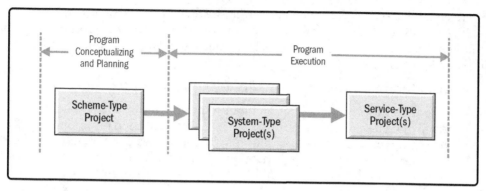

Exhibit 2.3.4: Basic Model of Program Architecture

of one scheme-type project, a number of system-type projects, and one or more service-type projects. It is not unusual for more than 10 system-type projects to be combined sequentially or concurrently in a program.

Although the basic form of a program is a configuration of the three types of projects, it is not always the case that all three must be present. When system construction is outsourced to an external contractor, it may often appear to the contractor as though it were a program without a service-type project, because use and operation of the completed system is usually transferred to the program owner. For the program owner, in contrast, there is no direct execution of system-type projects, just monitoring and control of their progress.

3.5 The Architecture Design Process

The program architecture design process requires inclusion of strategy, conformity to program lifecycle requirements, efficiency and reliability of program execution, and response to uncertainty regarding environmental changes, as explained in section 3.1.

(1) Inclusion of Strategy

Strategy, as defined strategic goals, is set as part of a program before the scenario development stage. In the program design process, the strategy must be carefully included through combination of feasible, effective, and efficient projects.

(2) Program Lifecycle

Program design defines program lifecycle along with each related individual project's lifecycle.

In program execution, phase gate management is implemented, based on program milestones, for timely confirmation and necessary control of the program's progress. Except for some cases, freedom in planning program schedules and milestones is very limited, due to factors including market competition; schedules for decision-making, budgeting, or financing on the customers' part; test-run periods; and business partners' situations. Obviously it is crucial that the program schedule and its milestones be coordinated according to the time required for each project. Program lifecycle is designed as a trade-off between internal/external factors and overall control based on a program execution strategy. If this trade-off does not work well, it may be necessary to make changes in project scope or the project execution organization. In some cases, change may be needed even in the program architecture, by adding or eliminating some projects.

Program lifecycle has to be designed considering two important aspects:

- Program lifecycle is a foundation for designing projects, and it should be comprised of phases for controlling program implementation duration properly.
- During the program lifecycle, phase-by-phase analysis of program attributes is important because these attributes (cost, cash flow, risk characteristics, environmental burden, etc.) tend to differ significantly from phase to phase (PMAJ, 2007, p. 124).

(3) Efficiency and Certainty

To capture higher value, a program must be equipped with systems for efficient and steadfast execution. Of primary importance is program architecture design, which creates a decentralized, autonomous structure and controls it. The purpose of autonomous decentralization is to delegate responsibility and authority to appropriate units of the projects, so that:

- The projects' activities can be carried out concurrently and autonomously.
- Each project is characterized by its own scope of expertise, enabling corresponding specialists to form its executing organization.
- Diseconomies of scale in management can be avoided as the span of control can be kept an appropriate size.

Concurrent activities ensure time efficiency. Expertise secures work quality, efficiency, and steadfast performance. Avoidance of excessively centralized management and a time-consuming multi-level reporting hierarchy improves managing efficiency.

Autonomous decentralization does not mean a *laissez-faire* system where rules are absent. Each project needs to be equipped with systems to monitor the status quo and proper measures to control deviations from the plan. More specifically, plans and contracts should stipulate systems and measures, including:

- Regular reporting and discussion on project progress
- Plans to identify and control the interfaces between interrelated projects
- Procedures of review, verification, and validation at program lifecycle milestones
- Other necessary systems and measures according to program content.

As is obvious from the ideas above, a program exceeding a certain scale may require a hierarchical structure where each project has some number of subordinate projects.

(4) Response to Environmental Changes

Program execution is made over a long period of time, during which the program environment can change in unpredictable ways. In general, response to this uncertainty is called risk management. Some environmental scenarios may indicate that future market trends are highly uncertain, and that incorrect positioning could result in catastrophe for the business entity. In such a case, it is important that measures to deal with the uncertainty be developed as part of program execution strategy. These must be incorporated into program structure. An example of this is to plan a program with optional strategies, assuming that the program architecture itself can be changed during program execution (see Chapter 3).

3.6 Modularization and Design Rules
(1) Modularization of Industrial Products

System architecture is a framework that enables structural independence and functional integration of system elements. In other words, it is a way to plan allocation of a system's overall functions to its physically independent components. In the manufacturing industry, the excellence of product architecture is the main driving force of corporate performance. Determination of this architecture takes place in the early stages of innovation, and is closely related to R&D (Garud, 2003, p. 117).

Modules are defined as units that are structurally independent, but which functionally collaborate in a larger system. Given the functions of a system, it is natural that one would think of breaking it down to appropriately independent functional units, or modules. How can a complex system be appropriately decomposed into modules? What are the clues to follow for delineating modules from the intricacy of correlations? These questions were not clearly answered until recently.

The 1990s saw progress in the study of product modularization. The idea of modularized design is quite helpful for designing a program, because the modules are in fact what we call *projects* in the program (see note below).

Note

As one example, in their "Design Rules," Baldwin and Clark (2000) presented a detailed and comprehensive discussion on the theory and effects of modularized design of multiple and intricately correlated subsystems and components typical of computer systems.

Those engaged in designing complicated systems are often stuck in circles going nowhere – design decisions for element A influence those of element B, which then influences element C, in turn influencing the design of element A. In such a situation, not only is a lot of time consumed before the designs of correlated elements are finalized, but also other parts of the system cannot be designed prior to that. The inevitable changes in any finalized designs could influence the entire system. The more complicated a system is, the more carefully this problem should be avoided.

This problem can be significantly reduced if an authority in charge of the entire system designates some design parameters in advance, facilitating the design of a hierarchical structure of block-type architecture, or modularized system architecture. Such pre-designation of design parameters may not be sufficient logically, for system optimization. However, as many have experienced, a system can be created better and more efficiently when individuals concentrate only on the focused task, clearly designated, instead of being dismayed by all the requirements displayed before them, which overloads individual capacity.

(2) Significance of Modularization Theory in Program Design

Seasoned program managers in general try their best to design a program's projects to be independent of each other as much as possible and free of mutual interference. The reason is that independent projects should be executed concurrently to reduce the entire period of program execution. Another important reason is because the significant interdependence that remains among projects implies a major risk that one project's trouble could spread to others. In the case of a large system-constructing program, where projects are subcontracted to different firms, it is probable that trouble with one project will arouse serious questions about who is responsible and how to share costs among the firms. This is exactly why a program structure comprising clean-interfaced projects that are highly independent with clearly-defined responsibility areas is called for, and program managers try hard to maintain interfaces in healthy condition. Therefore, if we regard projects as modules in a program, the independence of each module as discussed in the previous paragraph is already "professional common sense," beyond dispute among seasoned program managers.

This professional common sense is tacit knowledge learned from personal, and often bitter, experiences of failure during projcet management practices.. The significance of this theory on the modularity is that it clearly explains, in the form of explicit knowledge, the importance of what the tacit knowledge has been indicating. It more concretely specifies points calling out for attention in program design.

The other significance is that the theory has clarified, through its formalized concept of modularity, why designs should be examined, based in the assumption that "changes" can occur on a module level or sub-module level. This functions to optimize program design through progressive elaboration and response to environmental changes over the long period of a program's lifecycle. Freedom of design options – such as separation, exchange, deletion or addition – given to projects or sub-projects, can be considered an increase in program value.

3.7 Concept Plan Documents

The output of program design is called various things, including *concept plan document*, *basic plan*, or *system concept plan*. Such documents compile program objectives, the program's basic plans and scope, the basic plans of individual projects, as well as other items in the basic plans. They represent:

(a) Materials for assessing the appropriateness of concept plans as a program execution plan
(b) Basic documents defining requirements and baselines for overall program execution
(c) Basic documents defining requirements and baselines for each project's execution.

Basic documents (b) and (c) are prepared primarily as base materials for assessment (a) and are officially registered as basic documents for program execution after passing through assessment or undergoing amendment.

The contents of concept plan documents are as indicated in Exhibit 2.3.5, with variations according to project.

Categories		Main Contents
Program	Basic elements	Program objectives, background, executing organization
	Mission definition	Mission description (specified objectives and goals)
	Scenario development	Environmental scenario, scenario alternatives and selected execution scenario (including feasibility study)
	Program design	Program architecture, outline of individual project scope, lifecycle and schedule, executing organization, cost estimate, financial plan, investment recovery plan, main resources, quality and other issues, program execution strategy, risks, conditions, etc.
Individual Projects	Basic elements	Project mission, project scope, lifecycle and schedule, executing organization, cost estimate, main resources, quality and other issues, project execution strategy, risks, conditions, draft of RFP (when needed), etc.

Exhibit 2.3.5: Concept Plan Documents

3.8 Concept Plan Review

In the final step of the program concept plan phase, the designed program is reviewed for feasibility as to whether achievement of the given objectives of the program mission is ensured. According to the review, a decision is made on whether to execute the program. Participation by executives from the principal organization is crucial to this process, because a program has a significant impact on the business entity and its future operations, usually involving a huge amount of investment. The review meeting may take various forms—conference-type program reviews, discussions at boards of directors meetings, technical assessments by senior professionals, examination by the financial division, and combinations of all of these. The objective of these review opportunities is to properly and efficiently verify the designed program's effectiveness.

To achieve this objective, it is important that:

- The review materials (the concept plan documents indicated in Exhibit 2.3.5) correctly reflect the essence of the program's concept plan.
- Reviewers, whatever their offices and positions may be, are capable and willing to evaluate the concept plan accurately, based on their expertise and experience.
- The objectives and processes of each review activity are precisely laid out in advance so as to provide the required breadth of coverage.

4. Program Integration Management (3): Integration of Program Execution

4.1 The Processes of Program Execution Integration Management

Once an acceptable plan is approved, the program is launched, with each project executed in an autonomous decentralized manner. The basic example of execution is given in Exhibit 2.4.1, which roughly divides the process into two categories: (i) Program Execution Integration Management, carried out by the program manager in accordance with the program concept plan, and (ii) Project Management of individual projects, executed according to project-related basic elements (mission, goal, lifecycle, budget, etc.) defined in the program concept plan.

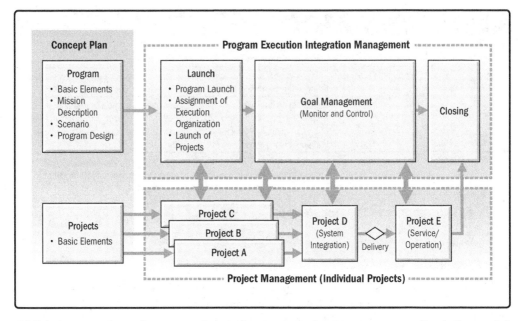

Exhibit 2.4.1 Process of Program Execution Integration Management (Basic Example)

This is the stage where qualitative change occurs. What has been a desk plan is now transferred to the real world, where many managers and staff members are mobilized. The first priority is to set up a program integration management organization. Executing organizations are determined for launching each individual project, and each project manager and executing organization is vested with authority and responsibility for proceeding.

The program integration management organization consists of the program manager and staff members. Its role is to monitor and control project activities so as to integrate the program toward the accomplishment of total program objectives.

Exhibit 2.4.2 shows the program manager's main duties, which can be largely divided into external and internal duties. The latter is further divided into relations to the program as a whole and to individual projects placed under it.

4.2 Program External Relations

Programs are businesses in themselves. The program manager represents a business called the "program" and bears full responsibility for conducting external negotiations. The program manager's primary duties of importance are to submit reports to, obtain approvals from, and coordinate with senior stakeholders, typically the program owner. These stakeholders may be (i) the division manager or the board of directors, when the program is planned in-house by a company, (ii) the counterpart of a client company, or (iii) a senior department with budgetary authority, in a government program. This duty vests the program manager with the responsibility for program execution, which is a duty of ultimate importance. Other duties of the program manager include public relations and negotiations with

Duty Categories	Outline		
External Duties	(a) Relations with senior stakeholders (report/approval, coordination, etc.) (b) Relations with third-party stakeholders (negotiation, PR, etc.) (c) Securing finance and other resources		

Internal Duties	Program as a whole	(a) Launch the program; create a program management organization
		(b) Prepare a program/projects execution environment
		(c) Goal management:
		  • Create a reporting/instruction system
		  • Monitor and control (holistic objectives, schedule, costs)
		  • Coordinate projects	

	Individual Projects	(a) Launch individual projects (e.g., set up or select executing organizations; assign or contract the executing authority; and determine project missions/goals) (b) Goal management (monitor, control, promote/assist) (Note: Responsibility for each individual project's execution rests on the respective project manager.)	

Exhibit 2.4.2: Main Duties of Program Integration Management (Execution Phase)

third-party stakeholders involved in program execution (e.g., administrative agencies, consumers, local communities, the media, etc.). Additionally, the duties include securing, or negotiating to secure, funds for program execution, as well as other resources essential to program operation, including raw materials and infrastructure (e.g., telecommunication networks, roads, harbors, etc.).

4.3 Internal Processes of Program Integration Management
The internal processes of program integration management can cover program relations and subordinate projects relations.

4.3.1 Program Launch
(1) Preparation for Program Execution Organization
Program execution requires individual project management organizations to cooperate with each other under a program management organization that integrates the entire program.

The project mission and other basic elements of individual projects are defined in the program concept and planning phase. For program integration management during execution, the first duty includes (i) specifying an organizational system to execute individual projects, (ii) assigning authority and responsibility to each organization, and (iii) launching projects in accordance with the basic requirements. The program management organization should be expanded and restructured, because the magnitude of work increases greatly in execution phase duties.

The organizations in charge of individual projects frequently require a major mobilization of human resources. Some such organizations are clearly specified in the concept and planning phase. However, it is common to reestablish an optimum organizational system by reviewing in-house organizational structures, or to introduce external resources for the projects through consortia, joint ventures, and procurement by RFP. Whatever the method, preparing such program execution organizations with clearly-defined authorities and responsibilities is important at the program launch stage.

(2) Shared Program Vision

A program involves a great number of people and organizations. To achieve strategic goals effectively, in spite of volatility in the external environment, all stakeholders must have a common understanding of the program's essence and be convinced of it firmly enough to unite their efforts in realizing the projects to which they are assigned. Shared vision requires a shared understanding of the program among all stakeholders. According to P2M, it is crucial that the stakeholders share a common understanding of the program mission's essence, and of the program architecture, to accomplish the mission (PMAJ, 2007, p. 92). This shared vision creates a shared perspective on judging value, allowing for justification of decisions made in the course of program execution. P2M points out the importance of a "community of practice" as a platform to ensure such a common understanding.

(3) Review of the Execution Plan

After the organizational system for project execution is determined, each project organization builds a reliable execution plan using methods most suited to their own experience and capacity. This is unnecessary if the execution plan has been developed carefully enough in the previous concept and planning phase. However, if the project organizations and project managers are newly appointed, the program manager should review the execution plans, taking into account the project organizations' capacity and procedures.

Missions, goals, schedules, budgets, and other targets and plans are defined in the concept plan documents as each project's basic elements, shown in Exhibit 2.3.5. The concept plan is reviewed or coordinated for the optimal assignment of duties, taking into consideration the capacity of and risks to the newly determined organization, before it is finalized as a plan of execution. Review and coordination activities cover the scope of each project, interfaces among projects (hardware, software, information transfer, and delivery schedules), milestones and their assessment plans, schedules, budgets, and technical risk measures (PMAJ, 2007, p. 136 [Detailed plan for execution]). To the extent that the project plan review (see Section 4.3.2) does not deviate from the concept plan (mission achievement, schedule, budget, finance, etc.), a modified program plan is drawn up to create a baseline for program goal management in subsequent processes.

(4) Arrangements for Total Optimization

Program architecture is designed to correlate projects to achieve the entire program's success or the program's total optimization. However, success is not guaranteed, because each project organization has its own objectives and interests. In a single company's in-house program, unification of purpose is easy and relatively manageable, compared to the case of a contracted-out program, where total optimization can be complex.

Responses to deal with this problem include forming a community of practice (see Chapter 5), and incorporating into contracts provisions for incentives and liquidated damages. In the latter case, certain goals (e.g., performance, cost, delivery date, etc.) for the entire program are determined in advance. When improved performance or early delivery, for instance, occurs in the execution phase, some extent of the profit increase in the service (operation) phase is returned to the contractors as a bonus. When the goal is not achieved, each contractor is charged for the loss.

In this way, incentives for achievement of goals are created. Many large-scale programs grant incentives for achievement beyond the goals set for the entire program, because success is a collective achievement; penalties, however, are charged to individual projects (PMAJ, 2007, p. 136. [Total optimization]; Koishihara, 2001).

4.3.2 Launching Individual Projects and Execution Systems

The first thing to be done when launching projects is to specify organizations (e.g., divisions of a company) or people (e.g., officers or directors) responsible for project execution. Project managers are appointed by these organizations or people. There are cases where project managers are appointed first, taking the entire responsibility for the project launch, including the appointment of executing organizations. In the case of outsourced projects, project managers are usually appointed by contractors, except when the program owner wants a specific person or group to be in the position.

As described in the previous section, it is important to make a review of the program execution plan and any modification of its details, if necessary, prior to starting execution. As programs are highly complex and lengthy, it is not unusual that implementation creates a task that does not fall under the responsibility of any project. To cope with such an eventuality, the program should set aside a contingency budget.

In this phase, it is also necessary to coordinate practices such as reporting, information exchange, negotiation and decision-making among the program and its projects. These should be clearly defined as operating rules and documented through contract or execution plan for smooth implementation.

4.3.3 Preparation of the Program/Project Execution Environment

Execution of programs and projects needs an appropriate environment. It is the responsibility of each project to prepare the execution environment, except for matters beyond the project's capacity, in which case those matters are the program's responsibility. Exhibit 2.4.4 shows typical examples, most of which should be dealt with well before execution occurs.

Categories	Duty Outlines	
	In-house	Contracted out
Project's Organizational System	• Appointment of responsible organization or person • Appointment of project manager (with assignment of authority) • Determination of project execution organization	• Selection of contractor (by appointment or tender) • Appointment (by the contractor) of project manager • Determination of project execution organization
Determination of Missions and Goals	• Confirmation (review, adjustment) of project missions and goals defined in concept plan • Finalization of execution plan	• Confirmation (review, contractual negotiation) of project missions and goals defined in concept plan • Finalization of contract and execution plan
Operational Rules	• Specification of reporting, information exchange and coordination systems (corporate rules and practices are usually employed)	• Specification of reporting, information exchange and coordination (usually newly stipulated in the execution plan and other documents)

Exhibit 2.4.3: Duty Outlines at the Stage of Individual Project Launch

Categories	Outlines
(a) Workspace	• Prepare physical or informational workspace, or grant authority to access or work in such spaces
(b) Coordination	• Coordinate cooperation to prevent conflicts between or among projects, systems, and stakeholders
(c) Resource-securing	• Secure or provide resources (funds, information, facilities, materials, etc.) that are difficult for a project to acquire through its own efforts or responsibility

Exhibit 2.4.4: Preparation of Program/Project Execution Environment (Examples)

A project may need to conduct a survey or install equipment within a customer facility or do work on customer information systems. If the program manager lacks the authority to allow access to such physical or informational space, he/she must get permission from the facility's administration for access.

Each project has a variety of interfaces with other projects or systems. For example, a project may need information on other projects for its own system design. For a project to be able to test its subsystem, it may be necessary that other projects have completed specific subsystems. A project may need a material sample being developed by another project. Administrative authorities' approval or license for system testing may be required, or consent from local residents for construction. If such matters cannot be dealt with by a project, the program must coordinate stakeholders or conduct negotiations. Additionally, when acquisition of funds, information, facilities, materials or other resources is beyond a project's capacity, the program should take over the activity.

In principle, such matters should be identified at the planning phase or at program launch. The project's assignments should be defined in contracts, execution plans, or specifications. Nevertheless, some matters do crop up as the program proceeds. In such instances realistic decisions are required.

4.3.4 Goal Management
The main tasks of project goal management in the program execution phase are (i) monitor each project's objectives and goals, schedule, costs, and so forth, depending on progress in the program schedule; (ii) monitor the program's overall objectives, goals, schedule, costs, and so forth, based on project monitoring results; and (iii) control the program or each project as necessary.

(1) Preparation of Information Communication Systems
Preparation of an information communication system in the broad sense is important as the basis for program monitoring and control. The system is intended to manage information within the program, such as reports and instructions, in a unified manner based on operational rules found in Section 4.3.2. *Information communication system* does not merely mean the electronic information network system. It covers a wide range, from the regular/irregular reporting/conferencing system, standardized methods of reporting for a variety of information types, including schedule progress and quality issues, terminology unification, or uniform formats for communicating, and so forth, all meant to contribute to shared understanding. Good preparation of such an information communication system provides the basis for goal management. For a project that needs detailed monitoring and close exchange of information, the program may send a senior engineer or manager to the project as a resident liaison.

(2) Monitoring and Control
(a) Monitoring

As shown in Exhibit 2.4.5, the program manager collects information on the program environment, progress data and the forecasts for each project and the entire program, as well as other information, on a regular basis or when necessary. Information and data are evaluated in comparison with plans to maintain necessary control. Data are facts from the past, and it is important for the program manager to evaluate them against the future path of program completion.

The primary purpose of monitoring is to identify such challenges as environmental changes, deviations from the plan, and quality issues. Even if evaluating the entire project by the earned value method, a localized problem potentially harmful for the whole is masked by overall complexity until its influence grows serious enough to be discovered. Most organizations try to fix trouble by themselves, and negative information is likely to be concealed, even without ill intentions. Therefore, just waiting for routine information often causes failure in timely acquisition of important information, as information can come to light too late. To prevent this, critical projects with such risk factors as difficult technical tasks or time-constrained subsystems, as well as critical items within the project, should be identified in advance and subject to special attention. Careful supervision is also important for solving problems in a timely fashion. Reliance on experts may be appropriate.

The program manager and the staff should visit the project site to see things with their own eyes, not merely rely on reports. They should be encouraged to expand their information sources to the project manager and other key persons.

(b) Facilitating and Advancing Execution

The project manager compares information and data acquired through monitoring with the goal plans, and controls each project, whether promoting, continuing, or altering its activity. Promoting a project means encouraging a project to catch up with its planned schedule or improving the speed of execution. Assisting the project is also a frequent practice of promotion.

The first step in encouraging improvement is to ask the project team to explain the reasons for delay or to have them present a list of problems with analysis of causes, and formally ask for plans for improvement. Often in the case of delay, upper-level managers of the contractor (or of the responsible organization if the project is executed in-house) are not aware of the problem, while those executing

Monitoring Items	Outlines	Methods
External Environment	Social and economic situation, market conditions, competition, technological innovation, regulatory changes, major disasters, affiliates' performance, shifts of key persons	Mass media, industry information, corporate information, personal relations, etc.
Project Progress	Project progress information and forecasts, cost information, quality/technical issues	Reporting (regular/irregular), conference (regular/irregular), sight inspection, etc.
Others	Critical projects, critical items, critical success factors (CSF)	Verification at milestones, experts' conferences

Exhibit 2.4.5: Main Monitoring Items of Program

the project may be too disturbed by it to make a level-headed decision. This type of situation can usually be saved through logical, analytical discussion involving contractor management, experts, and outsiders. When this does not work or when the project requests help, assistance from the program side becomes necessary. Assistance will include offering expert advice and information, lending machinery and other physical support, preparing the execution environment, removing obstacles, and coordinating relationships with other projects or stakeholders. Another popular response to the problem is to require the contractor to establish a scheme for shortening the schedule by improving its personnel system, specifically by reinforcing staff, relieving key persons from excessive workloads, and assigning staff to dedicate themselves to solving the problem, or to engage in schedule crashing.

(c) Project Autonomy

A high level of autonomy in individual project activities is an inevitable requirement for efficient implementation of a large, complex program. This, however, frequently causes difficulties in communication and controlling, because of the differences among project organizations in terms of attitude or execution style. For example, a technical term can be defined in different ways, and different terms can describe the same thing. There can be different views on scopes of responsibility. Differences occur frequently in attitudes toward contractual obligations; some may think meeting a delivery date a top priority, while others may think late delivery simply a matter of penalty payment. These are cultural differences among organizations, and they can cause problems among firms, particularly in cross-industrial or international business partnerships. These problems become obvious when serious problems occur, affecting quality, schedule, and/or costs.

Project autonomy should be respected in large-scale programs, but not left completely free. Projects should be controlled, keeping an eye on early signs of problems.

Adding to the above, controlling entire programs requires a viable approach to certainty in program execution (see Chapter 3, Section 3.3), and changes to programs and organizational systems as discussed in the next sections.

4.3.5 Program Change

A program manager should advance the program plan with firm conviction to achieve the desired mission outcome. However, if an environmental or other event is significantly beyond that originally envisaged, the program or projects will have to make changes in their original scope, schedule, or cost. Although program execution should not permit such changes easily, a delayed response would jeopardize the program mission. An important quality for a program manager is the ability to make a timely decision with flexible responses while strictly following the plan.

(1) Factors Leading to Program Change

If program objectives and goals are impossible to achieve, it becomes necessary to restructure and change the program. The thing that necessitates program change is, in many cases, failure of one or more specific projects. However, external factors, such as market conditions, are also important, because the program is related to business strategies, which usually require a long period of time for execution. Exhibit 2.4.6 shows examples of program change factors and Exhibit 2.4.7 specifies the items that are changed.

Factor Categories	Factor Examples
Customer's request/ Organization Strategy	• Reasons on the customer's part • Changes in business strategy
Changes in business management system	• Changes in business structure (M&A, etc.) or corporate strategy on the part of the principal organization • Shift in the program owner's position • Main stakeholders' change in policy, bankruptcy, conflict, etc.
Revelation of inconsistencies of objectives/ goals with market or market change	• Program objective revealed to be inappropriate • Program objective becomes difficult to achieve • Some projects fail to achieve goal or are seriously delayed • Team's capacity revealed to be inadequate
Significant changes in business environment, or miscalculation	• Unexpected situation at project site; insufficient or delayed construction of public infrastructure • Rapid market shrinkage (individual markets, economic crisis, etc.) • Arrival of strong competitor • Changes in legal system or state policy; wars/disturbances
Significant changes in core technologies	• Rapid spread of technical innovation • Material changes in existing technology

Exhibit 2.4.6: Examples of Program Change Factors

(2) *Procedure for Change Control*

Program change requires a formal procedure. The program plan, including overall objectives and the expected outcome, individual project missions, schedules, costs, and so forth, is reviewed and approved through formal examination procedures. Because a program change is a deviation from the program plan, it should be in accordance with formal change control procedures. Change control procedures must be arranged in advance as part of program management procedures. Program change control includes:

- Definition of the change to be handled through a formal change control procedure
- A change control organization (proponent, change control board or decision maker)
- An initiative for change (timing, procedure, etc., for proposing the change)
- Examination and decision-making methods regarding the change
- Delivery of the decision (documentation, communication to the parties concerned).

Forms of Program Change
(a) Termination of program before completion; postponement

(b) Program redefinition:
  • Changes in objectives/goals
  • Changes in program architecture

(c) Rearrangement of program management organization
(d) Changes in program budget/schedule
(e) Discontinuation, postponement or redefinition of some projects

Exhibit 2.4.7: Forms of Program Change

Change control is usually managed by a *change control board* (CCB) consisting of key stakeholders, including the program manager or his/her representative and the relevant project managers. Other forms are also possible, according to the size and nature of the program. In many cases, program owners and customers are directly affected by a change. When examining and making decisions, the CCB should include such stakeholders or those acting on their behalf, or otherwise coordinate their interests.

When a change is agreed among the parties concerned, program requirements are updated. Project monitoring and control is implemented to accommodate the change.

(3) The Role of Change Control Procedures
Formal change control procedures have two important functions:

Identification of the effects of the change: When a project change is required, and the influence of the change spreads beyond the project, achievement of the objective or the overall schedule may be affected in a chain reaction. Change control procedure provides all relevant parties an opportunity to examine whether the change is permissible or if some alternative method is required. This is the primary function of change control procedure for ensuring overall program success.

Consistency or maintenance of program performance quality: A program contains multiple projects and stakeholders in complex relationships. A slight change can have a serious effect on overall program success. Change control procedures stipulate that any unnecessary change in program mission should be removed. Necessary changes should be incorporated formally with an appropriate price, delivery date, and so forth, agreed upon by stakeholders, including customers. This is an important function of change control procedure, for contributing to the achievement of program objectives.

4.3.6 Early Program Termination
When continuation of the program will not yield sufficient value, the program should be terminated before completion. Such program termination is the most serious form of program change. Many reasons for termination are internal direct factors, although it is not unusual for external or combined factors to have strong impacts. Reasons for termination include:

- The expected outcome will probably not be obtained.
- It is obvious that the obtainable outcome will not be worth the investment, especially considering future investments.
- The expected outcome or technology has been impaired due to the market environment, innovation, and/or competition.
- Changes in business strategy have made the envisaged results obsolete.
- Core leaders and engineers have been lost.
- Management or customers are no longer interested in the program.
- Higher priority has been given to another program or activity.

Terminating a program before completion is unacceptable for those concerned, because they can be held responsible. Responsibility for the determination of program termination rests with senior management members, such as the program manager, program owner, and corporate executives. Program termination is expected to be advantageous, for instance, to avoid continuing ineffective investment and to divert technological capacity to new investment opportunities, or to rejuvenate organizational morale. Contractual penalties may be incurred and opposition from stakeholders may be aroused. Program termination should be justified by sound strategic judgment with all these factors taken into account.

Processes for a normal termination are given in Exhibits 2.4.8 and 2.4.9. These are also applied to early program termination, but with a few differences.

4.3.7 Organizational Rearrangement

For a program or project to survive extreme difficulties requires changes in personnel instead of changes in the program or project. Changing project managers or other leading personnel is often effective for salvaging the program or project. A new manager can view and comprehend the situation more objectively and develop a new perspective without being affected by the past. The new manager is not responsible for past investments and failures, and is less affected by sunk costs.

4.4 Closing Out and Evaluating Programs

There are many types of programs, such as strategic programs implemented to create new value, contracted programs that close when the contractor completes execution, and programs with long-term service projects carried out by the owner or PFI contractor. In this section typical processes are explained for closing and evaluating projects, before discussing program closing and evaluation.

4.4.1 Closing Out and Evaluating Projects
(1) Delivery and Closing

A contracted project is generally closed formally when its execution ends with official delivery of the system to the customer. This is an important process, through which the contractor's project responsibility is verified as complete and the project's operational appropriateness is ascertained. In-house projects, even if not contracted, should also employ a similar process. Exhibit 2.4.8 shows the process of project delivery and closing as viewed from the contractor's side.

Delivery means that property rights or administrative rights over the system are transferred to the customer. A common practice that precedes transfer is a completion inspection, which determines whether contractual requirements have been satisfied, including provision of all required documents, along with supplies like attachments and spare parts. The completion inspection is either witnessed testing or done through an inspection meeting. In some cases, system commissioning is required before or instead of a completion inspection.

Project closing occurs when the project side and the customer/project-owner side confirm that a project work package has been wholly completed. On the project side, it also means (i) evaluation and documentation of the course taken and the value obtained by the project, (ii) handling the residual equipment, materials, and other project assets remaining after delivery, and (iii) implementing contractual

Delivery	Project Closing

(a) Completion Inspection of Projects
  • Satisfy scope and specification requirements, including alterations and changes
  • Confirm documents, spare parts, attachments, and other supplies (mutual confirmation and documentation of the above)
(b) Transfer of property rights and administrative rights, etc.
	(a) Confirm completion of all work packages
	(b) Receive consideration
	(c) Evaluate and document projects (technically and financially)
	(d) Dispose of residual equipment and materials (by sale, disposal, or transfer)
	(e) Return rented facilities, equipment, and materials, and settle payments for them
	(f) Terminate subcontract agreements and settle payments
	(g) Submit Project Completion Report
	(h) Dismiss project staff and dismantle organization

Exhibit 2.4.8: Key Processes of Delivery and Closing (on the Contractor's Side)

obligations, including payments to subcontractors. In parallel with the project closing procedure, the project organization is gradually dismantled.

Although the project completion inspection and confirmation of work package completion partially overlap in content, the former focuses on achievement of objectives and goals and is mainly conducted by the technical department or the quality assurance department, while the latter places importance on implementation of contractual work obligations, which are usually handled by the sales or contract management departments.

(2) Project Evaluation and Documentation

To close a project, technical and financial outputs of the project are evaluated and documented as indicated in Exhibit 2.4.9. Some documents are submitted to the project buyer and others are used by the contractor to increase organizational capacity.

Items	Purposes
(a) Project outcome (satisfaction of scope and specification requirements)	• Confirm that technical and quality requirements have been met, and complete the project • Prevent future additions to requirements or disputes
(b) Deliverable system's requirements and design specifications, as-built drawings, actual measurement data, etc.	• Basic information for operation and maintenance of a deliverable system (to be supplied to the customer) • Improvement of design capability
(c) Financial outcome (budget and results)	• Project management information for the execution organization • Reference sources for future project plans, designs, costs, price negotiations, etc.
(d) Schedule (plans and results)	• Reference sources for future project plans and designs
(e) Remarkable outcome	• Reference sources (of competitive strategy, personnel affairs, etc.) for future business development of the company and the customer
(f) Lessons learned	• Filing of issues, failures and their countermeasures • Reference sources for future projects with horizontal dissemination to similar projects and technical fields

Exhibit 2.4.9: Project Evaluation and Documentation (on the Contractor Side)

The purpose of confirming project outcome, shown in line (a) of Exhibit 2.4.9, is to complete the project after both the project side and the project buyer's side have agreed that the project has met technical and quality requirements. For the project side, this process prevents future additional requirements or the risk of disputes. Information on the system outcome is not only necessary for its operation and maintenance after delivery, but helpful in designing other projects or improving organizational or personnel abilities. Although lessons learned are basically secret, the option to disclose some information needed by the customer is also important to win the customer's confidence and, consequently, to realize long-term growth in business.

(3) Other Activities

Enhancement of Customer Relationships: A company based on projects faces an important management challenge in expanding the business steadily and enriching personnel. Project closing is a pleasant milestone for both the company and its customer. Sharing with the customer confirms the significance of the project and of a positive outcome. Along with the sharing of other information, this is an important activity that creates continuous business and an enhanced relationship with the customer.

Management of Intellectual Property: Technical invention and ideas obtained in the course of project implementation, as well as know-how acquired through production or construction processes, should be secured by applications for patents, trademark rights, and so forth, as appropriate. Other useful know-how developed in the program should be transformed appropriately into explicit knowledge recorded in documents, drawings, or images for future internal use.

4.4.2 Program Closing and Evaluation
(1) Program Contractor

A contractor assigned to a program for plant construction or large-scale ICT system development has to manage more complicated processes than those of a single project. However, the closing and evaluation processes of a program are quite similar to those of a single project. Knowledge and experience obtained through program implementation, especially the ex-post evaluation of plans, forecasts, and results, should be properly maintained for future business development.

(2) Program Owner

If an owner of a large-scale system such as a petrochemical plant or a PFI program contractor wants to execute a service-type project, the completion of system development described above in (1) is an intermediate stage. This stage is important in the sense that the process to monitor and control the contractor is completed. The program manager confirms that planned targets have been fully accomplished, and then transfers property rights and control to the owner's direct authority. Then the program manager launches a service-type project as the subsequent step. This is still an intermediate stage, but appropriate action is required as the counterpart and superintendent of the contractor's program closing process.

The closing and evaluation of a service-type project is no different from what has been discussed above, although there is no tangible outcome. In closing such a project, it is important to make clear the financial results and to identify what the project has accomplished in terms of intangible assets (e.g., knowledge, know-how, credit, etc.) that could be useful in a future program. In service-type projects, these accomplishments are commonly evaluated and reported quarterly or annually along with other information. Summing up such information at the time of closing is helpful to the organization.

If a service-type project continues over a long time, it is a common practice to execute only the initial phase as part of the program until the operation gets on track. After this period of time for familiarization and improvements, the business is transferred to an operating organization.

(3) New Product Development and Related System Provision Program

When the program's objective is new product/service development or system provision for production or sales, program closing requires an evaluation to confirm overall accomplishment of performance, cost, and construction targets of related systems or sales channels.

(4) Strategic Programs

Strategic programs have vastly diversified objectives and architectures. These programs should be closed using processes explained above in Sections (1) to (3). Many strategic programs are executed over a long period of time, and many of them experience changes in their objectives and architecture. When closing them, lessons from this background are important, too.

5. Multiple Project Management

When a company or a division implements two or more unrelated projects concurrently, it is called *multiple project management* and not *program management*. Generally, a program integrates project outcomes to create a total value surpassing that of the total sum of all projects' value. Multiple projects obtain value only equivalent to the simple sum of project outcomes. Program management's interest is effective and efficient implementation of a program, and organizations to execute its projects are not necessarily limited to those within the company. On the other hand, multiple project management's interest is maximal use of the organization in executing different projects by efficiently sharing the organization's resources across tasks.

Program management and multiple project management are the same in that they both handle more than one project, though their perspectives are not identical. However, it is not unusual for a projectized company to engage in a large-scale system-type program and many other projects concurrently. In this type of organization, program management and multiple project management are integrated into one operation. In fact, management skills for these two have many things in common. This section outlines some things particular to multiple project management.

For the sake of long-term growth of business, projectized businesses represented by plant construction, IT solutions, space development, and the like require continuous and stable receipt of project orders and completion of projects on schedule and within budget. The following closely-connected challenges will arise in this kind of business:

- Stable and full use of specialist resources
- Increasing the quality of diverse specialist resources
- Stable project order backlog.

Management Elements	Outlines
Optimization of portfolio	Soundness, profitability, growth potential, efficient use of human resources
Maximization of productivity	Plan and operation for efficient use of human resources
Minimization of business risk	Monitoring and control across the organization
Enhancement of expertise by field	Foundation for competitiveness and growth

Exhibit 2.5.1: Key Perspectives on Multiple Project Management (PM/ENAA, 2005)

System development-type projects require different groups of specialists that work by turns as the project phases advance, for instance, as found in project planning, system design, subsystem design specialized in various technical fields, production and quality control of subsystems, system assembly and installation, and system testing. The time that the specialist groups (functional organizations in many cases) need for their jobs ranges from weeks to months, depending on the project phase and their responsibilities.

These jobs create a kind of value chain, with specialist groups generating value and adding it to the system in turn, one after another. If one company were to deal only with one link in this chain, it would require a continuous supply of projects of the same kind and size. If a company were to deal with the entire system, a continuous series of jobs done by different specialist groups would be necessary. If, for example, an annual workforce is provided only a 10-months' supply of work, the productivity of human resources decreases by 16.7%, a decrease that seriously affects profitability and competitiveness.

To enhance market competitiveness, the proficiency of these specialist groups must be increased. Proficiency is usually accumulated through continuous repetition of job implementation. It is therefore essential that an organization of this kind obtain multiple orders for programs and projects at staggered times to maintain the specialist groups' full and stable use in accordance with the lifecycles of the programs and projects, to provide the opportunity for improving worker proficiency. Such efficient use of human resources across multiple projects is also applicable to manufacturers who develop and make new products in-house.

In conclusion, multiple project business essentially requires stable and continuous orders for projects. Additionally, risk management for this kind of business is even more important, because trouble in a project creates unexpected impacts on staffing and a chain reaction of problems.

Considering all this, multiple project management requires the perspectives on management shown in Exhibit 2.5.1. Optimization of the program/project portfolio, among other things, is the high-level element of multiple project management with the strongest influence. An organization with excellent response to these management elements can enhance its competitiveness in project-based businesses. Therefore, it must be proficient in program implementation.

6. Contracts in Programs/Projects

In a sales agreement for mass-produced products, the products' specifications, performance, and costs are usually clear. Sales contracts for programs or projects are concluded without specifying systems or services to provide in detail, and therefore with an inadequate cost estimation based on many assumptions. This poses considerable risk to both parties to the contract. Contract conclusion is therefore a process for both parties to specify their rights and obligations as clearly as possible to minimize the mutual risk.

Traditionally, Japanese business culture has placed great importance on long-term commercial relationships, including sole-source ordering arrangements and restricting sourcing to companies that are members of the same *keiretsu* (corporate group). Many programs and projects even have been set up, based not on clear details but on the assumption that "good intentions" underlie the continuous transactions. This approach reduces transaction costs. However, in the modern environment of globalization with its severe business conditions, things such as shareholder litigation, an increasing focus on corporate governance, contract profitability, risk management, responsibility and indemnity for accidents, have grown in importance. Contract contents are now the concern not only of the legal, sales, or procurement department, but also of the entire organization.

6.1 Contract Types and Their Risks

A contract is basically a promise made between two or more private persons, and is, in principle, left to the broad discretion of the parties concerned. This has led to a variety of contract types, in terms of objectives, prices, and so forth, as illustrated in Exhibit 2.6.1.

Among these types, cost reimbursement contracts are where the selling party is paid a certain profit above actual expenses, which are reimbursed. This type of contract is no longer used much, as it tends to lead only to increased costs. Examples of contract types often used in system-type projects are listed in Exhibit 2.6.2. These include various types of contracts that are intended to enhance project outcomes by entitling the contractor/seller to incentives for successful improvement on contract objectives, such as in quality, costs, or scheduling.

	Examples	**Outlines**
Objectives of Contract	Work Contract	Execute contracted work with fixed specifications and deliver the outcome (development, construction, manufacturing, etc.)
	Service Contract	Perform specified service
	Sales and Purchase Contract	Transfer the property right and pay the price
Pricing Methodology	Fixed Price Contract, Lump Sum Contract	Price is fixed at contract conclusion
	Cost Reimbursement Contract	Actual cost is reimbursed after contract is executed (a.k.a. Provisional Payment Contract)
	Unit Price Contract	Unit price is predetermined; payment is made for the delivered quantity of commercial items, materials, or work performed
	Time and Materials Contract	Worker's labor-hour cost and cost of materials are paid under a service contract, etc.

Exhibit 2.6.1: Basic Types of Contracts (DoD)

Acronym	Titles	Outlines
FFP	Firm-Fixed-Price Contract	Price is fixed at the conclusion of the contract
FP/EPA	Fixed-Price Contract with Economic Price Adjustment	Basically equal to FFP except adjustment is based on prices of commodities
FPI	Fix-Price Incentive Contract	Basically equal to FFP but incentives attached
CPIF	Cost-Plus-Incentive-Fee Contract	Payment for actual cost plus incentives
CPFF	Cost-Plus-Fixed-Fee Contract	Payment for actual cost and fixed fees
T&M	Time and Materials Contract	Payment for actual work-hours and material cost, etc.

Exhibit 2.6.2: Examples of Practical Types of Contract (DoD)

Among these, the firm-fixed-price contract (FFP) provides for an amount that is fixed at the contracting stage, and unchangeable, minimizing the owner/buyer's risk and leaving it on the seller. Conversely, in the cost-plus-fixed-fee contract (CPFF) the seller is paid for costs, as well as a fixed fee, thus reducing the risk on its side while the owner/buyer is exposed to increased risk. The time and material (T&M) contract also has the same characteristics on buyer-contractor risk distribution.

Contract type is determined according to the project's objectives, predicted risks, the power relationship between the owner/buyer and the contractor/seller, and so forth. The Federal Acquisition Regulations (FAR) list 11 factors for contract type determination, including price competition, cost analysis, form and complexity of demand, urgency, contractor's capacity, nature of subcontract, and so forth (Department of Defense). There are many contracts containing a *liquidated damages* provision, which stipulates compensation in the case of failure to achieve a performance target, or of delayed delivery. For instance, a liquidated damages clause may stipulate a charge of 1/1,000 – 1/2,000 of the contract amount per day delay, up to 5–10% of the contract.

6.2 RFP and Outline of the Contracting Process

One of the most important contracts for both owner and contractor is the one for procuring the system that constitutes the core of the program or project. Exhibit 2.6.3 is an example of the contracting process for system outsourcing, with the upper part of the chart representing activities by the owner (ordering party), and the lower part the contractor (bidder). The owner starts by outlining the concept of a business proposal and then conducts a feasibility study of the proposed business. Once feasibility has been established, the owner begins detailed business planning. The processes so far, which are in a dashed-line oval in the exhibit, correspond to the mission profiling and program design stages of program management. These stages, where business objectives are planned and program structure is designed, are a scheme-type project on the part of the owner.

When the business plan necessitates outsourcing of important systems, the owner issues a request for proposal (RFP) to several companies. In a large-scale program or project, leading players in the industry usually know in advance about the proposal and are already examining viability and needed preparations from their

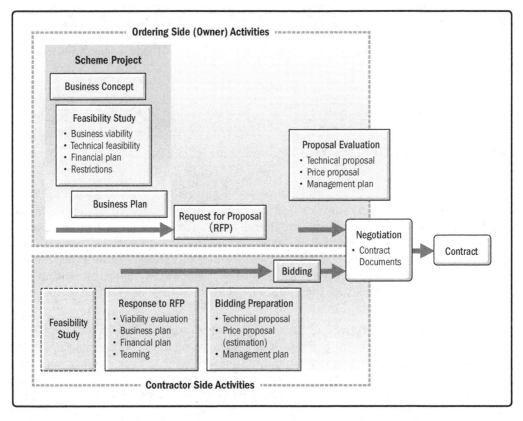

Exhibit 2.6.3: Example of Contracting Process for System Outsourcing

own perspectives. If satisfied with their examination, they respond to the RFP with a written technical and price proposal, based on a detailed technical study and cost estimation. A large-scale program or project may require plans from the bidders as well. When a part of the RFP's requirements is technically unachievable, or if there is any alternative method better than that specified in the RFP, the bidders may submit counterproposals. Bidding is often costly and in itself is a scheme-type project for them.

The owner evaluates the proposals, weighs them against each other and selects the best bidder to start negotiating with. During negotiations, evidence supporting feasibility and the probability of success is scrutinized before finalizing agreements on pricing and detailed management plans. The agreement is then memorialized in a contract. If agreement is not reached, the owner starts negotiating with the next best bidder. There are also cases where the owner negotiates with several bidders concurrently and selects the best resulting offer.

If there is a special relationship between the owner and the contractor, such as with a joint venture partner or some entity with which there exists a long-term relationship of mutual trust, tender bidding may be replaced with a negotiated contract or a sole-source contract.

6.3 Practice of Contract Documentation

(1) Contract Contents

While possible at least theoretically, a *complete contract* that describes all eventualities and provides guidance for all parties is a practical impossibility, particularly in the face of the complexity and deadlines involved in projects and programs. *Incomplete contracts* bring with them the risk of opportunism, which can create unpredicted risks for contract parties.

Assertion of one's own interests is natural. In a contractual relationship, both parties must carefully scrutinize the contract to mitigate risks in the joint business (the contract's primary purpose), seeking concerted mutual agreement from both sides. Because of risks stemming from environmental changes, accidents, business conditions, and the like, it is important that rules for dispute resolution, risk sharing, and contract amendment be defined in advance.

Although a contract is usually considered concluded and complete when memorialized in writing, it can be seen as comprised of three legally prescribed elements (Morris & Pinto, 2004, p. 682):

- Express terms: Items explicitly stated in a contractual document
- Implied terms: Items not stated in a contractual document but established as law, judicial precedent, or commercial custom and practice, including things like contractor responsibility for subcontractors and good faith efforts toward achievement of objectives
- Incorporation by reference: Items in secondary documents that are included in the main contract by virtue of its reference to them.

Many implied terms primarily represent the duty of both parties to perform in good faith when implementing the contract. This is particularly because the contractor's expertise and information about the target job are superior to that of the owner; implicit provisions in contracts can be understood as a customary practice to accommodate this asymmetry in ability and knowledge.

When a subcontractor is appointed on the contractor's option, the responsibility for the subcontractor rests wholly with the contractor. When the owner/buyer specifies a particular subcontractor, however, responsibilities regarding the subcontractor's performance should be clarified in the contract.

(2) Division by Lifecycle

Program/projects comprise significant uncertainties in their early stages, which will gradually be clarified as the lifecycle progresses. A practical solution is to divide contracts into several different forms, concluding them one by one in accordance with the progress of lifecycle stages. Initial surveys and concept planning should be entrusted to service providers using a time and material contract, while more substantial jobs at the system development stage should be handled using a fixed-price, fixed-fee, or incentive-type contract, thus optimizing the contracting method in accordance with program content and phases.

(3) Documents that Define Contract Details

As the contract defines a basic agreement between the parties, its details are usually set out in other related documents. Typical of these are (i) applicable documents or references stipulated as a part of a contract (e.g., industrial standards), (ii) contract annexes (e.g., technical specifications, execution plans, etc.), (iii) various types of intent agreements and/or memoranda of understanding (MOUs), (iv) proposals, (v) minutes of contractual negotiations, (vi) approved drawings, (vii) the owner's instructions, and (viii) minutes of various meetings.

To prepare a contract-related document, industry-standard model forms and general industry practice and standardized specifications should be followed to facilitate mutual understanding between the parties.

Inconsistency between provisions is dealt with through the following principles (Fisk, 2006, p. 521):

(a) Later provisions supersede previous provisions.
(b) Individual specific terms supersede general terms.
(c) A written agreement memorializing an oral agreement cancels the prior oral agreement.
(d) Peripheral words do not disturb judgments in keeping with the overall context and meaning of the document as agreed upon by both parties.

These are not written stipulations but general principles that may not apply in some cases. Take principle (b), for instance: inconsistency between specification requirements and statements in an attached detailed drawing are not readily addressed by this principle. If such problems can be anticipated, priorities should be set out in the contract.

6.4 Contracts in International Projects

International projects involve great differences of society, culture, legislative system, custom, and sense of values among the contractual parties. These differences should be taken into consideration when contracting in multinational projects. Important items to consider when contracting such projects are explained in Exhibit 2.6.4 (Saitoh & Kinumaki, 2001, p. 136).

Items	Outlines
Legislative System	• Compliance with the local legislative system regarding project job activities and deliverables (e.g., labor laws, trade/foreign exchange controls, environmental rules, competition (antitrust) policies, international taxation systems, etc.) • Measures against cost fluctuation or schedule delay due to changes in local laws
Standard Forms	• Use of industrial standard model forms that are globally accepted • FIDIC Contract Form from International Federation of Consulting Engineers • Model forms from Engineering Advancement Association of Japan (ENAA)
Governing Law	• Private contracts are under the rule of *contractual party autonomy*, and may determine governing law by mutual agreement. However, the governing law of the country where the work is done is adopted most of the time. • Also used are the Principles of International Commercial Contracts by International Institute for the Unification of Private Law (UNIDROIT).
Solution of Disputes	• Prior consent to the means for dispute solution, jurisdiction of international adjudication, international arbitration, etc.

Exhibit 2.6.4: Matters for Attention in Contracts in International Projects (Saitoh & Kinumaki, 2001, p. 136)

References

Aoki, M., & Ando, H. (2002) *Mojūru-ka: Atarashii sangyo ākitekucha no honshitsu* [Modularization: The essence of new industrial architecture]. Tokyo, Japan: Toyo Keizai.

Baldwin, C. Y., & Clark, K. B. (2000). *Design rules, vol.1: Power of modularity.* Cambridge, MA: MIT Press.

Chesbrou, H. W. (2003). *Open innovation.* Boston, MA: Harvard Business School Press.

Christensen, C. M. (1997). *The innovator's dilemma.* Boston, MA: Harvard Business School Press.

DoD (Department of Defense). *Federal acquisition regulation: Part 16 – Types of contracts.* Retrieved from https://www.acquisition.gov/far/current/pdf/FAR.pdf

Eisenmann, T., Parker, J., & Van Alstyne, M. W. (2006). Strategies for two-sided markets. *Harvard Business Review,* Oct. 1, 2006.

Fisk, R. F., & Reynolds, W. D. (2006). *Construction project administration* (8th ed). Upper Saddle River, NJ: Pearson Prentice Hall.

Fujimoto, T., et al. (2001) *Bijinesu ākitekucha* [Business architecture]. Tokyo, Japan: Yuhikaku Publishing.

Garland, R. (2009). *Project governance.* London, UK: Kogan Page.

Garud, R., et al. (Eds.). (2003). *Managing in the modular age.* Malden, MA: Blackwell Publishing.

Gawer, A., & Cusumano, M. A. (2002). *Platform leadership.* Boston, MA: Harvard Business School Press.

Kameoka, A. (Ed.) (2007). *Sabisu saiensu* [Service science]. Tokyo, Japan: NTS.

Koishihara, K. (2001). Eifutsu Kaikyou-tonneru Purojekuto niokeru Zentaisaiteki-ka no Jitugen [The achievement of total optimization for the Channel Tunnel project linking Britain and France]. *Journal of the Society of Project Management, 3*(6), 23.

Mintzberg, H. (1987). Crafting strategy. *Harvard Business Review,* July-August.

Moore, G.A. (2005). *Dealing with Darwin* New York, NY: Portfolio.

Morris, P., & Pinto, J. K. (Eds.). (2004). *The Wiley guide to managing projects.* Hoboken, NJ: John Wiley & Sons.

Ohara, S. (2004). Purojekuto manejimento no tenbou to hatten [Prospects and development of project management]. *P2M Journal 1,* Project Management Professionals Certification Center (PMCC).

PMAJ (Project Management Association of Japan). (2007). *New edition P2M project & program management standard guidebook.* Tokyo, Japan: JMA Management Center.

PM/ENAA (Subcommittee on Project Management of Engineering Advancement Association of Japan). (2005). *Maruchipurojekuto manejimento no kenkyu* [Study on multi-project management].

Rechtin, E., & Maier, M. W. (1997). *The art of systems architecting.* Boca Raton FL: CRC Press.

Saitoh, Y., & Kinumaki, Y. (2001). Kokusai purojekuto bijinesu [International project business]. Tokyo, Japan: Bunshindo.

Utterback, J. M. (1994). *Mastering the dynamics of innovation.* Boston, MA: Harvard Business School Press.

Van der Heijden, K. (1996). *Scenarios: The art of strategic conversation.* Chichester West Sussex, UK: John Wiley.

Yamada, H. (2007). Defacto sutandado no shinjitsu [The half truth of de facto standard]. *Diamond Harvard Business Review,* June 2007.

Chapter 3

Strategy Management and Risk Management

Chapter Overview

Chapter 3

Strategy Management and Risk Management

Chapter Overview

Exhibit 3.0 shows the conceptual relationship between strategy management and risk management from the viewpoint of program integration management.

As explained in Chapter 2, program implementation management is a series of processes from mission conceptualization to project execution. It starts with an initial program mission arising from the organization's strategic demands, then creates a concrete plan and a design for the program, ending with the execution of projects integrated by the program. These processes are executed through decisions made by managers at various levels, including the program manager. This chapter describes the knowledge required to make decisions about the management of program strategy and its related risks.

Strategy management develops a program mission into an organized concept and plan. In a program to create new value, uncertainty (i.e., risk) is unavoidable. In every process of strategy management, the program manager evaluates the risks of various alternatives, targeting strategic values and making appropriate decisions. Especially in the concept and planning phases, risks are thoroughly investigated, analyzed, and assessed. When uncertainty is high, the program architecture is amended to accommodate the risk parameters. Risk management in the concept and planning phases is executed implicitly as an intrinsic part of strategy management. In these processes, some risk elements are considered essential or acceptable. These known risks and unknown risks are handled in the execution phase, where risk management is implemented explicitly.

1. A General Outline of Business Strategy Theory

Readers of this book probably possess broad knowledge of business strategy theory. The term *strategy* is likely perceived very differently among the readership as it is used broadly, with a variety of definitions and perspectives. In order to share a common ground for discussing strategy management here, and to avoid misunderstanding, the following section provides a general outline of business strategy theory.

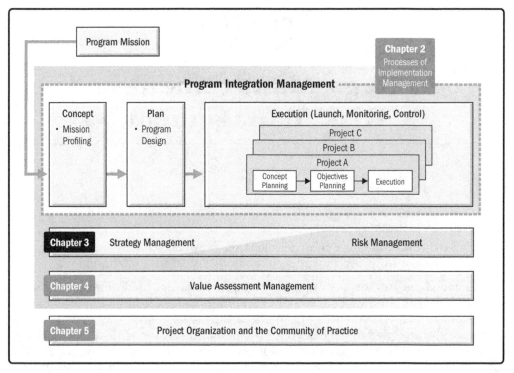

Exhibit 3.0: Strategy Management and Risk Management

1.1 What Is Strategy?

Business strategy has its roots in hierarchical military concepts of strategy, tactics, and combat. Many noted researchers have proposed definitions of business strategy. Ansoff (1968, p. 78) defined it thus: "Strategy is one of several sets of decision-making rules for guidance of organization behavior." Barney (2002, p. 6) said, "Strategy is defined as a firm's theory about how to compete successfully." He emphasized that a strategy is a "theory" as to how to compete successfully, always requiring implementation to verify its success. Mishina (2004, p. 11) stated: "Maximization of long-term earnings is the intrinsic function of corporate or business strategy. The objective to win the immediate battle is in the realm of tactics, however, strategy is located further back on the time axis." Despite these, and other, varying definitions, researchers share an understanding that strategy is the fundamental policy from which an organization sets out to achieve growth, profit maximization, and other long-term objectives.

1.2 Deliberative Strategy and Emergent Strategy

Mintzburg (1994, p. 23) explained two concepts of strategy. One says that "strategy is a plan" or "strategy is a set of future actions, directions and guideposts," while the other sees "strategy as a consistent pattern of actions made over time." The former is *intended strategy.* The latter is a behavioral pattern that is regarded as a strategy after it has been repeated by a successful firm. This is *realized strategy.* The realized strategy can be different from that which was initially intended. When a strategy is realized perfectly as initially intended, it is called *deliberative strategy*. When a series of actions with less-focused intention occur and create a consistent behavioral pattern, it is called *emergent strategy*. However, very few strategies are purely deliberative or emergent. Many combine characteristics of both. A major example is *umbrella strategy*. A firm sets up a large deliberative framework (an umbrella), which allows spontaneous or learning-by-doing behaviors to develop an emergent strategy. Mintzburg pointed out the other significant side of emergent strategy, noting that there can be different emergent strategies developed concurrently by various divisions within the organization. On the other hand, a deliberative strategy is implicitly premised on an organizational strategy formulated within the core of the organization.

A similar approach to explaining strategy is presented by Porter (1980, p. xiii), who referred to explicit strategy and implicit strategy. Explicit strategies are produced through strategic planning, while implicit ones are generated without any defined intention but as a result of the activities of various divisions. He states that an implicit strategy is rarely the best strategy for a firm.

Mishina (2004, p. 166) regarded strategies not as being deliberative but as part of a learning cycle. He argued that it is not appropriate to explain a strategy as a linear process with two phases, planning and execution. He proposed, instead, a cyclic process as illustrated in Exhibit 3.1.1(b) to execute a strategy. The cyclic process must start with a strong conviction that a correct strategy has been chosen which is then executed. Its results are assessed for important lessons that may lead to a revised strategy with consequent renewed conviction.

Likewise, Christensen (1997, p. 159) suggested that when innovation is commercialized, "guessing the right strategy at the outset isn't nearly as important to success as conserving enough resources (or having the relationships with trusting

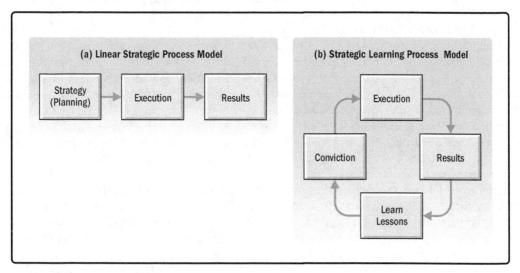

Exhibit 3.1.1: Strategic Process Models

Source: Mishina, K. (2004), *Senryaku fuzen no ronri* (Logic of strategy incompetence), Tokyo Japan, Toyo-Keizai, p. 166.

backers or investors) so that new business initiatives get a second or third stab at getting it right."

In a business environment where changes are drastic and unforeseeable, it is important to make an effective and appropriate choice from deliberative, emergent or cyclic strategic approaches.

Mintzburg's insights on emergent strategy are very intriguing for bootstrapping program management. Programs are not always implemented by the initiative of the firm's central organization, such as by a planning division. Rather, they can be implemented by organizations formed temporarily for program execution. A program is based on an initial strategic mission concept that is ambiguous. The first step is the mission profiling process, which clarifies the essence of the strategy. The primary organization provides only a general direction, while definition of the strategic details and goals (i.e., the mission profiling process) are entrusted to the team in charge of program execution. Programs are usually executed by adopting patterns from successful predecessors. A pattern accumulated through repetition is eventually recognized as an organization's program execution strategy. This is a hybrid umbrella strategy, where deliberative strategy and emergent strategy are combined. The former is formulated as a concept of the organizational holistic mission or strategy by the primary organization. The latter is developed and executed by the program organization to realize that concept.

1.3 Competitive Strategy

Strategy designed to create long-term profit maximization has a number of variations. From the corporate point of view, the most important are portfolio strategy and competitive strategy. The former focuses on "where to compete," and the latter asks "how to win the competitive edge." The following paragraphs outline the basic elements of competitive strategies, rather than describing portfolio strategies that vary widely from one firm to another, depending on environment, resources, and history.

1.3.1 Positioning and SWOT Analysis

Michael Porter's well-known competitive strategy theory is *positioning theory* and *SWOT analysis.* Porter first described the value chain concept for creating customer value and explained business activities in relation to this value chain. A business earns profit by full or partial participation in a value chain, where it inevitably meets competitors. Competitors could be from entirely different businesses. For example, the CD-ROM and USB key compete in the data storage industry, as do the postal service and the Internet (e-mail). No matter what the competitive environment may be, SWOT analysis is used to identify the firm's strengths and weaknesses, defined as threats and opportunities. Porter (1980, p. 4) defined five forces that drive competition and pose external threats to a firm in a competitive environment. They are (i) the threat of new entrants into the market; (ii) rivalry with existing competitors; (iii) the threat of alternative products; (iv) changes in buyers' bargaining power; and (v) sellers bargaining power. In response to these forces, Porter (ibid, p. 34) suggested three generic competitive strategies:

- Overall cost leadership by offering lower prices than competitors
- Differentiation by adding unique value different from competitors
- Focusing on market niches and targeted customers

Basic strategy for seeking opportunities differs according to industry structure. Barney (2002, p. 110), for example, categorized industry structures as follows:

- Fragmented
- Emerging
- Mature
- Declining
- International
- Network
- Hypercompetitive
- Empty core

Barney showed in each category a basic example of opportunities. In fragmented industry, for example, an opportunity can be created by consolidation, which leads to new economies of scale and alters ownership structure. In an emerging industry, opportunities lie in first mover's advantage, such as technological leadership, pre-emption of strategically valuable assets, and creation of customer-switching costs. Barney explains that every industry has a basic strategy suitable to its structure. Yet this is "basic," and the best strategy will differ depending on the firm's strengths and weaknesses, the competition, environmental changes, and future prospects.

1.3.2 A Resource-Based View of the Firm

A firm's competitive edge does not lie only in the way it copes with threats from industry and market structure. It also depends heavily on what resources the firm possesses. A *Resource-Based View* (RBV) of the firm focuses on strength and weakness (e.g., Barney, 2002, p. 155). RBV is based on the following principles:

- An excellent firm has distinctive capabilities, such as the competence of its CEO and leadership.
- Resource immobility: A firm's resources include those that are not obtainable or movable, no matter the cost.
- Resource heterogeneity: A firm is an assembly of productive resources based on people, and such resources are highly diverse among individual firms.

Even in the same business, Toyota and Honda, for instance, or Panasonic and Sony, each have different resources marking their strengths. This is resource heterogeneity. Resource immobility, on the other hand, means that business resources include those that are too costly to reproduce or copy, or which lack price supply elasticity, such as competent engineers or a highly advantageous business location. RBV is a proposition that the heterogeneity and the immobility of business resources constitute the most important sources of competitiveness.

Barney (2002, p. 159) focused on the VRIO framework of business resources or capabilities that a firm should have for a competitive advantage. VRIO stands for Value, Rareness, Inimitability, and Organization. *Value* means that the business resources and capabilities of a company should be valuable enough to pose an effective response to threats or opportunities in the environment. *Rareness* means that only a limited number of companies possess such resources. *Inimitability* means that it is difficult for other companies to copy or imitate the business resources. *Organization* means that the company has a system to use the valuable, rare, and inimitable resources. With all these four elements, a company can attain a sustainable competitive advantage and produce superior economic performance. If a company has valuable and rare resources that could be copied at low cost, its short-term economic performance might be very good, but its competitive advantage would be only temporary. When resources are valuable but not rare, a company could gain competitive parity, but not a competitive edge.

If a business resource is valuable and scarce, the passage of time can diminish its value and the diffusion of knowledge can degrade its worth. Companies must make continuous efforts to gain and improve resources or capabilities to maintain their competitive edge. Examples of technologies with high initial prices that are now affordable and used broadly abound, including digital image processing (DIP), global positioning systems (GPS), and flat panel displays (FPD). Other technologies like hybrid cars, radio frequency identification (RFID) chips, and solar cells are becoming common and their prices can be expected to fall rapidly. As Barney (2002, p. 171) pointed out, R&D efforts would be in vain if a company did not have a system to market its technological innovation. A well-known example is Xerox Corporation's failure to take to market many of the products developed at its Palo Alto Research Center. These included Ethernet, graphical user interfaces (GUI), and the computer mouse, as well as object-oriented programming (OOP). Examples where R&D results were a success in the market include Sharp's improvement of its LCD technology, Toyota's hybrid car commercialization when the innovation was considered too costly for mass production, and Xerox PARC's own invention of laser printing. To sustain competitive advantage, business resources or capabilities should be unique and not easy to copy. Technologies are easy to copy, no matter how complicated. It is internal dynamics that optimize an organization's performance, and people's thought/behavior patterns that are difficult for outsiders to imitate. A good combination of complicated physical technologies and internal, socially complex skills in an organization are effective at sustaining a competitive edge (Barney, 2002, p. 169).

Business managers themselves are also very important strategic business resources. A distinctive example of this is the late Apple CEO, Steve Jobs. Executives like him, even if not well-known, are found wherever there is an industrial community, regardless of whether it is a developed or emerging economy. Mishina (2004, p. 163) made a comprehensive study of the strategic accomplishments of Japanese companies. His research covered 40 years of business performance from 1960, of all the First and Second Section companies listed on the Tokyo, Osaka, and Nagoya stock exchanges. The First Section companies included 163 firms in the electric and precision industries to the year 2000. According to Mishina's findings, 21 of the 163 firms retained a ratio of operating profit to sales of over 10% for 30 years. All but one of these 21 companies, including Keyence and Fanuc, were led by the same CEOs, unchanged for at least 14 years. Of these CEOs, 76% had held the position for more than 20 years. This is a powerful illustration that a good manager is the most important business resource.

2. Program Strategy Management

2.1 Structure of Program Strategy Management

Project management focuses on processes (i.e., "how to make" or "how to build") to achieve a series of tasks bundled as a project. The complexity of a project is solved by a simple approach – breaking the project down into hierarchical modules called work packages, which are themselves further broken down into elements of processes. Close and careful attention to these process elements can then move the project to successful completion.

Program management is not so simple. Although a program can be broken down into concrete measures called projects, its initial strategic mission is often very ambiguous, with multiple meanings. Program management translates this strategic mission into concrete objectives and goals, deciding "what to make" or "what to build." Other than dividing the program into a group of projects, it has to determine whether the configuration of projects is consistent with the strategic mission's nature when viewed as an integrated whole. It should even question if the mission's nature is correctly understood. Program objectives and goals can now be detailed through mission description and scenario development. With such clarification of specific goals, the program is divided into a hierarchical architecture of projects.

Program strategy management can be divided into two parts, as illustrated in Exhibit 3.2.1. The first part is strategic goal management, which breaks down a business strategy into the most effective and realistic goals. The second part is execution strategy management, which drives the program toward successful completion. In other words, strategic goal management focuses on "what to implement" and execution strategy management focuses on "how to execute." Risks are analyzed and assessed through these processes, and the result is reflected primarily in strategic goal management.

This section covers strategic goal management and execution strategy management. The relation between program strategy management and risk management will be covered in section 3.

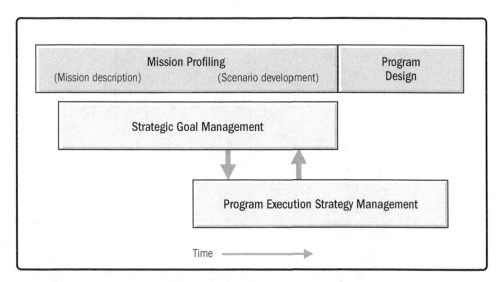

Exhibit 3.2.1: Framework of Program Strategy Management

Source: Shimizu, M. (2010), "P2M ni okeru senryaku to risuku Manejimento ni kansuru ichi-kousatsu (On Strategy and Risk Management in P2M)" *Journal of the International Association of Project and Program Management (IAP2M)*, 5(1), 129.

"Doubling the sales of product X within two years" is not a strategic goal; it is a statement of a wish. A strategic goal is a declaration such as: "Develop a high performance product that sells double the amount of our current product," "Create a high efficiency production system that doubles current capacity," or "Build a sales and service system that will double revenue." A strategic goal should be clear and concrete, describing how to enhance the organizational system's capabilities and strengths to prepare for the future.

2.2 Strategic Goal Management

The most important criteria for program goals subject to strategic goal management are effectiveness, growth potential, and certainty of execution. This section discusses the effectiveness and potential of program goals. *Program goals* are a set of goals determined through the mission description process, illustrated in Exhibit 3.2.2. *Strategic goal* is used as a generic term. Strategic goal management is to divide the business strategy into segments, incorporating the segments into program goals.

2.2.1 Effectiveness of Program Goals

Mission profiling determines program goals that maximize the effect of the strategic mission, developing scenarios to conceptualize the mission. The following three judgment factors and perspectives are particularly important:

- Effectiveness and efficiency
- Time
- Uniqueness of value

(1) Effectiveness and Efficiency

Management pursues effectiveness and efficiency. According to Drucker:

> *The administrative job of manager is to optimize the yield from those resources. This, we are usually told, means efficiency. It means focus on costs. But the optimizing approach should focus on effectiveness. It focuses*

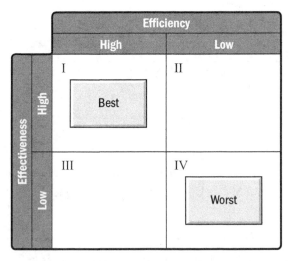

Exhibit 3.2.2: Effectiveness and Efficiency

Source: Sakakibara, K. "*Keieigaku Nyumon (Jou)* (Introduction to Business Management vol.1)" Tokyo, Japan: Nikkei, 2002, p. 32.

on opportunities to produce revenues, to create markets, and to change the economic characteristics of existing products and markets. (1974, p. 5)

Later, his point was condensed into the famous phrase: "Efficiency is doing things right; effectiveness is doing the right thing."

Effectiveness is the compatibility of program measures with the environment, and efficiency is the ratio of output to input. The emphasis Drucker placed on the difference between effectiveness and efficiency does not mean that they are mutually exclusive, as both are important. Exhibit 3.2.2 compares the combination of effectiveness and efficiency. The combination in box I is the best choice – high effectiveness and high efficiency. If either box II or III has to be selected, the exhibit recommends II, giving effectiveness priority over efficiency (Sakakibara, 2002, p. 32). Efficiency improvement often leads to effectiveness, but business without effectiveness would never be good, no matter how efficient. Braun-tube display production of the highest efficiency still had to surrender to the effectiveness of LCD technology. Being without effectiveness, in the worst case, can threaten the survival of the business itself. Being effective means being adaptable to a market, or being able to create a market. Therefore, it is most important that program goals be judged and selected in relation to customer and market needs. It should be kept in mind, however, that the selection be prone to efficiency, as this evaluation is easier than the identification of effectiveness.

(2) Time

A strategy's effectiveness can also deteriorate over time in a competitive environment. But even if a strategy is less effective, its early execution can be relatively effective. A high performance product may be effective, but if its manufacturer falls behind its competitors in releasing it, its effectiveness could be greatly reduced. Conversely, a product of lower quality may have an advantage if it is marketed at an earlier date. Effectiveness should be judged in relation to time. Program goals should be determined, with constant consideration of time, as to whether to aim for a high goal quickly or go step by step, achieving smaller goals one by one.

(3) Uniqueness of Value

Uniqueness means that the value created by the program has a distinctive strength that other companies cannot copy easily. This strength ranges from special attributes of the product to a unique position in the market and an effective organizational system. But if the value created is identical with that created by others, it will produce nothing more than competitive parity at best, that is, a situation where no advantage occurs. Uniqueness of value may be realized in combination with the characteristics of the organization or may evolve through accumulated program experience. The major element of uniqueness of value corresponds to the uniqueness of the product's customer value and the uniqueness of the organization's business resources and capabilities.

Examination of strategy includes factors such as (i) understanding the relationship between the strategy and major trends of external change; (ii) in-depth knowledge of the market, customer, and value chain, as well as of core technologies up to the present; (iii) thorough study of future possibilities and uncertainties; and

(4) insight into the regional environment and human nature. It is not easy to address all of these. To do so requires extremely complicated trade-offs among factors, requiring significant time and money. As a strategic mission is to create something unique to the organization within given time and resource constraints, decisions must be made to neglect or abandon some of the above factors instead of trying to fulfill all of them. The three perspectives described above provide criteria for decision-making.

2.2.2 Growth Potential

Continuous growth is most important for organizations, especially for those engaging in business. Growth potential is therefore a critically important element of a program.

Program growth potential has two aspects. One is program scalability. Scalability requires designing a program architecture that can grow an existing program or that can start a new program to lead to further success. A follow-on program (or project) expands the success a step further. A company will move to the second phase of a program, such as building a factory, launching a sales network in an emerging market, or developing a natural resource, because the first phase was successful. How to make good use of the lessons from the previous program phase in the next phase is a very important subject. At the time of project completion, a project contractor company in such industries as construction, plant engineering, or ICT solutions is far into the learning curve, and its knowledge and experience is at a peak, giving it great advantage over competitors. Strategically, it is very important that this momentum be continued in the follow-on program. Without follow-on business or a similar program, the hard-won accumulation of capable human resources, organizational knowledge, and technologies will likely dissipate and be lost.

Another aspect of growth potential is acquiring new business resources and capabilities through program execution. While the primary purpose of program execution is achievement of the strategic mission, execution of a program can be an opportunity for an organization to acquire business resources or competence, such as (i) rare resources, (ii) new markets and customers, (iii) enhanced organizational and management competence, (iv) new financial channels, (v) credibility, and (vi) brand power. These are advantages that can be broadened after program completion. This is especially important for Japanese companies that emphasize organizational continuity.

Growth potential is very important in business strategy, but it cannot be achieved as an independent objective. From the program management point of view, growth potential provides an additional perspective on post-program issues.

2.3 Perspectives of Strategic Goal Management

In a large-scale system program the targets of individual programs are different from each other, although program stakeholders share a more or less common understanding of "what to make" (i.e., they share knowledge of strategic missions and program goals). Strategic missions for strategic programs (or programs that P2M defines as *creative-type* or *innovative-type* programs) vary widely, and so do the program environments and resources. This section discusses the major perspectives of strategic goal management in strategic programs.

A creative-type or innovative-type program is one that an organization has never experienced before. Commercial firms carry out such programs in response to their competition strategies; they are creations or innovations that are made to gain advantages with unique products or entirely new markets. In strategies based on RBV, these types of programs are important to acquire valuable and scarce business resources.

Exhibit 3.2.3 is an outline of perspectives on strategic goal management. There are two domains of competitive market strategy: (i) competitive strategy of products and (ii) business portfolio strategy. "Basic Strategy," in the second column of the exhibit, shows competitive strategies for an existing market, such as cost leadership, and new market creation. It is common that several strategies are combined to form an overall strategy – for instance, differentiating a product to create a new market, or creating a market while retreating from an existing one (i.e., scrap and build). The purpose of each strategy is to acquire competitive advantage through use of sources of competitive advantages in the third column, which includes economies of scale, economies of scope, and other items. Effective combination of these items is important. The items listed in the "Basic Strategy" column are generic expressions of strategic missions that are assigned to programs. In many cases a program's strategic mission corresponds with one (or a combination of two or more) of these items. Similarly, the items for "Source of Competitive Advantage" are generic expressions of program goals. A program goal, which is actually defined through the mission definition process, can be one of these items, restated to conform to the program.

Strategic Area (business strategy)	Basic Strategy (corresponding to strategic mission)	Source of Competitive Advantage	Focuses & Measures

[Market Strategy]
 • Competitive strategy of Products
  ▪ Response to threat
  ▪ Use of opportunity
 • Business portfolio strategy
  ▪ Expansion business area
  ▪ Terminate unprofitable business
	• Cost leadership
	 • Differentiating
	 • Focus
	 • New market creation
	  ▪ Novel products
	  ▪ New customer market
	  ▪ Diversification
	 • Withdrawal
	  ▪ Business termination
	  ▪ Business sellout
		• Economies of scale
		 • Experience curve
		 • Economies of scope, synergy
		 • Quality (function, performance, design)
		 • Network externality
		 • Niche
		 • Sales channel
		 • Service
			• Value chain
			 • Transaction cost
			 • Innovation
			 • Products
			 • Market
			 • Production engineering
			 • Focusing market characteristics (customer segment, region)
			 • Facilities
			 • Organization
			 • M&A, alliance
			 • Production engineering
			 • Investment for efficiency improvement
			 • Finance
			 • Information

[Resource Strategy] • RBV (VRIO) • Resource efficiency enhancement	• Organization capability • Scarce resource acquisition • Process efficiency	• Efficiency enhancement • System focusing • Parts/element focusing • Distinctive technology • Unique internal processes • Supply chain	

Exhibit 3.2.3: Perspectives of Strategic Goal Management (Strategic Programs) (Shimizu, 2010)

Source: Shimizu, M. (Sept. 2010), "P2M ni okeru senryaku to risuku Manejimento ni kansuru ichi-kousatsu (On Strategy and Risk Management in P2M)" *Journal of the International Association of Project & Program Management* (IAP2M) 5, (1), 129.

In preparing a program with concrete measures, discussion should proceed from various perspectives, major examples of which are shown in the last column, "Focuses & Measures." Consider a situation where a company sets a goal to achieve through economies of scale. The company has to design its business execution system to include details regarding "facilities" and R&D investments ("Innovations"), considering the span of the "value chain" and related "transaction costs." As a result of these processes, the program architecture for execution comes to be defined.

In the RBV area of the exhibit, it is important to determine which organizational capability needs reinforcement. In some cases capability is not obtained through projects but through long, continuing business operations conducted through small group activities. Such accumulation of activities made a great contribution to the development of the Toyota Production System (TPS or "lean production system") and to quality control capabilities in many companies. If other companies wish to introduce the system however, they would need program or project activities. "Scarce resource acquisition" covers a vast diversity of resources to gain competitive advantage, including rare raw materials, a good downtown location for a branch shop, talented researchers or designers, and a controlling share in an entrepreneurial venture with distinctive technology.

"Resource efficiency enhancement" is a strategy to improve costs and physical resource use efficiency. It is typically implemented by developing a new plant or restructuring the system of operation. It is also important to clarify business direction: for example, whether to build an integrated system, or focus on segmented elemental technologies of modules, parts and materials, or on unique technologies that are difficult to copy, or on proprietary internal processes.

2.4 Execution Strategy Management
2.4.1 Purpose of Execution Strategy Management
As already described, execution strategy management focuses on "how to execute the program" or "how to build the products" in an effort to enhance program value. More specifically, execution strategy management objectives are to increase the certainty and efficiency of program execution, as well as to enhance product competitiveness. Certainty in program execution is discussed in relation with risk management in the next section. Enhancement of product competitiveness is one of the core elements of strategic goals. However, in manufacturing industries where product improvement is almost routine, designing the competitiveness of products is often a matter of program design or individual projects, rather than a theme of mission profiling, which is to determine strategic goals. The importance of mission profiling is obvious where discovery of new value is critical in commercializing new products, but it is not emphasized when minor changes to existing products are intended. To improve product competitiveness, emphasis is placed on strategic goal management in the case of strategic programs. But, in many large-scale system-type programs it is included in execution strategy management, where strategic goals are rather obvious.

2.4.2 Focuses and Measures in Execution Strategy Management
Execution strategy for strategic (or creative and innovative-type) programs varies so greatly that its focus can hardly be typified by generalization. The following is

a discussion of execution strategy management for a large-scale system program, which is also applicable to some types of strategic programs.

In industries such as construction, plant engineering, ICT, space systems, and pharmaceuticals, programs and projects are routine, with similar, but not exactly the same, efforts repeated. Programs carried out in the drug discovery and development industry are very creative by nature, but in most cases their processes are also nearly routine. In these areas, a program or a project itself is usually a business, and business strategies overlap with program strategies. The perspectives and strategies in this category are summarized in Exhibit 3.2.4.

In a large-scale system-type program, business growth through enhancement of competitiveness and acquisition of new customers is also important. And even more important here is a perspective of steadily increasing sales and organizational efficiency improvement by smoothing out operating rate fluctuations through continuous execution of programs. This is quite similar to multi-project management (see Chapter 2, Section 5). The organizational efficiency attained by combining internal resources with outsourcing or business alliances is important. Such efforts to enhance organizational efficiency lead directly to competitiveness, including improvement in employee capabilities and process efficiency based on work experience, job specialization, and division of labor.

An order backlog that falls short of the organization's capacity is obviously a problem. However, a backlog that far exceeds capacity is likely to cause excessive workloads, leading to schedule overruns and increased failures, which would result in large losses. This indicates the importance of order selection while taking the current backlog into account. In Japan, where laying employees off is difficult, an

Strategic Area (execution strategy)	Basic Strategy (program organization, operation)	Focuses & Measures
• Efficiency of organizational operation • Product competitiveness	• Multi-programs/projects • Developmental group technology, or modular technology • Pipeline management • Selective order acceptance, Project portfolio (unprofitable order acceptance) • Alliance (consortium, joint ventures, others) • Core technology	• Reduce operating rate fluctuation (improvement of operational cost efficiency, stability of quality and lead time) • Shared use among projects (improvement of operational cost efficiency, modular design) • Specialization, division of labor (efficiency improvement of human and facility resources, alliances and outsourcing, improvement of marketing capabilities) • Market requirements and strategic technology development (product technology, process technology)

Exhibit 3.2.4: Focuses and Measures in Execution Strategy Management (Large-scale system-Type Program)

Source: Shimizu, M. (Sept. 2010), "P2M ni okeru senryaku to risuku Manejimento ni kansuru ichi-kousatsu (On Strategy and Risk Management in P2M)" *Journal of the International Association of Project & Program Management* (IAP2M) 5, (1), 129.

unprofitable contract may in some cases be accepted just to maintain a certain operating rate. If such contracts increase, the business or organization needs to be restructured.

In the electrical and automotive industries products are continuously improved and sold as new products. Efforts in these fields are creative- or innovative-type programs if the novelty of the improved product is exceptionally high. However, if the products are improved routinely, the programs are more of an operational type. In Exhibit 3.2.4, "Developmental group technology" aims at synergy in product development efficiency, which occurs when products are viewed as a group. In industries engaging in a single product family with a number of product varieties, a manufacturer develops modular-type components or sub-systems that are common to its products so that efficiency is optimized and economies of scale are brought to bear in production. Unlike businesses that sell modular products widely to external users, the objective of developmental group technology is to improve quality, costs, lead times and related technologies of end system products by massive use of common intermediate products developed as modules. "Pipeline management" is a method typically used in the drug industry, where one effective medical agent is selected from hundreds of candidate substances through multiple selection stages. This method optimizes the number of candidate substances stage by stage so that the workload will level off.

Broad areas of technology are required for large-scale system-type programs dealing with system products. To improve a competitive edge, strategic use of high-quality external resources through alliances and so forth is very important, in addition to advancement of internal core technology.

3. Strategy and Program Risk

3.1 Strategy Management and Risk

Execution of a strategy generally means bringing innovative change to the organizational status quo. Therefore, strategy and its execution are always accompanied by the uncertainty, large or small, in innovation, which is inherently the risk itself. Strategy and risk are two sides of a coin. Ambitious strategies increase risk. An ad hoc, or haphazard strategy could in the long run put competitiveness at stake, no matter how certain its execution. Program strategy management is a process that embeds the strategy into the program by mission profiling. Response to strategic-level risks is also incorporated into the program. Next, the strategy mission and its risks are evaluated as an integrated whole, designed as a final program that reflects all of these. Until the program design phase, risk management is done within the scope of strategy management; it is not recognized as risk management per se. In this phase, risks are identified and analyzed, and goals or architecture are changed so that the risk becomes acceptable.

Meanwhile, at the program execution phase, the mission of each individual project is clearly defined and established. Its risks are the uncertainties in the course of project execution. Risk management is generally explained as an independent process that identifies, evaluates, and responds to risks lurking in the project. The risks arising from the program execution processes integrating the projects are treated as part of program management. Exhibit 3.3.1 illustrates relations between strategy management and risks in a program.

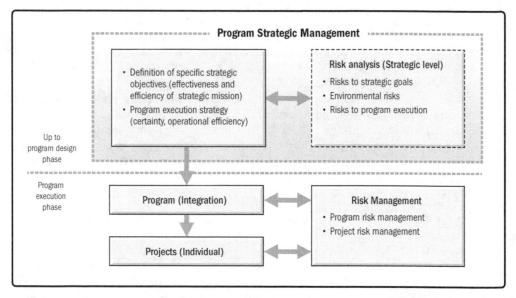

Exhibit 3.3.1: Program Strategy Management and Risk Management

Source: Shimizu, M. (Sept. 2010), "P2M ni okeru senryaku to risuku Manejimento ni kansuru ichi-kousatsu (On Strategy and Risk Management in P2M)" *Journal of the International Association of Project & Program Management* (IAP2M) 5 (1), 129.

There are two kinds of risks. One is pure risk, which comprises the probability of loss. The other, a speculative risk, contains the probability of both loss and gain of profit. In many cases, the goal to accomplish in an individual project is clear, and project management focuses on pure risk with the primary concern being achievement of the goal without defects or failures. However, up to the program design phase, including the design of strategic goals, the focus is primarily on profit maximization, which could therefore be called speculative risk – though the term might sound slightly inappropriate. Thus, in the practice of mission profiling, where a manager's main concern is to investigate achievable program goals, risks remain *dependent variables* in the investigation.

3.2 The Relation between Strategy and Risks – a case study

Case:
Company A's market share is the largest by a narrow margin, due to its high efficiency in assembling processes and its reputation for quality. Company B has a somewhat lower reputation for product quality. Armed with its low pricing, however, Company B is increasing its market share. Company A plans to build a factory with a production capacity five times as large as its current one in order to gain an overwhelming competitive advantage with its cost-leadership strategy, responding to a forecast of rapid market growth.

What kind of strategic risks will Company A take on as it promotes this "economies of scale" strategy? The first question is: Are market growth and Company A's position in the future market estimated appropriately? Second: Will the strategy successfully compete with Company B? These are the risks of the uncertainties relating to the market.

To operate the new factory with a capacity five times larger, a stable supply of parts and materials is necessary. Company A's core competence is its assembly line process. Whether the upstream processes should be outsourced or vertically integrated in-house may become an important strategic issue. The cost of establishing such processes in-house can be burdensome if market growth is lower than expected. Additionally, Company A lacks experience, and production quantities will fall behind those of manufacturers specializing in the work. Company A will incur the risk of a production-cost disadvantage compared to Company B, at least during the early stages.

On the other hand, if Company A outsources to Company C, a parts manufacturer, for the quintupled volume of production, Company C will need a new factory, which may pose a high investment risk. Company A may encourage Company C to build a new factory by guaranteeing the order volume for three years, for example. If Company A commits to the transaction with Company C so that Company C can recover the investment in three years, the price would have to be too high. If Company C's products exclusively designed for Company A cannot be sold to anyone else, its new factory would not operate beyond the three-year guarantee period if Company A stops ordering the product. Company C would have a risk of accepting unprofitable orders if Company A pushes Company C. This is an example of *opportunism risk* for Company C. But if the market expands greatly after Company A's three-year guarantee, Company C could extend its sales to Company B as well. Company C would have a stronger competitive position and Company A could face higher transaction costs or tougher competition. In the past, Japanese companies used to solve problems of this kind by "pseudo" vertical integration with *keiretsu* companies, a type of hierarchical corporate group. With global competition, however, transactions limited within *keiretsu* may be losing cost competitiveness.

These are examples of the risks when a company takes a cost-leadership strategy. To adopt this strategy and execute it through a program, it is essential to examine many possibilities to gain a competitive edge. Strategy management must define goals that take into account program risks.

The sample case above offers a variety of possibilities. For risk related to market growth, strategy to expand business step by step can be a solution. For risks related to transaction costs and opportunism, business alliances such as collaborative ventures could be a solution. There are many options, depending on the relationship between Company A and Company C. Strategies to prepare for uncertainties caused by competitor Company B should vary responding to the situation. Solutions should be considered based on Company B's capacity, capabilities, and behavioral patterns. Program architecture varies, depending on the kind of risk judged acceptable and how it is incorporated in the program.

3.3 Risk Elements and Program Certainty
A program is meant to include uncertainty because it creates new value. On the other hand, program managers are expected to achieve program goals with certainty.

If program goals are easy to achieve, program certainty naturally increases, while the overall effect might be less. Program certainty would be low if a goal is chosen that is difficult due to the capabilities of organizational resources, even though a large return is expected with success. The degree of certainty is influenced not only by management, but also by the external environment, such as markets, customers, competition, and social infrastructure. Levels of uncertainty contained in program goals can often be reduced by re-examining program architecture and the executing organization.

3.3.1 Strategic Risk Elements of Program

The risk elements that can influence program uncertainty are listed with counter-measures in Exhibit 3.3.2.

"Inappropriate goals" create risk caused by failures in the mission definition process. Risk at this level is the most serious, because it comes from insufficient effort or lack of capability for the most essential level of program implementation. "Market uncertainty" arises from market forecasts and changes; external risk factors are significantly large in this risk area. Transactional opportunism is the risk arising from the interrelations among business partners and/or collaborators. Risk of this nature requires full attention to program architecture or organizational structure. "Defective or insufficient resources" create risk from a lack of human,

Risk Area	Risk Elements	Countermeasure Examples
• Inappropriate goals	• Ambiguous goals • Goals too big or too distant	• Establishment of proper governance system • Mission redefinition
• Market uncertainty	• Uncertainty of scale or growth • Complexity (Interaction between products and market; development of new technology, etc.) • Market volatility; environmental changes • Product lifecycle (Chasm; Death Valley)	• Phased decision making (option strategy), real option • Quick response cycle • Accomplishment in niche markets
• Transactional Opportunism	• Transaction specific contract • Asymmetrical future value	• Countermeasure by transaction contract (spot transaction; complete contracting; sequential contracting; use of relationships) • Vertical integration (internal market) • Collaborative venture
• Defective or insufficient resources	• Organizational structure • Deficiency of human resources (e.g., engineering staff) • Physical resources (e.g., facilities, materials) • Funds	• Enhancement of organization • Acquisition of resources • Personnel management; recruiting • R&D • M&A; alliance; collaboration: outsourcing • Public assistance (low-price site provision; subsidy; tax exemptions; public loans)
• Threats from other companies	• Five forces (see Porter, 1980) • Disruptive innovation	• Individual countermeasure suitable for individual threats

Exhibit 3.3.2: Strategic Risks and Useful Countermeasures

Source: Shimizu, M. (Sept. 2010), "P2M ni okeru senryaku to risuku Manejimento ni kansuru ichi-kousatsu (On Strategy and Risk Management in P2M)" *Journal of the International Association of Project & Program Management* (IAP2M) 5(1), 129

physical and financial resources for program execution. "Threats from other companies," in the last line, vary greatly. The threats are not only from direct competitors but also from events affecting business partners, such as forward- or backward-vertical integration. Individual programs require various countermeasures, depending on the nature of the threats. Risks identified in the planning phase are treated by countermeasures developed by reexamining plans. When risks are unacceptable, reexamination should be made again, going back to the mission definition phase.

3.3.2 Risk Elements and Countermeasures

Risks can be identified by methods described in Section 4.2 of this chapter. Risks are analyzed and evaluated in detail by financial and business environment investigations, technical design reviews, or numerical simulations. Risk surfaces in various patterns. It is important to incorporate countermeasures in program design, based on the essential nature of the strategy. The following are brief summaries of some typical strategy-level risks and countermeasures that should be incorporated in the program.

(1) Program Goals and Risk Elements

Setting program goals as strategic goals is the responsibility of mission definition. The method of execution greatly affects the certainty of goal achievement. Examination of risk elements is important in processes of scenario development and in program design. Risk elements are usually analyzed together with the method of mission execution at the program scenario phase, which is more abstract and simple compared to the detailed program design phase. When risk is at an unacceptable level, the mission definition must be reexamined. Through this iteration, the program manager becomes more confident of success. Finally, at the program design phase, it must be confirmed that no risk remains unacceptable or unrecognized in the scenario.

(2) Establishment of a Governance System

Ambiguous or overly ambitious goals lead to program failure, regardless of the execution process. Executing a long-term program often becomes a goal in itself, or creates interest groups. The larger the problem, the more difficult it is for an executing organization to change direction. It is essential that the leadership has a clear recognition of the strategic mission. A governance system must be established so that program reviews and decisions are made properly and at the appropriate time, based on such strategic mission recognition. Bootstrap program management should not be misunderstood to dump top management's responsibilities onto program management. To execute a program aligned with strategic goals, a governance system is essential.

(3) Option Strategy/Real Option

Option strategy is a method to cope with program uncertainty. This method is used to decide continuation, alteration, or discontinuation of the program, based on interim results. Many programs have uncertainties that are too great to start with a large investment. Risks are mitigated by starting from some limited program areas that have fewer uncertainties or that need smaller and less risky investment. The program proceeds to the next step when the prediction of achieving the final outcome is one of success; otherwise the program is reformulated or terminated.

The risks include not only market uncertainty, but also those of various other categories, such as technological uncertainty in a broad sense, or business areas, like in mining, where success is only a matter of probability.

This approach is applied in many fields, such as trial production of a new product, test marketing, step-wise expansion of a factory, mining rights options, film rights options, among others. Of these, step-wise execution of a program may start as a compromise between disagreeing executives or program managers. In many cases this ends up in failure and should be avoided. In the option strategies, an option scenario should be established beforehand, based on a risk evaluation, in order to avoid failure from lack of proper decision-making or repeated haphazard resource inputs. It is essential to define beforehand the conditions for continuation and what to do with sunk costs if a program is discontinued.

Real option is a method to evaluate the option effect numerically at first. Investment in a real asset, such as a new factory or a new large-scale facility, is evaluated on the premise that the decision about optional investment is postponed until information with a higher certainty (i.e., of lower risk) is obtained. Real option enables more precise and effective risk evaluation, compared with the simple NPV method. In some conditions, the real option procedure makes it possible to evaluate a program as feasible, even when NPV would not judge it feasible. The concept of the method is outlined in Chapter 4.

(4) Quick Response Cycle

Swiftness is strength. When a drastic market change occurs, excessive forecasting effort is useless if the prediction does not become reality. Being prepared in advance to detect the phenomenon is important, enabling frequent rapid response. It is also important to prepare appropriate responses, allowing deviations from predictions. For example, the basic idea behind Toyota's *Kanban* (Just-in-Time) method is not to forecast demand, but to have real demand trigger rapid responses in upstream processes. This methodology is widely applied in inventory control by retailers, including convenience store chains and large supermarkets, which quickly respond to hot-selling products.

These examples are not projects themselves, but the idea of quick response has wide applications in business strategy. As an example, despite decreased demand for oil after the 1973 crisis, oil plant construction projects were not discontinued. The world's refinery capacity continued to increase for the next eight years. As a result, the oil industry suffered from operating losses for a long period of time. If a company had responded more quickly than its competitors, it could have gained a large competitive advantage. Shell Oil learned from this, and began aiming to cultivate organizational awareness and adaptability to ensure the quickest possible responses to environmental changes, rather than attempt to rely on perfect predictions (Van der Heijden, 1996, p. 4).

(5) The "Chasm" in the Product Life Cycle

It is common in manufacturing to develop and market product lines corresponding to each product's life cycle. This requires innovations at each stage of that life cycle. When developing an unprecedented, innovative product line, it is difficult to introduce immediately to a general market even if it proves to be successful in an early-adopters market. Between a preceding market and a large-volume general market, there exists a big "chasm," as Moore (2000, p. 19) pointed out. Programs to merchandize new and innovative products require built-in measures to cross the chasm between early adopters and the general market. In many cases, it is said that success in an appropriate niche market can appeal to the sense of security of the large variety of users in the general market, supporting their adoption of the product.

(6) Countermeasures against Opportunism

Opportunism means to take advantage of a situation for selfish motives, and often by means not thought to be ethical. Suppose that Companies A and B are cooperating in business; if B invests in a certain asset that is inapplicable or worthless for any other purpose than the transaction with A, such investment is called a *transaction-specific investment.* Once such an investment is made, B has no choice but to continue operating the invested facilities or equipment so as to obtain returns on the investment. Since B has no other customer for the products of the asset, it is possible for A to gain profits by imposing unjustly low prices on B's products. This is an example of opportunism in a transaction, taking advantage of a partner's weakness.

Countermeasures against opportunism are necessary when execution of a program depends on a contract with an external organization. It is necessary to select proper contracting methods, including *spot contracts*, which are applicable only for a certain period of time, or *complete contracts*, which define minor details in preparation for all possible future eventualities. As complete contracts are usually very difficult to make, they can be substituted with *sequential contracts*, which cover only the foreseeable period and are modified at any time when a change in situation occurs. Organizational or personal relations can be also adopted to prevent opportunism (see note below).

When a company has within itself a vertically integrated part of a necessary value chain, the threat of opportunism is eliminated, but in return the risk of undesirable enlargement of an organization, or deterioration in efficiency, is shouldered. One solution, when there is a mutual fear of a partner's opportunism, is a joint business such as a joint venture (Barney, 2002, p. 197).

Note

In Japan it used to be common that a business contract did not go into excessive detail, but, instead, included a gentleman's agreement-type provision that would read like, "Should any problem occur, both parties shall sincerely cooperate with each other to resolve it." These agreements recognized and emphasized the importance of long-lasting business relationships. Obviously, if opportunistic thinking motivated either party, such an agreement would become ineffective. In the modern world of highly competitive globalization, it is increasingly important to be careful about contracting methods.

(7) Expansion of Business Resources

When a company lacks business resources to accomplish program goals, it is necessary to judge whether to redesign them or to expand the business resources. Apart from funding, the organization's technology and capability are usually the most important things, and if they cannot be obtained simply by procurement or service contracts, such business arrangements as technology licensing, consortium, alliances, or M&A should be used as part of the program. However, in the event that the scale or importance of such an arrangement is more significant relative to the program, or that the span of time required by the arrangement exceeds the program duration, it is necessary to examine if the issue should be addressed by the program or be treated as part of business to be handled concurrently with the program by a corporate or superior business unit.

(8) Unifying Force and Driving Force

One big engine for completing programs with certainty and efficiency is highly motivated program organization members. The implementation methodology of the program, and leadership by the top executive, play the major role in encouraging motivation.

A well-known example is the Apollo Project led by President John F. Kennedy, who successfully unified program organization members throughout the project by declaring his resolution to attain the program goal. Dramatic visualization of early-stage accomplishment of program goals is tremendously effective at focusing an organization's energy upon program implementation. An excellent example of this is the "Nissan Revival Plan" executed by Carlos Ghosn, who successfully reconstructed the business after publicly committing to a V-shaped turnaround.

Another approach is to incorporate a driving force into the program surely and efficiently. Examples include reorganizing the production process into a lean production system as part of the program, or, introducing a new system to support sales channels. This last measure should be handled with care, since it could increase uncertainty in the program if understanding and preparation were insufficient.

4. Program Risk Management

The *PMBOK® Guide* explains six basic processes in project risk management: risk management planning, risk identification, qualitative risk analysis, quantitative risk analysis, risk response planning, and risk monitoring and control. The approach itself is essentially the same in program risk management, but the reach of each process is very different.

As already explained, risk identification and risk analysis are incorporated in strategy management processes up to the program design phase. Consequently, the designed program is embedded with permissible or controllable risks, many of which are allocated to individual projects and the rest becoming the risks of the integrated overall program. This is why there are two kinds of risk management in the program execution phase – program risk management and project risk management. The former covers the program as a whole, and the latter deals with risks in individual projects.

In this section the discussion is mainly on a general outline of risk identification and analysis and on program risk management. Risk management in individual projects is detailed in the *PMBOK® Guide*, P2M, and elsewhere.

4.1 Basic Processes of Risk Management

4.1.1 Risk and Risk Impact

(1) Speculative Risk and Pure Risk

Generally, risk is understood as uncertainty in doing business or in engaging in other activities. Traditionally it has been understood as something that imparts a negative influence on accomplishment of the activity's objectives. This is called *pure risk.*

On the other hand, there is uncertainty that can work both negatively and positively. This type of uncertainty includes foreign exchange fluctuations for trading companies and oil prices for electric power companies. This is called *speculative risk.* Every investment is an activity with speculative risk, as typified by investment in the stock market or in other companies' businesses. Execution of a business strategy such as investing in a new business is of the nature of speculative risk, which pursues a positive outcome, taking the risk of ending with a negative result.

Exhibit 3.4.1 illustrates schematically the relations between speculative risk and pure risk in a commercial program. A program is planned to achieve a certain level of expected earnings, which consists of two parts: one is the minimum

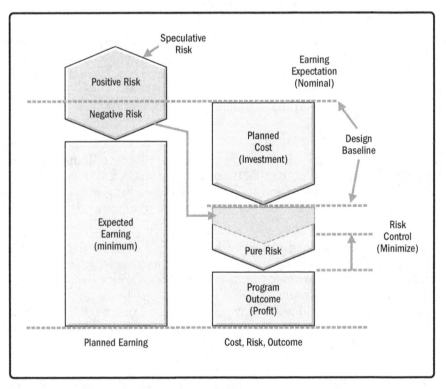

Exhibit 3.4.1: Speculative Risk and Pure Risk

Source: Shimizu, M. (2011), "Senryaku puroguramu ni okeru risuku manejimento (Risk Management in Strategic Program Management)" *Journal of the Society of Project Management (Japan), 13* (4), 20

expected earning, considered to be a high probability result, and the other is the speculative risk, estimated with uncertainty. The positive and negative influences of a speculative risk are expressed in the exhibit as "Positive Risk" and "Negative Risk," respectively. "Earning Expectation (Nominal)" is the expectation of earnings including the expected value of the speculative risks. In an actual program, the program outcome, which is obtained after subtracting the necessary costs and the pure risk expectation from the nominal earning expectation, is designed to be substantially positive as the baseline. Risk management in program execution is to minimize pure risks, including negative risk, and maximize the positive risk. Speculative risks with positive and negative risks are treated as a whole in program strategy management, as explained by examples in Section 3.3.2. In the program design process, some negative risks are allocated to individual projects as acceptable (negative) risks in program execution. During program execution, pure risk management is conducted for nominal earning expectations. The following discussion deals with the risk management of pure risks, unless noted otherwise.

(2) Risk Impact

Various uncertain factors exist as risk events in connection with execution of a project. Each individual risk event may or may not surface by project completion time. This probability is called *risk event probability*. The influence or impact from surfaced risk is diverse, ranging from financial loss to schedule delays, depending on the risk's nature. The risk of a program or a project is expressed as a total sum of the products of the impact and the probability of individual risks.

$$\text{Risk} = \sum_{i=1}^{n} (\text{impact } x \text{ event probability})_{\text{risk event } i}$$

The impact of individual risk events is much different, depending on the timing of the event becoming visible. For example, when design errors or software bugs are discovered during the design or module production phases, their impacts are usually not very large, but when they are found in the final test phase or after operations have started, it is not unusual for a small error to cause a huge loss.

Exhibit 3.4.2 illustrates the relationship between risk and risk impacts in a program. Up to the program design phase at the left, risks are contained in the processes of mission profiling and program design as design parameters to optimize the realization of the strategic mission as described in Section 3. Generally, program risk is reduced to a minimum insofar as the strategic mission is achievable. But in some programs, a higher risk is accepted intentionally, aiming at a higher strategic effect. This would be a management decision, but the decision would need to be made with sufficient understanding of the risk.

In the execution phase of programs and projects, investment piles up over time. In accordance with progress in planning or execution, uncertain elements (i.e., risk event probabilities) decrease. Accordingly, total risk generally decreases as the program progresses, although a portion, small as it may be, remains until the program is closed. Meanwhile, corrective steps and countermeasures become larger in scale as risk events surface in accordance with program progress. Thus the possible impact of risk increases with the passage of time, reaching its maximum when the system-type project is at its completion. In the operational or service period after

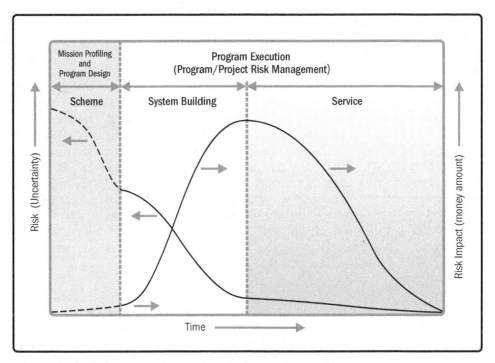

Exhibit 3.4.2: Risk and Risk Impact of a Program

completion and handover of the system, risk continues to exist. However, both risk event probability and risk impact decrease over time.

4.1.2. Program Risk and Project Risk

Exhibit 3.4.3 shows the basic process of program risk management. The exhibit's left side, ending with "up to program design phase," illustrates the mission profiling and program design process. It is where program-related risks are identified and reduced to an acceptable level by reviewing program goals and program architecture. After program design is completed, the risks are divided into two categories, as shown on the right side of the exhibit. One is the individual project risks, which represent the risk of each individual project's failure. The other is program risks, which should be treated by the program as a whole, not by separate projects.

Goals assigned to the individual projects are all project-specific, and therefore, accomplishment of these goals constitutes the reference criteria for the project risk assessment. When the program is to sell a new product, for instance, goals given to a project in charge of product development are to meet specific functions, performance, and development deadlines of the product. The risks for this project are the uncertainty that it will successfully achieve these product development-specific goals. Risks differ project by project among the projects within a program. There may be a risk of failing in the business because of a mistake made in coordinating the distribution network of the product and service. This is a risk in the project in charge of distributor coordination, not in the one in charge of product development. Risks also differ between projects and programs. There may be a risk of losing the

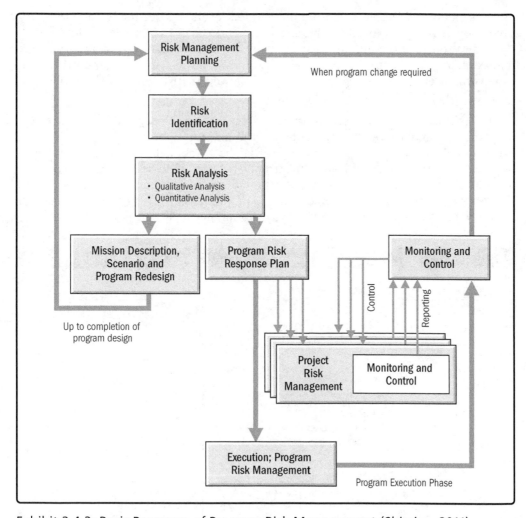

Exhibit 3.4.3: Basic Processes of Program Risk Management (Shimizu, 2011)

Source: Shimizu, M. (2011), "Senryaku puroguramu ni okeru risuku manejimento (Risk Management in Strategic Program Management)" *Journal of the Society of Project Management (Japan)*, 13, (4), 20

validity of the goal itself because of wrong recognition of economic changes. This last is not a project risk but a program risk of setting the wrong goals or misreading the business environment.

Each project manager is responsible for managing these risks by implementing risk management processes, which include risk identification, risk analysis, risk response planning, risk response execution, and risk monitoring and control. This part in the diagram is simply indicated as "project risk management." When a risk event surfaces in a project, it is recognized by the monitoring and control processes of the project and reported to the program.

Program risk management consists of two processes. The first one is a process for planning and execution of program risk response related to the entirety of the program, and the second process is for risks to goal achievement in individual projects. As far as a project can handle the risk event within itself, the program's involvement is not required. When a risk event surfaces in a project and threatens the achievement of the program's strategic goals, it is a program risk. Program risk management should then engage in additional activities, such as promoting goal achievement efforts of the project, giving renewed instructions to the project, or coordinating it with other related projects.

Exhibit 3.4.4 shows objectives, main matters of concern, and main risk areas of program risk management in the concept and planning phase and in the program execution phase. In the concept and planning phase and up to program design completion, risks are estimated from a macro perspective, such as an overall risk level for individual projects. Also, it is important to identify high-risk projects or risk elements of vital importance for the entire program. Special care should be taken for such risk items in scenario development or program design.

Program Risk Management		Risk Management of Individual Project
Up to Completion of Program Design <included in program strategic management>		
Objectives	• To define the optimum program goals • To select a secure program scenario and architecture	N/A
Main matters of concern	• Overall risk level of each project • To identify high risk projects and high-risk elements • Risks of integrating programs	
Main risk areas	• External risks • Capability of project organizations (including resource supplying capability)	
Program Execution Phase <Program risk management and risk management of individual projects>		
Objectives	• To monitor and control projects • To respond to exposed risk events affecting program objectives • To deal with risks of integrating program	• To eliminate or minimize project risk • To maintain project risk within an acceptable level
Main matters of concern	• Progress status of projects • Information relating to major external risks (environment, market and stakeholders, etc.) • Early recognition of notable risk events • Corrective action required	• Overall risk level of the project • Planning and execution of responses to individual risks • Progress status of project • Corrective action required
Main risk area	• Status or outcome of projects • Risks in project interrelation • External risks (market environment, economic and social environment, natural environment and disaster) • Contracts • Funding • Competitors' moves	• QCD of the project • Technical risks • External interface • Human errors & accidents

Exhibit 3.4.4: Program Risk Management and Project Risk Management
Source: Shimizu, M. (2011), "Senryaku puroguramu ni okeru risuku manejimento (Risk Management in Strategic Program Management)" *Journal of the Society of Project Management (Japan)*, 13(4), 20.

In the execution phase, there are program risk management and individual project risk management. From reporting and monitoring the progress of individual projects, the program makes early recognition of possible risk events that threaten program objectives, and gives necessary instruction to the project, or directly responds to the threat by the program itself. The key to preventing problem expansion is that the program takes the initiative in handling risk events that make it difficult for individual projects to make decisions or respond. It is also important for the program to pay attention to external risk events derived from the external environment.

4.2 Risk Identification
4.2.1 Systematic Risk Identification

Risk identification is a process to clarify potential risks that exist within a program or project. There should always be a good number of risks, even in smaller projects, if they are examined closely. Risk identification is done by systematic classification of the overall project to avoid passing over important risks. There are two basic perspectives: one is to trace back from work units (i.e., work packages, subsystems, etc.) where the risks are possibly substantiated; the other is to examine the sources or origins of risk that can possibly arise.

The former is to identify possible risk events, including contingent accidents and errors that would affect costs, schedules, quality, and so forth of the entire project and each work package, and then examine possible causes. The latter is a method to examine the possible risk elements within the categories of internal and external risks, for example. Another example is to classify risk elements by the focus area of risk management, such as risks related to the target system, organization, external environment, and customers. Apart from the above, there are different classification methods used uniquely by specific companies or within certain industries. It should be noted that risk impact varies greatly depending on the timing when the surfacing of the risk is reported and recognized.

Examples of such risk classification are summarized in Exhibit 3.4.5. The risk elements of external and internal risks are also summarized in Exhibit 3.4.6.

In further explanation of Exhibit 3.4.5, note the following: "Organization and personnel affairs" in "Risks related to organization" means cases such as a drastic organizational reform or sudden replacement or resignation of a key person. These may result in significant degradation of technology or management capability and could lead to cancellation of working-level agreements, which lead to grave risks. "Information transmission" suggests that care must be taken because inadequate information transmission within organizations can create risks. "Requirements and the changes to them" in "Risks related to customers" means that ambiguity in customer requirements is a well-known risk element for various projects. In long-term programs, sometimes program value or customer interests may deviate from the original requirements because of changes in the environment. "Customer technical capabilities" implies the risk of incurring necessary friction with the customer at a later stage due to lack of explanation beforehand when, for instance, their own technical requirements definition is insufficient, or, their technical understanding is relatively low. Even though cost impacts may be small, sometimes the perception gap between both parties could become a trigger for another large risk. "Delay of related infrastructure" in "Construction projects" refers to risk

Perspective	Classification Method	Examples of Risk Results or Elements
Risk Results	Systematic classification by overall, work packages, etc.	• Termination or change of overall or part of a program/project • Risks for goal accomplishment of cost, schedule, quality, etc. • Contingents accident or failures
Sources of Risk	Internal risks and external risks	• Risks which program/project can control or have influence over • Risks which program/project cannot control or do not have influence over
	Classification by management areas	• Risks relating to target systems (technical, fund raising, execution processes, external interfaces, etc.) • Risks relating to organization (capabilities, resource volume, organization and personnel affairs, information transmission, etc.) • Risks relating to the environment (market demand, competitors, economic or social environments, laws and regulations, etc.) • Risks relating to customers (requirements and changes to them, contracts, funding, technical capabilities, etc.)
Unique to Industry (Example)	International program of plant construction (Saito & Kinumaki, p. 100)	• Country risk (war and civil conflict, nationalization, policy, laws and regulations, approval and license, variations of economic or social environment, exchange rate fluctuation, environmental assessment policy, etc.) • Risks of construction work (delay of completion, cost, delay of related infrastructure, etc.) • Operational risks (raw materials, energy, logistics, technology, operation and maintenance, management skill, additional investment, sales market, etc.)

Exhibit 3.4.5: Systematic Classification of Program/Project Risks

events, mostly in developing countries, such as a delay in construction of public infrastructure, including roads, electricity, and seaports, which is a responsibility on the customer's side.

4.2.2 Methods for Risk Identification

The objective of risk identification is to make a list of risk items that are likely to have a negative influence on the project. The influence on the project means either a risk impact of a certain level of significance with high probability, or a high-risk

Large Classification	Intermediate Classification	Areas of Risk Elements (Examples)
External risks	Environment, Customer	Country risk, economic or social change, exchange rates, laws and regulations, approvals and licenses, environmental regulations, market competition, trend of dominant technology, trend of demand, customer requirements, customer satisfaction, management of customers or cooperative firms, accidents and natural disasters
Internal risks	System/Technical Risks	Requirements and specifications of deliverables, designing technology, modeling and simulation, production engineering, production facilities, production capabilities, tests and inspections, operation, operation launching processes, internal accidents
	Management Risks	Organization, leadership, contract management, funding, budget and cost, schedules, production control, quality control, human resources, procurement and logistics, information control, stakeholder relationships, license agreements, intellectual property, disputes and lawsuits

Exhibit 3.4.6: External Risks and Internal Risks

impact with low probability. Risks with large impact and high probability should be eliminated beforehand. Risks whose probability and impact can both be judged low should be omitted from further examination because detailed examination would be unnecessary extra labor.

In the risk identification process, it is also important to have people with different standpoints or experiences examine risks to avoid oversights or biased judgments. The following methods are applied widely to risk identification, including combinations thereof:

- The checklist method
- The tree method, matrix method
- Judgment by experts, knowledgeable persons and customers (interviews)
- Creative thinking methods (e.g., the KJ method, brainstorming, Delphi method)
- Hypothesis method, failure scenario method (i.e., judge by assuming occurrence of a specific situation)
- Trend analysis, analogy
- Application of risk identification from similar projects, use of experience.

A checklist prepared in advance, or a matrix table consisting of risk elements and the work packages that might possibly incur risk events, is used to list risks, reducing the chances of oversights. The tree method is used for the same purpose, using a tree-shape diagram. However, these methods are not sufficient to avoid oversights in new projects. Judgment by experts, creative thinking methods, and hypothesis or failure scenario methods, by which risk impact is judged supposing certain environmental changes, are the methods to prepare for such risks. The failure scenario method resembles FMEA (failure mode and effect analysis) in reliability management. The plan of a program/project is based on a scenario of a chain of successes or accomplishments of certain successive events. The failure scenario method examines the influence of an element's failure on such a chain. This is effective to find implicit assumptions or pitfalls in group thinking creeping into the scenario (see note below). Other important methods are to examine technology or market trends, or to judge from analogy by other companies' failures or successes.

Naturally, time and cost are required even for risk identification alone. The application of previous experience from similar projects is very important to improve risk management efficiency.

Note

In March 2011, huge earthquakes and a gigantic *tsunami* hit Fukushima Daiichi Nuclear Plant. This resulted in a serious accident, with complete power failure of the reactor cooling system and subsequent meltdown of three reactor cores. In the plant, the risk element "all power cut for reactor cooling" had in fact been identified, but the power company had had a very long record of extremely stable power supply, with people in charge carrying a tacit assumption that "recovery of external electricity would be possible within a few hours." Sufficient countermeasures against such a disruptive disaster had not been prepared.

4.3 Risk Analysis

Risk analysis is a process to clarify the nature of identified risks, along with the causes and conditions for their surfacing, and their impact once they have occurred. In earlier phases, results of the analysis are used for redefinition of the program scenario or design. Results are also used to make risk response plans for the subsequent part of the program execution phase. Risk is calculated as the product of its impact and its probability. In many cases, the surfacing of a risk is subject to some causal relation between elements; for example, a risk can become an actual event under a coincidence of certain conditions, but cannot under other conditions. In such a case, probability is still an important factor to take into account. It is very common that the level of risk significance differs largely even between similar program execution organizations, depending on the experience or capabilities of their members, availability of information, or usefulness of various resources. In short, program/ project risk is in inverse correlation to the capability of the execution organization. The capability of the organization here means the total of technology and management capabilities, resources in hand and the maturity of its risk management. Each organization has its own methodologies or criteria for risk management, especially for risk analysis and assessment, depending on its risk management maturity.

4.3.1 Qualitative Risk Analysis

Qualitative risk analysis of a project is affected by analyzing the nature of the risk. Its purpose is to assess the level of risk by judging whether it should be treated as a risk with high impact probability on the project, or whether its impact would be almost negligible, or whether it is controllable with reasonable attention. There are two areas in qualitative risk analysis, as shown in Exhibit 3.4.7.

Qualitative analysis does not mean exclusion of numerical evaluation. The actual objective of qualitative analysis is to know the level of risk significance by a five-leveled classification, for instance, of overall and individual risk elements. The individual risk elements judged to be high-level are eliminated or mitigated by revision of the project plan or optimization of resource allocation. The overall project risk elements classified as high-level are dealt with by redefinition of the project mission or project goals, modification of the project organization, or other changes to the overall project plan. In addition, risk is further controlled through vigilant monitoring in the execution process.

Area	Objectives
Assessment of individual risk level	• To assess probability and impact of individual risk events of each work package or task included in the project. • To classify each risk level and categorize the risk response policy, such as "needs response with priority" or "no need of response."
Assessment of overall project risk level	• To assess the overall project risk level, whether the project can be executed as a whole with certainty, or whether it has large potential risks

Exhibit 3.4.7: Areas of Qualitative Analysis (Shimizu, 2011)

Source: Shimizu, M. (2011), "Senryaku puroguramu ni okeru risuku manejimento (Risk Management in Strategic Program Management)" *Journal of the Society of Project Management (Japan)*, 13, (4), 20.

(1) Assessment of Individual Risk Level

The probability impact matrix (PMI, 2000, p. 187) is a typical approach for individual risk level assessment. In this method, a matrix table is made with five impact levels of risk events, from *minor* to *very significant* on the horizontal axis and five levels of risk event probability on the vertical axis. The level of risk impact expectation of individual risks is expressed on this two-dimensional matrix table to indicate the level of risk response necessity. Similar methods, including "Risk reporting matrix" (Department of Defense, 2006, p. 11) and "Risk assessment matrix" (Kendrick, 2003, p. 167), are used in this area.

(2) Assessment of Overall Project Risk Level

Overall project risk level is evaluated using the answers to tens to hundreds of risk-related questions prepared beforehand. Such assessment is usually summarized using computer software, because the questionnaire includes a good number of questions, each of which is weighted appropriately. Such questionnaires are unique to each industry or corporation in terms of the weight and criteria given to the questions. Companies in projectized businesses have their own risk assessment models.

For a complicated technical risk assessment with many risk elements, the evaluation of an individual element's risk level is made using simple methods, such as the "technical risk quantification model" (Branscomb & Auerswald, 2001, p. 36), or the probability impact matrix referred to in the previous paragraph. The data are then summarized for an overall risk level analysis. The "technical risk quantification model" is used to assess the risk level, according to the technical maturity in such a manner as, for example: (i) the success probability of improving the existing technology is 90%, and, (ii) that of unproven new technology is 30%.

The "Project Definition Rating Index (PDRI)," developed by the Construction Industry Institute (CII), is a method to rate how perfectly defined is project scope at the initial phase of a project, which is highly influential to project success (Gibson & Dumont, 1996). PDRI makes a five-step evaluation for each of 70 items relating to program planning, with their total value indicating whether the project is well-defined. The items are weighted by their significance of influence, so that those with higher risk are noticeable by their high scores. The 70 items are devised to reach a maximum 1,000-point score, and the project plan designed to achieve a sufficiently low score. PDRI has three different standards, which correspond to three areas: architecture, civil engineering, and plant engineering.

An example of the unique-to-a-company approach for risk level assessment is "Project Risk Management – Pre-self Assessment Sheet," which was developed by Toyama and Minamino (2002) for the information system division of Hitachi Ltd. This self-diagnosis tool uses 247 items, selected based on the company's experience, making an item-by-item assessment regarding their ambiguity, and summarizing the results in an overall estimation of the project risk level. The score for each item is weighted by the significance of the influence on the project. What is characteristic to this method is that the scored points are adjusted by the "project profile diagnosis score," which is determined by the nature or features of the project. Another feature of this method is that the "criterion line" is designed to come down, i.e., the criterion score decreases as the project progresses, in correspondence with the decrease of uncertainty. The assessment starts from the estimation phase, and is repeated at every milestone to control the scores, keeping them below the "criterion curve."

4.3.2 Quantitative Risk Analysis

Quantitative risk analysis is for analyzing expectations of impacts on the program/project by using a quantitatively assumed probability of major risk events and their impact. Because of the large amount of work required, quantitative analysis is conducted only on important occasions, such as when selecting a program scenario, planning a system's basic design, or selecting an important material supplier or key technology. While qualitative analysis often focuses on filtering risks that do not require risk response efforts, quantitative analysis' concern is to find the way to minimize primary risk, which is itself usually impossible to eliminate.

Typical methods for quantitative analysis include (i) sensitivity analysis using a simple spreadsheet in something like Excel format; (ii) decision trees; (iii) numerical simulations such as the Monte Carlo method; (iv) investment value estimation using net present value; and (v) the real option method. These methods are the same as those used for the program value assessment. The outlines of ii to v are described in Chapter 4.

4.4 Basics of Risk Response

Basic risk response can be roughly divided into risk control and risk finance. Risk control is to eliminate or mitigate risks prior to execution, by elaborating technical measures, including project architecture, execution methods, and execution organization structure. Risk finance accepts risks as they are, exercising financial countermeasures to prepare for when risk events will surface. Practical methodology for risk control is explained in many books, and this book provides a summary, as illustrated in Exhibit 3.4.8.

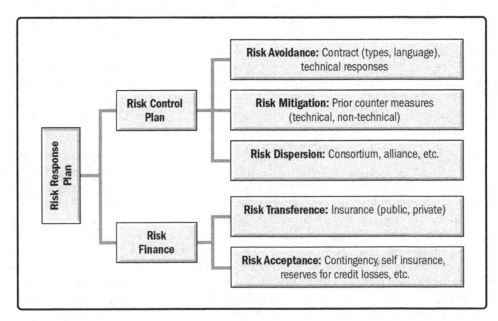

Exhibit 3.4.8: Outline of Risk Response Plan

Basic methods for risk control are risk avoidance, risk mitigation, and risk dispersion. Risk avoidance is to eliminate risk elements by changing contract type or contractual provisions, or by using certain technical methods. There are a number of methods relating to contract, which include (i) using step-wise contracts; (ii) appropriate use of cost-reimbursable contracts and fixed contracts; (iii) customer supply of materials with risks; (iv) changes or clarification in scope of work; and (v) management of intellectual property. Technical methods for risk avoidance are (i) changes of system design; (ii) use of high performance or proven components; (iii) introduction of backup systems; (iv) changes of technical requirements; (v) changes of delivery and its conditions; (vi) changes of organization structure or subcontractors; and many others.

Risk mitigation is to reduce the probability or impact of risk events to acceptable levels, using technical or non-technical measures. The essence of risk mitigation is the same as risk avoidance in nature, except that complete elimination of risk is not attainable by risk mitigation. Indeed, many practical methods are identical between risk mitigation and avoidance. Other than such methods, technical methods for risk mitigation include (i) test production; (ii) sequential execution methods, including the real option method; (iii) introduction of technology; and (iv) technical information provision from customers. There are non-technical methods, as well, such as: (i) critical path improvement by resource reinforcement; (ii) reexamination of procurement schedules or prices; (iii) step-wise procurement; (iv) procurement option; (v) revision of funding plans; and other various methods and their combinations.

Risk dispersion is to distribute risks to related stakeholders by reexamining the project organization, even when the risks cannot be eliminated. Technical or financial capabilities are improved by organizing a consortium or a joint venture. If participant companies have capabilities to handle technical risks, funding risks, or customer- or market-particular risks according to their specialty, it mitigates the risk of collective as well as individual loss.

While risk control plans are proactive countermeasures made in the project planning and design phases, risk finance is to prepare for possible surfacing of risks that are difficult to respond to in advance by risk control plans or that have been judged as not needing a response.

Risk transfer is to make insurance contracts with other companies at a certain price to cover losses in case the risk event surfaces. Insurance includes public trade insurance and private accident insurance underwritten by insurance companies, such as marine insurance and fire insurance. Insurance covers only the area of pure risks, where probability can be estimated statistically.

Generally in projects, there exist a number of risks of low probability and small impact. The costs for responding to such risks one by one can, in many cases, exceed the profits obtainable from such measures. Risk acceptance is a policy to accept risks as they are, not exercising reactive measures. It would be fortunate if no risks surface; generally, however, a certain portion of them actually do, incurring costs. Contingency and other risk budgets are prepared at the planning phase to respond to such and other unknown risks.

In addition to the above, risks can be hedged by futures trading, for example, risks in foreign currency exchange rates and various market commodities, such as fuels and metals. Also effective for risk finance are various financial techniques, such as option trading to buy the right to make a certain deal on foreign currencies or interest rates at a specific future date. Generally, however, these are executed as part of corporate financial strategy, not program strategy.

4.5 Risk Management Maturity Model

As already discussed, risk impacts tend to be smaller when the organization's capabilities are high. Higher project management maturity means higher risk management capability in general. The risk management maturity model is focused on assessing the project's or business organization's capabilities at risk management. Conversely, organizations make efforts to improve their risk management maturity to deal with their programs/projects more safely.

Hopkinson (2011, p. 93) presented an example of this by explaining the Project Risk Maturity Model, in which 50 questions relating to project management are used. In this example, maturity in the following six areas is examined by a four-level evaluation to assess overall risk management capability. The areas are project stakeholders, risk identification, risk analysis, risk response, project management, and culture. The organization risk maturity is evaluated using four levels for each area: Naïve, Novice, Normalized and Natural. In this way overall risk management capability is rated.

References

Ansoff, H. I. (1968). *The new corporate strategy.* Hoboken NJ: John Wiley.

Barney, J. B. (2002). *Gaining and sustaining competitive advantage* (2nd ed.). Upper Saddle River, NJ: Prentice Hall.

Branscomb, L. M., & Auerswald, P. E. (2001). *Taking technical risks.* Cambridge, MA: MIT Press.

Christensen, C. M. (1997). *The innovator's dilemma.* Boston, MA: Harvard Business School Press.

Department of Defense. (2006). *Risk management guide for DoD acquisition, sixth edition* (version 1.0).

Gibson, G. E., & Dumont, P. R. (1996). Project definition rating index (PDRI), research report 113–11 to Construction Industry Institute, Austin TX: University of Texas at Austin (June 1996).

Hopkinson, M. (2011). *The project risk maturity model.* Farnham, Surrey, UK: Gower.

Kendrick, T. (2003). *Identifying and managing project risk.* New York, NY: Amacom.

Mintzberg, H. (1994). *The rise and fall of strategic planning.* New York, NY: Free Press.

Mishina, K. (2004). *Senryaku fuzen no ronri* [Logic of strategy incompetence]. Tokyo, Japan: Toyo Keizai.

Moore, G.A. (2000). *Crossing the chasm.* New York, NY: Harper Collins.

PMI. (2000). *A guide to project management body of knowledge.* Newtown Square, PA: PMI.

Porter, M. E. (1980). *Competitive strategy.* New York, NY: Free Press.

Saito, Y., & Kinumaki, Y. (2001). *Kokusai purojekuto bijinesu* [International project business]. Tokyo, Japan: Bunshin-do.

Sakakibara, K. (2002). Keieigaku nyumon [Introduction to business management]. Tokyo, Japan:Nikkei.

Toyama, H., & Minamino, T. (2002). Risuku souki chuushutu jiko-sinndann-hyo no kaihatu to katuyo [Development and utilization of "project risk management-pre-self assessment sheet]. *Journal of the Society of Project Management (Japan), 4*(6), 40.

Van der Heijden, K. (1996). *Scenarios.* Chichester, West Sussex, UK: John Wiley.

Chapter 4

Value Assessment

Chapter Overview

Chapter 4

Value Assessment

Chapter Overview

A program, the purpose of which is the creation of value, starts by asking, "What specifically should the target value be?" This question is answered through the mission definition process. Value creation, however, cannot proceed without asking how to assess the value. In Chapter 2, the implementation management process in the program integration phase is described in accordance with the program's life cycle. Chapter 3 illustrates the strategy-risk relationship, and management during the program's conceptualization, planning, and execution phases. In the course of these processes, the program manager and program organization managers are required to make proper decisions depending on the situation. The foundation beneath these decisions is the value assessment. Without proper assessment of value, program management might, in the end, be worthless.

Chapter 4 starts with a brief study of the natures of value and value assessment from a program's point of view. This is followed in Section 2 with a description of the process of value transformation, where resource value is transformed into customer value. The section studies the relationship among physical, financial and intangible assets, as well as comparison of value perspectives that vary by program area.

Section 3 describes the purposes of value assessment conducted in the different program phases, and Section 4 presents various value assessment methods. Corporate accounting methods are important for commercial programs, where the value of a sum of money can differ depending on timing or uncertainty. The section outlines the methods to assess present value or calculate expectations based on uncertainty. Value assessment of intangible assets is also described here, as these assets, including technologies and brands, have become increasingly important for sustainability of corporate growth.

Finally, Section 5 introduces examples of value assessment in non-commercial programs, which have major difficulties different from those of commercial programs.

1. Value and Value Assessment

A program is an activity to create and capture some value that constitutes a strategic objective of the organization.

Value is often classified as utility value and exchange value. Diamonds have very high exchange value, though their utility value is not so high. On the other hand, water is essential for life and its utility value is very high, while its exchange value is very low. However, when water is contained in a small plastic bottle, it becomes more expensive than gasoline because it now has the utility value of portability. If we add some flavor and chill it in a refrigerator, the exchange value increases even more. A price of one or two dollars then represents not the bottle but the utility value of portable, cold, flavored water. The price is the exchange value in the market determined by three factors: customers' sense of value regarding what they are willing to pay for the transformed cold water, cost, and competition in the market.

The essence of business management is gathering things of low exchange value ("resources"), transforming them into things called commercial goods of high utility value for customers, and then exchanging them at a good price in the market in an organized way. The difference between the sum of the exchange value of the resources used and the exchange value of the goods produced is the profit. It is common that the exchange value of similar things, whether resources or goods, varies depending on location. The activity of moving things from places where exchange value is low to places where it is high is called commerce or trade. The relationship between the utility value and the exchange value at each place is the reason for the price difference. A fundamental issue in business management, therefore, is how utility value and exchange value are recognized for commercial goods.

The knowledge, wisdom, or skill to respond to such questions as "What kind of goods should be produced?" or "How best should resources be combined?" are intangible assets of suppliers. The exchange value to be found in the goods is dependent on customers' value judgment. Although all of these elements are difficult to value in monetary terms, they play an essential role in the process to create goods of high utility value by bringing resources together.

A program is a part or a form of business management. Programs, therefore, have the same nature: for instance, efficiency is important in the transformation from resources into commercial goods. Programs, however, have the following additional characteristics in comparison to repetitive commercial operational businesses:

(a) Non-repetitiveness: There is little information for assessing the utility value for customers, achievement of which is the objective of the program in terms of exchange value, because programs are not repetitive but one-off structures.
(b) Pricing difficulty: The customer utility value of many programs has characteristics that are difficult to transform into exchange value. In some cases, it is hard to know the market exchange value, because it is hard to determine who the customers themselves are.
(c) Future value: Even with predicted value, it could be far in the future that the utility value is realized. Because of this, future value needs to be evaluated by discounting into present value.

Characteristic (b) is applicable to such public programs as national security, disaster prevention, public infrastructure projects, and basic scientific research. National security and disaster prevention have only limited utility value in ordinary times, but their tangible and intangible values are tremendous during emergencies. Although the overall exchange value of such public programs is hard to describe in money terms, it is common that the execution activities for constructing systems with such program objectives are handled as large commercial projects. In the private sector as well, future exchange value at the time of program accomplishment is difficult to predict in some programs, for instance in basic scientific research, even if everyone is aware of its importance. Another example is a program to build a certain organization or system inside a company: it would be useless for other companies, and the exchange value of such a program is not assessable. The challenge with these programs is the extreme difficulty in determining, first, what the optimum objectives of the program are, and second, how much money should be invested when exchange value is indeterminable.

It is the mission definition process to identify the specific value the program aims at, and it is the scenario development process to determine how to realize that value. Meanwhile, various costs (investments) are incurred in implementing the program, and various risks (uncertainty) are run trying to attain the desired value. Program managers are responsible for designing and executing the program according to the target value, considering cost and risk. Value assessment is the fundamental activity for making appropriate decisions required of program managers throughout the program lifecycle process.

Although this book maintains that value creation for the organization is made by programs, there are indeed a good number of independent projects that aim at creation of certain value. In such a case, the discussion on programs is obviously applicable to such projects. In today's complex social and industrial environment, however, it is difficult to realize a large value by an independent project, such as to develop one new product, to open one new store, or to build one infrastructure system. For project success, it is necessary to combine projects, such as installing a system for volume production, running a promotional campaign, or preparing a system for operating new infrastructure. This is exactly the significance of programs. Individual projects are discussed henceforward on the premise that each will contribute their own relevant part to the program.

2. The Value of a Program
2.1 The Concept of Value Transformation
(1) Commercial programs
In commercial programs, the executing organization essentially aims for value as monetary profit. In general, companies provide customers with a specific value and are paid for providing customer satisfaction. In programs, every participating stakeholder should end up satisfied, and only receive satisfaction in the form of a reward for their activity or sales, when customer satisfaction is realized.

Exhibit 4.2.1(a) illustrates a value transformation scheme in a program. The organization transforms its assets into customer utility value through a system-type project, and then provides or sells the value to customers through a service-type project. In return, consideration for the provided value is received and added to the organization's financial assets. Today, customers place higher value on utility value in usage, rather than in possession, even when they purchase tangible products. Organizations cannot transform the resources they possess (capital and materials) into customer value directly, so they commonly transform their resources into new assets, which constitute some system for providing value to customers.

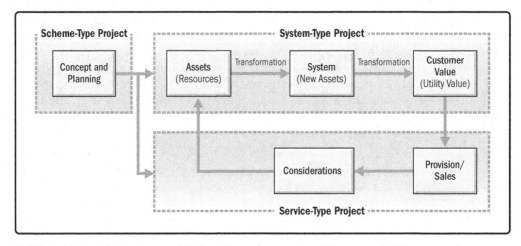

Exhibit 4.2.1: (a) Concept of Value Transformation (Commercial Programs)

Systems that provide customers with value include manufacturing plants, communication service networks, transportation networks, retail shop networks, liquefied natural gas plants and power plants. In this diagram, from the financial point of view, the value of assets originally owned by the organization stays the same when transformed into a new system (the vendor's profit and interest on money being neglected). The profit that the organization can capture depends on how much customer value can be created by virtue of the new system. In other words, the assets required (i.e., costs) for transformation into the new asset (i.e., system) should be kept as small as possible, as long as the same customer value can be created. In service-type projects, minimization of cost related to selling customer value is an important issue. It is a scheme-type project that conceptualizes how to efficiently enhance the transformation of input assets, taking the whole process into account, and designs the program with a concrete set of projects.

The most important things for a commercial program manager are management of how to increase customer value, which itself can hardly be expressed in financial terms, and how to decrease the resources (i.e., costs) for accomplishing the system. Such efforts lead to good financial outcomes.

(2) Non-commercial programs

Exhibit 4.2.1(b) illustrates the case of non-commercial public programs. In principle, the system-type projects involved do not differ much from those in commercial programs. In some services, customers (i.e., citizens) pay usage fees, such as portions of medical expenses, school tuition or highway tolls. Other than things like these, taxes and social insurance premiums are intended to take care of public expenses and investments, including road construction, national defense, policing, public health, welfare, promotion of industry, science and technology, as well as maintaining the various branches of government. Public investments and various promotional investments are expected to be recovered eventually through taxes. In Japan's case, the roads and industrial parks constructed during the high-growth period were highly effective and contributed greatly to tax revenue.

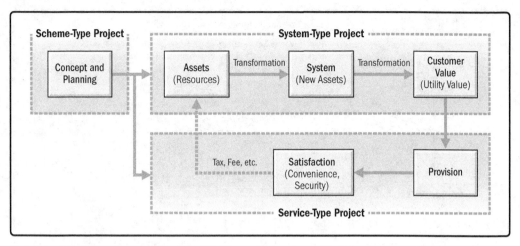

Exhibit 4.2.1: (b) Concept of Value Transformation (Public Programs)

Because public assets and revenue come from a variety of sources, and the purposes for expenditures are widely diverse, it is inappropriate to discuss them in the same way as commercial programs. Given today's financial circumstances the world over, however, public programs are also required to try to reduce costs for the provision of services by enhancing efficiency within the objectives of each program.

2.2 Intangible Assets

Itami (1984, p. 47) pointed out the importance of "invisible assets" as business management resources, such as efficient business organization, accumulated expertise and skills, and a good sales network. Invisible assets are those that do not appear explicitly as figures in financial reports like the balance sheet or profit-and-loss statement. *Immaterial* is another word of the same meaning, though *intangible* will be used here.

Because intangible assets do not appear in financial statements, it is impossible to know their presence from the outside. They are created by people's own efforts and are not something money can buy. Long periods of time are required to build them up and they are difficult for competitors to imitate. As intangible assets are essentially information-oriented, they can be applied to other purposes without incurring additional cost, once they are established. Intangible assets also have the characteristic of being created and accumulated as a result of business activities. On the other hand, however, many intangible assets become obsolete and lose value when they are left unimproved. For these reasons, persistent effort is very important to accumulate and renew intangible assets continuously for the sake of the organization's competitiveness and its continuous growth.

Program value is assessed differently depending on the program area, taking intangible assets into account. Typical aspects of program value are summarized in the next section for various program areas. Prior to the discussion, a detailed relationship of assets and values in a commercial program is illustrated in

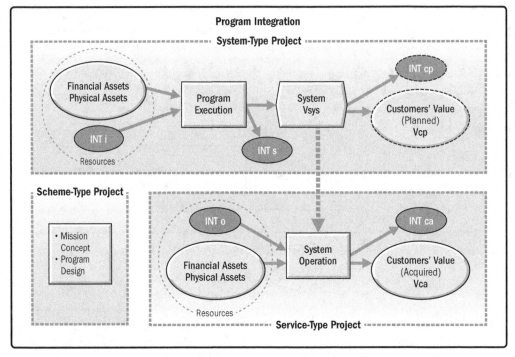

Exhibit 4.2.2: Concept of Value Creation Processes and Program Integration

Exhibit 4.2.2. In the execution of system-type projects, financial assets, physical assets (materials), and intangible assets *INTi*, including technology, knowledge, and organized activity, are put in as program input resources. As a result, the output includes the *System Vsys* and the intangible assets *INT s*, including the increased and newly captured portions. The planned system is assumed to create a specific size of *Customers' Value Vcp*, as well as to capture, through system operation, new intangible assets *INT cp* relating to customers, markets, and sales skills. A service-type project is a process to realize "planned" *Customers' Value Vcp* as "acquired" *Customers' Value Vca* by obtaining the price of services. In this process, financial and physical assets (funds and materials) are combined with the intangible asset *INTo*, which is used for system operation. In many cases, however, *Vca* is limited as a small portion of planned *Customers' Value Vcp*, due to competition, lack of sales skills or errors in prediction. New intangible assets *INTca* are acquired in this process, relating to customers, markets and sales skills.

2.3 Program Categories and Value Perspectives

How is value interpreted at each phase in the various program categories? Examples are summarized in Exhibit 4.2.3. In this exhibit, the system value is the sum of *Vsys* (tangible system value) and *INTs* (acquired intangible value) in the system-type project, as shown in Exhibit 4.2.2. The program value is the sum of (a) "value of system" and (b) "target of system operation" in the exhibit, during the scheme-type project phase and the execution phase of the system-type project. The value after system completion is (c), the outcome of system operation.

Area of Programs	Commercial Programs		Public Programs		Potential Value Programs	
Program Examples	• New business development • New product development • Facilities investment • Projectized business	• Merger & acquisition (corporate, business) • Private equity investment (restructuring)	• Road • Airport • Urban infrastructure	• Defense & security • Disaster prevention • Public health and welfare • Environmental protection	• Basic research in a private firm • Change of corporate culture	• Education • Scientific research • Official development aid
(a) Value of System — Tangible Assets (Vsys)	• Physical assets (acquisition cost)	• Corporate, business, business organization	• Physical assets (acquisition cost)	• Same as on the left, or no residual asset	• No or very small tangible assets	• Same as on the left, or transferred to other party
(a) Value of System — Intangible Assets (INTs)	• System design & acquisition KH • Technology & KH	• Business execution KH • Market Power	• Owner (government): small amount of KH accumulation • Contractors: System design & acquisition KH, Technology & KH		• Technology & KH • Execution KH	• Technology & KH • Execution KH
(b) Target of System Operation — Tangible Assets (Vcp)	• Business profit	• Business (operational) profit • Profit on corporate sale	• Public financial benefit • Social benefit (follow precedent, do what others do)	• Political judgment • Political leading	• Potential value (Future possibility to gain profit indirectly)	
(b) Target of System Operation — Intangible Assets (INTcp)	• Customer & market KH • Operation efficiency KH	• Transfer of KH (intake) • Organizational capability enhancement	• Not many cases to assign significance to INTs		• Knowledge • Capable human resources • Corporate culture	• Knowledge • Capable human resources
(c) Outcome of System Operation — Tangible Assets (Vca)	• Business profit	• Business (operational) profit • Profit on corporate sale	• Ex-post assessments are not made in many case • (Negative valuation when problems occur)		• Potential value (achieved indirectly)	
(c) Outcome of System Operation — Intangible Assets (INTca)	• Customer & market KH • Operation efficiency KH	• Transfer of KH (intake) • Organizational capability enhancement			• Knowledge • Capable human resources • Corporate culture	• Knowledge • Capable human resources

Exhibit 4.2.3: Examples of Value Perspectives

Note: "KH" stands for "know-how."

In commercial programs, the completed system produces a financially evaluated asset value, which is usually expressed as equivalent to acquisition cost, and a variety of intangible asset values acquired during system construction. The tangible part of the operational outcome is the profit that equals the price paid by customers less the cost of the program.

In mergers and acquisitions, value for the buyer is the assets of the acquired business unit and increased intangible assets, such as additional know-how or a larger market share. The intangible asset at the time of acquisition is the value of goodwill. The customer value of the acquired intangible assets is generally estimated by movements of stock prices, which reflect corporate performance. However, the general market environment and other factors make it difficult to isolate any particular part as contributing to corporate performance (Ito & Kagaya, 2008). In the case of private equity investment acquiring underperforming firms, the acquiring party profits from selling the business after restructuring or reforming it; the target or outcome here corresponds to the profit on sale.

Public programs are generally divided into two categories: one provides economic benefits for the general public, such as roads, airports, or urban infrastructure construction programs; the other has the objective of maintaining social stability – typically national defense, policing, public health and welfare, as well as environmental protection. Huge investments are made in all these areas by central and local governments. Intangible assets relating to this type of investment, including design know-how and cost reduction measures, tend to be less prone to accumulation for the owner (i.e., government), compared to commercial programs. For programs that provide economic benefits, customer value is evaluated in a manner similar to commercial programs in the planning phase. In other areas of this category, there is no such criterion. The investments are made according to political judgments, and their legitimacy is examined in the legislature. In contrast to commercial programs, the outcome of many public programs is not assessed in detail. However, if the occurrence of a disaster or accident is attributable to the program deficiency, the legislature or public would give a negative assessment. Given this possibility, investments tend to be excessive compared to commercial programs.

Potential value programs in the third category of the table aim for potential value that might be realized in the distant future, and are not intended to achieve immediate profit. This category includes basic research and corporate cultural reform, and in the public sector, education, scientific research, and overseas economic aid. Value assessment in this category requires long-term insight and strong will on the part of the leadership. Being difficult to evaluate in a short period of time, it calls for two simultaneously contradictory policies: persistent continuation and clear-cut judgment to avoid fruitless investments.

2.4 Assets and Resources

Boulton, Libert, and Samek (2000, p. 27) discussed corporate value using five asset classes: (i) physical assets, (ii) financial assets, (iii) employee and supplier assets, (iv) customer assets, and (v) organization assets. These are then broken into 25 smaller segments. Corporate value has traditionally been assessed by the assets listed in the balance sheet and other financial statements. Boulton, Libert, and Samek stressed the importance of valuation including factors that are not reflected in financial statements. Value created by intangible assets such as leadership, organizational structure, relationships with suppliers, and the effectiveness of the workforce, some of which are usually regarded as costs, are examples of such factors.

Ohara et al., (2003, p. 167) listed six resource categories: (i) physical resources, (ii) financial resources, (iii) human resources, (iv) knowledge resources, (v) information resources, and (vi) infrastructure resources, which he divided into 24 segments. Infrastructure resources include external resources such as transportation networks, electricity and other energy supply infrastructure, the Internet, the legal system and various social systems, as well as internal resources such as internal networks, accounting systems, common engineering tools, and project management information systems. External infrastructure resources are like air to breathe: indispensable for business operations, but their value is not usually evaluated. Though the major part of program resources to be evaluated are those owned by organizations, they produce value only when they are used. Physical assets and intangible assets lose their value over time when they are left unused. It should be noted that in assessing value, appropriate use is assumed.

3. Value Assessment

3.1 Objectives of Value Assessment

Value assessment in program management has the following three objectives:

- Decision-making in management
- Assessment of financial outcome (profit or loss)
- Applications for organizational learning

Many decisions are required in various phases of the program or project life cycle. These include options for better profitability, size of investment, and what kind of outcome to expect. The basis for such decisions is always the expected value of results against the cost of investment. Such value assessments for management decisions are important in defining concepts while planning in the initial phase, selecting specific measures in the execution phase, and for appropriate decision-making in program or project change management.

At program or project closeout, the outcome is assessed by financial valuation of input costs and profit generated. It is important to assess tangible assets and intangible assets at various phases in the lifecycle, to accumulate knowledge to refer to for future decision-making.

3.2 Value Assessment for Decision-making

Decision-making in programs is classified into two areas: investment decision-making for the overall program prior to its startup, and decision-making in the program execution process. Decision-making is hierarchical. Important decisions are made by program or project managers or their seniors, while less important decisions are made by junior managers responsible for work packages.

(1) Investment decisions

To make an assessment for investment decisions, estimations are required for financial value to be retained, intangible asset capture, and input costs. Investment is acceptable, in principle, when the total value expected to be captured exceeds predicted cost. In commercial programs, the expected financial value should exceed the predicted cost and probable risk impact. The value must be converted into present value considering future expectations (see section 4.2). Some intangible assets, including knowledge or know-how, can be acquired only through program execution. Such capabilities are directly related to the future competitiveness of the organization. Assessment of these elements is a very important issue in investment decision-making.

Program value expectations also vary depending on uncertainties, that is, risks. In assessing program value, an important element is the cost of funds, which corresponds to the expected rate of return for the fund providers who take the risk. The risk level acceptable to fund providers, and the rate of return consistent with that risk, is the financial basis for program formation.

(2) Internal process decisions

Decisions internal to the execution process are made by individual project or work package managers. Decisions will be made to create and capture program value, but it is extremely difficult to know specifically how much each decision impacts the program during program execution. This is why such process-internal decisions are made with reference to project or work package criteria, such as quality, cost, and schedule. These criteria are selected so as to achieve program value in mission profiling, program design, and project planning. Value assessment procedures for these decisions are briefly discussed in Section 4 of this chapter.

3.3 Assessment of Financial Outcomes

Needless to say, financial assessment of program or project outcomes is one of the most fundamental and important management activities, having been done for hundreds of years. *The Merchant of Prato* by Origo (1957), for instance, showed late 14th century business records. Today it is easy to calculate project earnings and costs by aggregating monthly accounting data and preparing profit-loss analysis of individual projects. But in practice, analysis of financial outcomes, or recognition of failure of a project, is often insufficient or left unfinished.

Assessments of corporate activities are made annually or quarterly according to rules and regulations. A program or project term often does not conform to such time periods, and assessment is based on project lifecycle. In multi-year programs or projects, financial assessment is made on a percentage-of-completion method.

3.4 Applications for Organizational Learning

It is important to advance organizational learning in order to improve the organization's capability and outcomes. Organizational learning means (i) to evaluate for such things as the outcome obtained, how success was achieved, or what caused failure, and (ii) to share the resulting evaluation as explicit knowledge in the organization. Numerical value assessment makes it possible to ascertain the degree of success or failure, and to compare different programs with one another. Numerical knowledge and information is objective and highly effective; it is important to accumulate it for future decision-making.

These processes will advance the organization's systems and strengthen personnel capabilities, building intangible value inside the organization that is difficult to copy. These merits can be obtained only through executing a program and are very important elements for an organization's growth.

4. An Overview Of Value Assessment Methods

4.1 Corporate Accounting Methods

(1) Financial accounting and management accounting

Financial accounting and management accounting are basic methods of value assessment in business. The former is used primarily to provide information to people outside the company, such as stockholders, creditors, and the tax authority, as well as employees and the general public. Its main function is to allocate profit and adjust priorities among stakeholders. The latter is for internal management. Its main function is to provide information for management control.

Financial accounting information is externally defined by law. It provides methods and formats for financial statements: balance sheets, profit and loss statements, and cash flow statements. In contrast, management accounting is done internally using private accounting methodology, which is largely divided in two: decision-making accounting for management strategy, and performance control accounting through break-even analysis and budget planning and control.

(2) Financial accounting information and business analysis

Financial accounting information is most fundamental in business management and plays a great role in making business decisions. It can be used for strategic planning and program management. This information is scheduled on an annual or quarterly accounting period. Accordingly, it is often pointed out that management judgment based solely on this information is risky, as the data is essentially from the past, without current or future information.

A fundamental approach for judging the future standing of a company is to examine cause-and-effect between its analysis of its financial statement and its corporate activities. However, it is difficult to judge the management based solely on the data of the company by itself; a cross-sectional analysis of the industry, or of a similar industry, is important. A good approach is to use time-series analysis to compare data chronologically. Ratio analysis methods are used to compare ratios rather than absolute numbers, eliminating the effect of company size. Exhibit 4.4.1 outlines important financial analysis methods, including safety, efficiency and productivity, profitability, and growth analyses, as well as overall assessment (Ito, 1994, p. 568).

(3) Management Accounting Information

Management accounting gathers numerical accounting data to measure business performance and to conduct analysis and evaluation in order to make judgments and decisions for business management. Its contents and methods are very broad and differ from company to company, business to business. In this context, the analytical financial information explained above can be seen as a management accounting method. A conceptual example of management accounting methods is shown in Exhibit 4.4.2, for which management uses accounting perspectives for business strategy planning.

4.2 The Value of Money

Value assessment of a commercial program is an estimation of how much cash flow will be obtained by the program. For instance, the true value of a hypothetical $100 changes, depending on the following four conditions as described by Benninga

Category		Outline
Safety analysis	• Short-term solvency • Long-term solvency • Interest coverage	• Current ratio, quick ratio • Capital-to-asset ratio, debt ratio, etc. • Interest coverage ratio
Efficiency and productivity analysis	• Efficiency of asset use • Productivity	• Total asset turnover, tangible fixed asset turnover, inventory turnover, receivables turnover, etc. • Labor productivity, equipment productivity, capital intensity of labor
Profitability analysis	• Return on sales (ROS) • Return on investment (ROI) • Return on equity (ROE)	• Ratio of sales versus gross profit, operating profit, current profit, before-tax profit or after-tax profit • Ratio of total capital versus profit. Usually, business profit (i.e., operating profit plus interest and dividend income) is treated as profit • Ratio of equity versus net profit after tax (rate of profit from shareholders' perspective)
Growth analysis	• Growth of sales • Growth of current profit • Growth of total capital • Growth of equity • Growth of payroll	• Growth rate of each item, relative to the value at a given time. Time-series variation is analyzed and evaluated by management, using the variation of each item or the ratio among items; for example, if growth of profit exceeds growth of sales, business management is improved.
Overall assessment	• Various methods are proposed, such as the index method by A. Wall. This method has seven financial data points (the current ratio, debt ratio, receivables turnover, etc.), and are weighted so that their sum will produce an index with 100 points when all conditions are fulfilled.	

Exhibit 4.4.1: Business Management Analyses using Financial Accounting Information (Ito, 1994, p. 568)

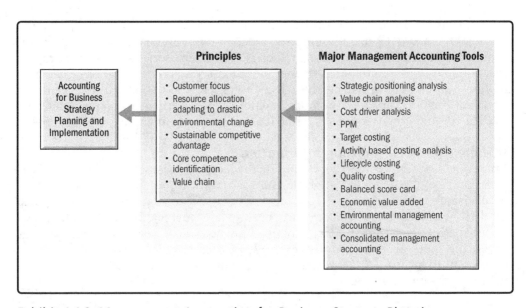

Exhibit 4.4.2: Management Accounting for Business Strategy Planning
Source: Okamoto, K., *Kanrikaikei* (Managment accounting), Tokyo, Japan: Chuo-keizaisha, 2003, pp. 17.

and Sarig (1997), and many others. These must be taken into account in business value assessment:

- Timing
- Risk of uncertainty
- Purchasing power
- Liquidity

The present value of $100 is not equal to that of $100 received one year from now. If $100 is invested at interest rate r for one year, one will get $100 \times (1 + r)$ as the return, one year later. In other words, the present value of the $100 obtained at the end of the year is $100 / (1 + r)$ dollars. The present value of $100 to be received in two years is $100/(1 + r)^2$. Cash flow in a future time should be evaluated at present value, as described in the next section.

Uncertainty is an unavoidable companion of programs. A variety of methods are employed to incorporate uncertainty into value assessment. Several are explained in Section 4.4.

Purchasing power incorporates the effect of inflation. Value assessment is made to maximize cash flow obtained. But cash flow is essentially a translation of value, and value should be measured by purchasing power, that is, how many units of goods or services can be obtained. Here, the purchasing power is an average for a whole country or region, not for particular products or industries.

In value assessment, an asset's value is based on its market value as determined by trade in the open market. Assets with unclear market value, such as securities issued by an unlisted company, should be examined in detail. Assets with such an unclear market price are less liquid and more difficult to sell. Discounting is required to offset liquidity disadvantages.

4.3 Present Value

(1) Net present value

Assume that a project predicts a cash flow of C_1 at the end of one year, C_2 at two years later, and C_t at t years later in the same manner, with an initial investment of C_0 today. The Net present value (NPV) of this project is expressed by the following formula:

$$\text{NPV} = \text{present value of predicted cash flow - investment}$$

$$= C_0 + C_1/(1 + r)\ 1\ C_2/(1 + r)^2 + \cdots + Ct/(1 + r)^t$$

$$= C_0 + \sum_{t=1}^{n} (C_t/(1 + r)^t)$$

C_0 corresponds to "- investment" in the first line of the formula, expressed as a negative value.

The method of discounting future cash flow to present value in this way is the core concept of discounted cash flow (DCF). Rate r is typically described as the interest rate, that an investor would expect. It is also called the rate of profitability, discount rate, or capital cost.

(2) Payback period

The payback period is the time period in which the investor can expect to receive a return equivalent to the amount invested. An investment of $100 that provides a return of $25 annually yields a payback period of four years. This method is often used for convenience. A more realistic tool is the discounted payback period, which incorporates the time value of money. In our example here, the discounted payback period would be 5.6 years, instead of 4 years at a discount rate of 10%.

(3) The internal rate of return

The internal rate of return (IRR) is a derivative of NPV that determines whether to proceed with a project by calculating a discount rate r for NPV=0, using r as a variable. The internal rate of return means the discount rate, which makes the present value of the total future cash flow of the project lasting for n years equivalent to the amount of the initial investment.

$$\sum_{t=1}^{n} (C_t/(1 + r)^t) - C_0 = 0$$

(4) The competitive environment and NPV

If investment efficiency is very low in a harshly competitive market in which the profitability of a competitor's investment is superior, the competitor's profitability may decrease to NPV=0, which leads to a negative own NPV. When evaluating an investment in a severe environment, assessing the competitor's NPV is also required (Brealey & Myers, 2000, p. 297).

4.4 Uncertainty and Value Assessment

4.4.1 Expectation

Suppose an investment that has a predicted certainty of attaining an outcome of 200 at 60%, and an outcome of 100 at 40%. The value of this project is expressed as an expectation that has been weighted for each outcome, and is calculated as 200 × 0.6 + 100 × 0.4 = 160.

If there are a number of possibilities n, and the possibility of the i-th cash flow and its probability are denoted as C_i and p_i, respectively, the expectation is expressed as follows:

$$\text{expectation} = \sum_{i=1}^{n} (C_i \times p_i)$$

A payoff table or decision matrix is a method using expectations for decision-making. When there are several options, such as when deciding to purchase some volume of goods for stock, a simple approach is to select the best choice by calculating the profit expectation table based on uncontrollable external conditions, such as demand for the goods.

4.4.2 Decision Tree

A decision tree is a method of making a decision to select the most preferable choice from two or more candidate plans for resolving strategic policy or business development problems. In a decision tree, multilevel decision-making and possible events occur along each decision. These are described in a tree-like chart for each candidate

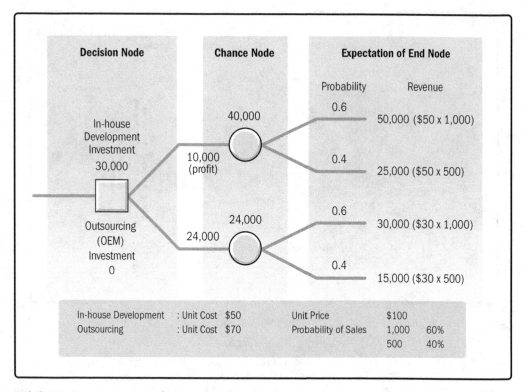

Decision Node	Chance Node	Expectation of End Node	
		Probability	Revenue

In-house Development Investment 30,000 — 40,000 — 0.6 — 50,000 ($50 x 1,000)

10,000 (profit) — 0.4 — 25,000 ($50 x 500)

Outsourcing (OEM) Investment 0 — 24,000 — 24,000 — 0.6 — 30,000 ($30 x 1,000)

0.4 — 15,000 ($30 x 500)

In-house Development	: Unit Cost $50	Unit Price	$100	
Outsourcing	: Unit Cost $70	Probability of Sales	1,000	60%
			500	40%

Exhibit 4.4.3: Concept of Decision Tree

plan. The outcome and its probability are predicted for all possible outcomes arising from each decision. The expectation of achieving each plan is calculated and the results are compared to each other to select the most effective execution plan.

Exhibit 4.4.3 is a basic example illustrating decision tree methodology. Take the example of a business retailing a product priced at $100. A strategic decision-analysis is made to determine whether to invest $30,000 in in-house development or to outsource manufacturing as an OEM to an outside manufacturer. The in-house manufacturing unit cost is $50, and the unit cost purchased from the OEM manufacturer is $70. The probability of selling 1,000 units and 500 units are 60% and 40%, respectively. The profit expectation for in-house development is $10,000, while the expected profit in the OEM case is $24,000. As a result, the OEM is expected to produce a better profit. If the investment is less than $16,000, then in-house development is a better choice.

In a decision tree, each uncertainty factor is expressed as several branches of a chart. The method is intuitive. The complexity of the model is limited by the diagram's format, though decision trees can be used for more complex analysis using specialty software.

4.4.3 Monte Carlo Simulation

Monte Carlo is a simulation method using random numbers. PC software has become readily available, making this a popular tool. In Monte Carlo simulation

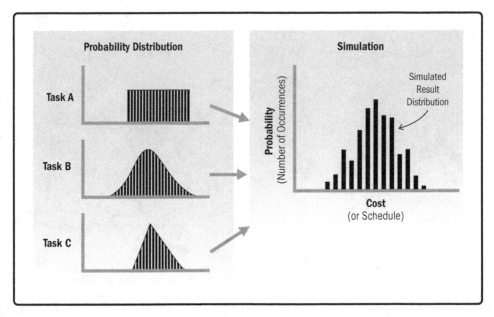

Exhibit 4.4.4: Concept of Monte Carlo Simulation

the conditions of each element of the system computation model are represented by random numbers, subject to the appropriate probability density function of each element. Random probability density numbers can be generated for each element, even if there are many elements. The simulation is made by integrating trial results numerous times. In every trial, random numbers representing the conditions of individual elements are generated. The system outcome is calculated using those random numbers to give one sample value representing one possible outcome. The simulation is repeated from 100,000 to a million times. The expected system outcome is obtained in the form of a statistical distribution by integrating the trial samples.

Exhibit 4.4.4 shows the concept of the Monte Carlo simulation. In this diagram there are tasks A, B and C with respective probability distributions for cost. A random value is generated independently for the cost of each task in accordance with the respective probability distribution. The overall cost is calculated using the random values. By repeating this calculation many times, the resulting statistical data simulates the probability distribution of the total cost of the system. The same procedure can be applied for the schedule estimation.

4.4.4 Real Option
In the common NPV or decision tree method, the outcome of a project is evaluated with the assumption that it will be executed at the present time by a discounting process. The decision to go ahead is decided by the results of the evaluation. The evaluation is an expectation of the outcome based on the given conditions, with uncertainties in execution included as probability values.

However, in practice, decisions are not always made this way. Management might provide additional investment if the market is growing or might retreat if miscalculation occurs. Real option is a method for assessment in the planning phase that takes into account possible changes during execution, rather than reconsidering the plan at a time when there are deviations.

Real option assessment is always better than a conventional NPV assessment, in principle, as it incorporates possible changes in the course of execution. This is possible because real option uses new information obtained at an appropriate point in time to make decisions. The difference between real option assessment and fixed strategy assessment in business execution is "the value of strategic freedom." With real option it is possible that some projects that would have been abandoned by conventional NPV evaluation are executable.

Exhibit 4.4.5 illustrates the basic concept of real option. Suppose a project that is projected to have a cash flow of 400 or 100 with a possibility of 50% each, after two years. The total investment required is 200. The capital cost is 12%. The market prospect will become clear in one year.

The NPV estimation produces an expectation of a negative cash flow value of -0.7, making the project a loss. On the other hand, if the final decision for making the investment can be made one year later, a positive cash flow of 42.4 is expected, making the project viable. In this example, 25% of the total investment is supposed to be made at the outset, and the project can be canceled one year later without making further investments if there is no hope for success. The initial investment of 50 can be viewed as the cost of gathering information.

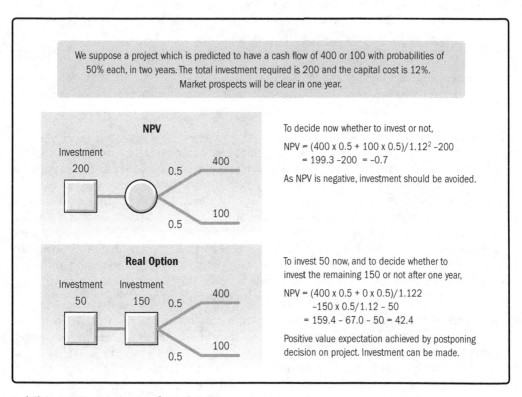

Exhibit 4.4.5: Concept of Real Option

4.5 The Cost of Capital

4.5.1 The Weighted Average Cost of Capital (WACC)

When evaluating a company by means of NPV, the weighted average cost of capital (WACC) is used as the discount rate. WACC is calculated in the following formula using the expected cost of capital, including dividends for equity E, and the cost of debt.

$$WACC = Re \times (E/(E + D)) + Rd \times (1 - T)(D/(E + D))$$

where E is equity (total market value),
D is total amount of debt with interest,
Re is capital cost (rate of dividend and others),
Rd is debt cost (interest rate), and
T is tax rate.

Cost of debt is the interest rate of debt. As no tax is imposed on the interest, its amount is deducted from the cost of debt, as the cost of debt is shown in the second term in the formula.

Cost of capital is the return expected by shareholders in exchange for the risk of equity investment. Main revenues for shareholders are dividends and rising share prices. Cost of capital Re is calculated by the following capital asset pricing model (CAPM), although it is a more complex calculation, compared to the cost of debt.

$$Re = \text{risk-free rate} + \beta \times \text{risk premium}$$

Here, the risk-free rate is the rate of a very secure investment, such as a long-term government bond. The risk premium is then the expected return on an asset (such as from the whole stock market) – the risk-free rate. The variable β is the ratio of the volatility of an individual stock versus the volatility of the whole stock market.

4.5.2 The Cost of Capital for Projects

The risk structure of a program or project is much different from that of a corporate investment.

(1) Risk and discount rate

The discount rate r of a project increases when risk or uncertainty increases, requiring a larger risk premium. The present value of a project decreases as the execution period lengthens, even if the discount rate remains constant. An investment (e.g., $10,000) would be relatively secure if it were for the business expansion of a product whose demand is growing. The investment would be high risk if it were for new product development, even if using a mature technology. Developing a new market using a revolutionary new technology is very high risk. It is important to use an appropriate discount rate when valuing such a project. Some companies set specific hurdle rates as their internal standard based on experience, such as 30% for venture-type projects and 20% for new product development.

The most basic procedure for programs and projects is phase-by-phase, progressive elaboration during the lifecycle. Uncertainty decreases as a program or project progresses. The investment for the uncertain initial phase is very small in relation to the overall investment. It would be irrational to apply a high discount rate throughout the whole lifecycle, even for programs with high uncertainty, as far as the programs are governed appropriately (Boer, 1999, p. 113).

To execute a high-risk and high-return project is risky, but if several similar projects are executed simultaneously, overall portfolio risk is reduced to medium risk and medium return. This way capital cost can be decreased. A typical example is the strong move toward increasing scale in the pharmaceutical industry through M&A.

(2) The hurdle rate

The hurdle rate is the rate of profit that allows an investment to go ahead if the project's rate of return by NPV estimation exceeds the capital cost (WACC). This is often explained as equal to the cost of capital. In practice, however, a higher rate of profit is used as a criterion for determining the value of an alternative investment. Many companies set hurdle rates or such criteria. If a project yields a 15% profit in the market, less profitable projects cannot be approved. This would effectively constitute a hurdle rate in the capital market. To investors in multiple high-risk projects, like venture capitalists and incubators, the average resulting profitability of investments corresponds to the hurdle rate, so that the risk premium of individual project investments is usually set very high.

On the other hand, in an environment of extremely low interest rates like in Japan of late, low-profit projects may be tolerated in companies having less growth potential. Continuous efforts are required to improve the quality of business investment.

4.6 Valuing Intangible Assets

(1) Intangible assets and accounting

Intangible assets are generally defined as assets with no physical substance, excluding financial assets. Examples include knowledge assets, including R&D results, patents and know-how, brands, data on customers, capability of human resources, organizational power, and various rights granted by government or obtained by contract. Research on intangible asset evaluation has been done in the United States for corporate acquisitions since the end of the 19th century. The value of such intangible assets that does not appear in the balance sheet is called "goodwill" in total. In current corporate accounting, some intangible assets are expected to be placed in the balance sheet appropriately as depreciable intangible fixed assets, to give a fair valuation to corporate assets.

In corporate accounting, valuing intangible assets requires that the assets are identifiable from other assets and can be evaluated independently. Examples include computer software and patent rights. Assets such as R&D accomplishments, organizational capability nurtured by personnel training, and brand value earned by efforts are difficult to quantify. These are not treated as intangible assets in accounting, except those which are clearly included in purchased goodwill in the course of M&A. Intangible assets are treated somewhat differently, depending on a country's accounting rules.

Another objective of assessment of intangible assets is to focus on the specific effects of technology, brands, and organizational capability for purposes of enhancing corporate strategy or competitiveness. Evaluation of intangible assets in program and project management is mainly for competitiveness and especially its future improvement.

(2) The increasing importance of intangible assets

If corporate value is considered to be the corporation's exchange value and equivalent to total market value, the value of intangible assets is largely equal to the market value less the net assets. Ulrich and Smallwood (2003, p. 10) pointed out that the percentage of intangible assets in corporate value in the United States was 38% in 1982, and increased to 62% in 1992 and to 85% in 2000. A variety of elements contribute to this proportion of intangible assets. The progress of industrial computerization and increasing global market competition have much to do with the increase.

Brynjolfsson (2004, p. 24) surveyed several hundred large projects, such as ERP systems installations. He found that computer hardware was less than 5% of the average total investment of $20 million. Software accounted for about 15%, so that hardware and software combined accounted for only 20% of total project investment. The major part of total cost is for such areas as business process reconfiguration and user training. Upon surveying many similar projects, he discovered that investment for intangible assets is about nine times that of computer hardware investment for large projects. This indicates that the improvement of business efficiency is not supported by computers but rather by related intangible assets.

(3) Historical lessons from electric technology

Brynjolfsson (2004, p. 53) pointed out another interesting fact on intangible assets. It was long said in the United States that productivity improvement was not realized even though IT investments were made actively since the 1970s. It was in the 1990s that productivity improvement became evident in the United States. It takes time for effectiveness to be evident even for such revolutionary technology that is highly advantageous. For example, it took 30–40 years until effects came to be realized in actual productivity after steam engines were displaced by electric motors 100 years ago.

In the age of steam engines, power was transmitted by shafts and gear trains. The large mechanisms required a great deal of energy and had to be located close to the engines. In factories, larger machines were placed around the steam engines, and smaller machines farther away, or even set three dimensionally, for better efficiency. When electric motors came into use, people bought motors of larger power merely as replacements for steam engines. Factory layouts, accordingly, changed little for about 30 years. A generational change in managers was needed before new types of factories became popular where many small motors were set along assembly lines and jobs and materials spread out on the shop floor. This, at last, dramatically improved efficiency in new factories.

The story of steam versus electric motors is comparable, in the form of distribution architecture, to today's ICT technology, though less important in comparison. The value of intangible assets is not very large in the technology itself or in its direct applications, but is far more significant in practical application, or in people's adaptation to new processes surrounding the new technology The mission of programs or projects is not merely to build something new, but to create new intangible assets, such as new applications or adaptive technologies for new processes, and to put them into practice.

4.7 Assessing the Value of Intangible Assets

Successful implementation of a program requires insight into intangible assets and their continuous assessment.

Due diligence with regard to intangible assets at the time of M&A is put into practice in various ways. The intent is to evaluate the total value of the target organization expressed as present monetary value. Financial accounting aims to fairly disclose the company's financial status for shareholders and investors. Objectivity is required so that different assessors produce the same result.

In contrast, the purpose of assessing the value of a program's intangible assets is to judge the relevance of activities that focus on future achievement, including program success (e.g., output maximization) and improvement of organizational capabilities. Assessment is made in various ways, not necessarily only to show a total amount of money, and it contains a significant amount of subjective judgment. An example is estimating how much value managers find in their organization's capabilities.

There may be two forms of assessment. One is quantitative with numerical criteria. The other is qualitative, non-numerical assessment (e.g., "good," "bad," etc.). In practice, quantitative assessment is a methodology of objective evaluation. Subjective assessment is strongly characteristic of qualitative efforts. In this section, quantitative and subjective assessments are discussed from the program management point of view.

4.7.1 Quantitative Assessment

Quantitative assessment using a numerical scale provides objective criteria for assessment, within a defined range. To help efficiency in controlling program activities or sharing knowledge among stakeholders, a variety of methods are employed to convert intangible values into numbers. It is important to clearly define objectives and assess criteria in order to avoid differences in perception among stakeholders.

(1) Indicators of quantitative assessment

A generic process of management based on quantitative value assessment of intangible assets is as follows:

- Define the intangible value of the program or project
- Specify the methodology, including the system for measuring intangible value
- Set numerical targets for management
- Measure the value and control the program or project referring to numerical targets

Value that cannot be defined in words is virtually non-existent, and value that cannot be expressed numerically is hard to control, except possibly in very small organizations. Defining the value of intangible assets is to clarify what the intended asset is, as well as clarify whether the condition of the asset is of high value. To specify assessment methodology is to define what method and what kind of value indicator are to be employed. In most cases, it is impossible to quantify intangible assets, such as an organization's capabilities, competitiveness, or knowledge. Evaluation is usually done by one of the following indirect methods:

- **Indirect value indicator:** Indirect evaluation is based on a criterion that can represent a target attribute partially or comprehensively. Typical examples are task processing rates, number of VE (value engineering) proposals, number of patents pending, failure counts, customer satisfaction metrics, quality indices, and brand recognition ratings. Other examples would be capability maturity models, which provide ratings-based evaluations of the level of management systems or members' proficiency. These are then put on a numerical scale to indicate the quality of the maturity in an organization.

- **Substitute value indicators:** This measures using inputs instead of outcomes (i.e., accomplishments) because measuring outcome is too complex. Research expenses, advertising expenses and the number of customer visits are examples. Substitute value indicators are based on the assumption that output is proportionate to input given the same level of management capability, though there is no guarantee that output will be greater with a larger input.

- **Numerical value indicator for comparison:** This method sets a numerical value indicator by comparison with the market or with other companies, such as market share ranking or benchmarking. Another example of this method is to evaluate temporal differences to show an increase or decrease from previous evaluations.

- **Statistical value indicator:** Individual customer opinions, good or bad, do not have much significance. Service quality can be evaluated with confidence if statistical values from a sufficiently sized sample are obtained. Many indirect value indicators and substitute value indicators are statistical value indicators.

(2) Problems with Management by Objectives

Objectives are often controlled by setting numerical targets. Such targets contribute much to the improvement of management processes. These do not provide final targets in numerical form, but are themselves indirect or substitute indicators of value. Therefore it is very important to make efforts to set appropriate objectives and maintain stakeholder understanding. If such efforts are neglected through excessive emphasis on the targeted value, the true objective behind the figure may be forgotten. For example, when production efficiency is emphasized as production units per hour, product quality could be neglected. This is an example of "goal displacement." Swiss (1991, p. 91) provided an example of an English bus company that compelled its drivers to keep strictly on time. As a consequence, buses would sometimes skip stops where many passengers were waiting. For the same reason, in Japan a railway company had a bad accident when a commuter train full of rush hour passengers overturned at a sharp corner, resulting in a large number of casualties.

As is often said, "you get what you measure." If something is controlled only by numerical assessment with the essential nature of the objectives forgotten, either the target number will be achieved independently of its essential meaning, or stakeholders will view the measurement as senseless and neglect it altogether. Control is required to avoid deviation from the true objective by appropriately combining qualitative and quantitative evaluations.

4.7.2 Subjective Assessment

The essential nature of intangible value is dependent on people's subjective view of the world. Many intangible value-based programs are understood as important, but their value is difficult to express numerically. An important role for a program manager is to create a way to share common understanding of the value among stakeholders.

Today's science and technology would have never been accomplished without the numerical expression of all phenomena. The modern economy could never have developed without the driving force of the numerical value indicator "money." On the other hand, the richness of life or the feeling of contentment is impossible to express numerically. It is, however, possible to judge that "A is more important than B" even if there can be no numerical measurement of the two as variables.

Many intangible business assets have to do with the improvement of organizational capability. As previously discussed, numerical assessment is important here, but subjective and qualitative value judgment is even more important. A manager's sense of value or philosophy is an example. The image of an ideal organization would be another. Every business organization has its history and its own environment. Managers of different organizations are expected to make decisions based on their own judgment, and to see things in different ways, even if positioned in the same market at the same time. For example, Honda or Suzuki may examine Toyota's strategy as a reference point in responding to a market shock, or in preparing for the coming ultra-low emissions revolution. They would never adopt the same strategy, because their organizations and environments are different. Individual judgment is highly important.

Subjective assessment is qualitative. It is easily treated in an ad hoc manner by a manager, and if assessment is merely set at "good" it is hard to motivate people to improve to "better." Numerical evaluation by an indirect or substitute value indicator may reduce this problem. Without a numerical value indicator, a leader would be required to issue messages repeatedly on the importance of the value. When subjective assessment is adopted for controlling organizational activities, the following points are useful: (i) the items to be assessed should be clearly focused, avoiding the "this and that" manner that causes stakeholder misunderstandings, (ii) assessment criteria should be consistent, (iii) the assessment process and its results should be fair and free from ambiguity, and (iv) fair and convincing principles exist as the basis of the assessment.

Typical ways for managers to clearly demonstrate values are:

- Reward and punish (admire, recognize, promote, give bonuses, honor, rebuke, etc.)
- Words (organization philosophy or value, use of slogans and aphorisms, positive and negative tones of voice, etc.)
- Action (initiative, being a role model, leadership from in front, etc.)

4.8 The Balanced Score Card

The balanced score card (BSC) is a method to assess the value generated by business activities as a whole for improving performance.

Program value consists of targets the business strategy aims to achieve and value that program activities will bring to stakeholders. These values may also be categorized as financial value that can be assessed in terms of profit or loss, and intangible value that affects the organization's competency. BSC evaluates intangible assets along with financial value, and is now widely used to assess organizational strategy and to support its execution.

Perspective Category	Scope
Financial Perspective	What is required for investors to achieve business success?
Customer Perspective	What needs to be offered to customers to accomplish the business vision?
Internal Business Process Perspective	Which business processes are best for customer satisfaction?
Innovation and Learning (Growth) Perspective	How should the organization learn and improve to accomplish the vision?

Exhibit 4.4.6: Four Perspective Categories of the Balanced Score Card (Kaplan & Norton, 2001, p. 75)

BSC sets separate targets and quantitative indicators in four perspective categories: (i) financial perspective, (ii) customer perspective, (iii) internal business process perspective, and (iv) innovation and learning perspective. The last category is sometimes referred to as the growth perspective (Kaplan & Norton, 2001, p. 75).

For example, "survival" and "success" are used as targets in the financial perspective, with specific indicators used for each, such as "cash flow" for "survival" and "quarterly sales growth rate and operational profit" for "success." In the internal business process category, several specific targets are used for intangible assets, mainly for achieving a competitive edge, and their quantitative value indicators, include processing time, failure cost, and design lead time. Many of these are indirect or alternative value indicators.

As strategies and targets differ depending on the organization, BSC activities are unique, even between two business units within the same company. BSC can also be applied to programs. In programs, the weight among the four categories should be adjusted, and targets and value indicators should be determined in accordance with the program phase or the project type (i.e., scheme, system, or service).

In P2M (Ohara et al., 2003, p. 68), a "Total value benchmark" provides indicators for areas of value called the "Two A's and Five E's," including acceptability, accountability, effectiveness, efficiency, ethics, ecology, and earned value. Like BSC, detailed sub-indicators are required in practice. The seven indicators can be tailored to individual programs or organizations by including more items or eliminating less important ones.

5. Assessment of Non-Commercial Programs

Non-commercial programs, such as public programs or potential value programs, are classified in Exhibit 4.2.3. These may be difficult to assess in monetary terms. Public investments include roads, airports, and urban infrastructure. It is necessary to explain the economic effectiveness of these investments. Programs in disaster prevention, health and welfare, and the like should be accountable for justifying the investments they represent by providing an assessment of their effectiveness.

Even in areas such as defense, environmental protection, and potential value programs, which are generally beyond the scope of this book, cost-effectiveness analysis of their elements may be used to determine the best options and solve problems. But monetary value assessment of overall investments using cost-benefit analysis or other methods is not wholly suited for these areas. Planning is based on the professional judgment of experts and managers in accordance with the higher level strategy and vision of the nation or corporation. Put another way, in such areas, the strategy or vision as the nation or corporation should be of extreme importance.

5.1 Policy Assessment

Budgets for central or local governments are discussed in the legislature. This is an important political process for confirming an investment's legitimacy and to maintain fiscal discipline. It is very difficult to evaluate in money terms an investment's effectiveness vis-à-vis its budget, as previously noted, so policy assessment employs indirect methods.

Methods of policy analysis differ, with two basic types: a single value indicator, and multiple value indicators. Choosing a suitable method depends on timing – prior assessment or ex post assessment. Here, popular methods are discussed for cost-benefit analysis, cost-effectiveness analysis, and input-output analysis. Additionally, efficiency improvement of public programs is discussed (Nakai, 2005, p 14).

Policy assessment significantly differs, country to country, in its basic approach and application. Care should be taken when putting an assessment method into practice.

The difficulty with public programs arises from the value judgments of public officials or lawmakers participating in decision-making. Different from commercial programs, cash flow is not necessary a primary matter of concern to public officials. Their success criterion is budget maximization. It is of no use to consider this an ethical problem with individual officials. Viewed the other way, eagerness to secure as large a budget as possible for responsible projects can be seen to constitute a conscientious attitude among government departmental officials. For example, if an official is responsible for road construction, he/she should not be blamed for being eager to get a big enough budget to complete the task. Unlike bureaucrats, lawmakers have the responsibility to assess central or local government projects and budgets, but their judgment is likely to be affected by the next election.

Determining budget priorities is the most important governance issue in public choice, though a more in-depth discussion is beyond the scope of this book. It is important to note that public program or project budgets are inherently prone to the expansion called *scope creep*.

5.2 Cost-Benefit Analysis

Cost-benefit analysis serves to estimate potential benefits, and compares them with the investment plan. Intended benefits cannot be expressed in dollars directly, so they are converted into monetary amounts by a variety of methods for analysis. Typical examples are shown in Exhibit 4.5.1 (Morita, 2003; NILIM, 2004).

5.3 Cost-Effectiveness Analysis

Contrary to *benefit* in cost-benefit analysis, *effectiveness* in cost-effectiveness analysis is for cases that cannot be measured in money terms. For instance, data, such as the decreasing rate of pollution, mortality rates, proportion of smokers and numbers of casualties are evaluated by comparison to relative costs. The analysis is used for both ex ante and ex post assessments (Nakai, 2005, p. 49).

Category	Main Example of Method	Notes
Revealed Preference Methods	**Replacement Cost Method:** The target of valuation is compared with similar goods or services of known monetary value.	Example: Evaluation of a forest water conservation system's capacity by comparison with the cost of a dam of the same capacity. Sometimes it is difficult to find an appropriate substitute good or service.
	Travel Cost Method: The value of recreational facilities is estimated indirectly by estimating the number of visitors and their travel costs.	Applicable to sightseeing or recreational facilities
	Hedonic Approach: Value is estimated based on the hypothesis that the value of environmental or social capital transfers to land prices and such effect can be isolated from the land price.	This assessment is considered to be objective and reliable because it is based on land prices in the market.
Stated Preference Methods	**Contingent Valuation Method (CVM):** Evaluates value by asking people about their willingness to pay (WTP) or willingness to accept (WTA) the supposed change.	Applicable to various areas, in theory. Problems arise from inaccurate answers due to poorly targeted questions, and the possibility of indicating higher WTP for purposes of project promotion.
	Conjoint Analysis: Estimates the value of individual attributes in a profile by asking for preferences about profiles that have multiple attributes.	Allows evaluation of profiles by individual attribute, by statistical analysis of combinations and answers

Exhibit 4.5.1: Major Examples of Cost-Benefit Analyses (Morita, 2003; NILIM, 2004)

Cost-utility analysis is a similar concept. It is used for assessment that measures quality in addition to quantity. For example, the longevity of a certain quality level of patients (e.g., functional capacity to work) is evaluated, instead of mere years of survival as measured in a cost-effectiveness analysis.

5.4 Input-Output Analysis

Input-output analysis studies the inter-industry relationships within a country or a region, to see what propagation effect the output of an industry has on the production of other industries. The input-output table consists of three Excel-type spreadsheets: Basic Transaction Table, Input Coefficient Table, and Inverse Matrix Coefficient Table (Nakai, 2005, p. 56).

The Basic Transaction Table illustrates the interrelations of transaction values among industries, and the production output and gross value added by individual industries. The Input Coefficient Table indicates units of inputs from raw material industry required for each industry to produce a unit of output. The Inverse Matrix Coefficient Table is a table of the direct and indirect multi-stage propagation effect of demand for each individual industry in response to the unit final demand of an industry. The data is prepared for each country or region and is publicly available. Input-output analysis provides prior assessment of production's propagation effects or the influence of a policy or project. It also can provide assessment of the effects or influence of executed projects by comparing ex ante and ex post assessments.

This method is widely used for public construction projects. It is also applied to assess economic propagation effects on a local economy for projects such as expos or popular TV drama series where the story takes place in a specific region (Expo 2005; KER, 2008).

5.5 The Efficiency of Budget-Based Programs and Projects

The programs and projects of a government or other public institution are in principle not-for-profit. This does not excuse inefficiency in providing services (i.e., excessive spending). The financial deficit of the Japanese government stands out among advanced countries. Improvement in the efficiency of public programs is indispensable, even though many are carried out after confirmation of their legitimacy through cost-benefit analysis, cost-effectiveness analysis, or input-output analysis.

Public programs or projects are essentially implemented on a budgetary system funded by tax money, not on a profit-or-loss basis. They are legitimized in a budget, which is allocated after political discussion. It is the obligation of public officials to execute them when the budget comes into effect. Drucker stated,

> *Results in the budget-based institution mean a larger budget. Performance is the ability to maintain or to increase one's budget. Results, as the term is commonly understood, that is, contributions to the market or achievement toward goal and objectives, are, in effect, secondary. The first test of a budget-based institution and the first requirement for its survival is to obtain the budget. And the budget is not, by definition, related to contribution but to good intentions.* (Drucker, 1985, p. 142)

Conversely, public program management should be reorganized into something resembling a private business. Drucker cited three types of public organizations: (i) natural monopolies, (ii) budget-based service organizations, such as schools and hospitals, and (iii) administrative organizations, including national defense and the judiciary. Natural monopolies are better if managed in the private sector and regulated, rather than if nationalized. In the case of Japan, services were significantly improved through competition by dividing and privatizing formerly public corporations, which operated telecommunications and railways. The country's current challenge is efficiency improvement of toll highways, the postal service, airports, seaports, and the water supply. The government's reorganization initiatives for independent administrative institutions and national university corporations are improving efficiency by instituting management autonomy, partially detaching the institutions from their traditional strict budget systems.

Situations vary significantly, country by country. Though Drucker's explanation may look too simplistic today, it is quite acceptable as a generality.

These explanations may be weak for enthusiastic believers in the market economy who are convinced that economic efficiency is optimized when government participation is minimized. However, the very concept of *intangible value* in business management does not square with an economic theory that evaluates everything in money terms. It is an irony that strong government measures are required to stabilize the volatility in a globalized and deregulated financial market. Much of the technological basis for today's manufacturing and service industries, including financial services, arose from creations supported by military and government programs. Development of the Internet by DARPA is such an example. Super express trains that run at 300km/hour would never have been developed in Japan if the railway corporation had not been state-owned. Genetic technology will probably create tremendous social and economic value in the near future, promoted largely by use of public funds. The role of the public sector in creating social value should be considered when taking into account the essential nature of the technology or the service and its industrial level of maturity. It is very important to make clear the target value with public programs, which cannot be expressed in money terms.

PFI (private finance initiatives) are a way to bring private sector efficiency to public programs. Public programs often use private companies to design, construct, or provide services. PFI provides a much wider range of private participation. PFI has a long history in the U.K. There are three major types (DBJ, 1998, p. 928):

- Service provider: The private sector provides construction and service operations, paid by the public sector.
- Independent: The private sector provides construction and service operations, receiving a fee from users directly.
- Joint venture: The private sector provides services while government provides investments, subsidies or facilities.

PFI is a very important method for implementing public programs efficiently. There are a variety of approaches in practice and a large body of literature.

Budget-based activities in private corporations have characteristics similar to the public services described above. Typical examples are basic research, advertising, publicity, and market research. Closer investigation into such activities indicates that some parts will become far more efficient if outsourced, while some particular parts are vital for the company's future and should never be outsourced. While both approaches are necessary for value creation through a program, it is very important to create a program concept with deepest insight into effectiveness.

References

Benninga, S. Z., & Sarig, O. H. (1997). *Corporate finance: A valuation approach.* New York, NY: McGraw-Hill.

Boer, F. P. (1999). *The valuation of technology.* Hoboken, NJ: John Wiley.

Brealey, R. A., & Myers, S. C. (2000). *Principles of corporate finance* (6th ed.). New York, NY: McGraw Hill.

Brynjolfsson, E. (2004). *Intangibulu asetto* [Intangible asset]. Tokyo, Japan: Diamond-sha.

Boulton, R., Libert, B., & Samek, S. (2000). *Cracking the value code.* New York, NY: Harper Collins.

DBJ. (Nihon Kaihatsu Ginkou) PFI Research Group. (1998). *"PFI to jigyouka shuhou* [PFI and method for business operation]. Kinzai Institute for Financial Affairs.

Drucker, P. F. (1985). *Management: Tasks, responsibilities, practices.* Harper Colophon.

Expo 2005 (Japan Association for the 2005 World Exposition). Ai-Chikyu Haku no Keizai-Koka nikansuru Hyouka-Houkokusho [Assessment report on the economic effect of Expo 2005 Aichi Japan]. Retreived from http//www.expo2005 .or.jp/jp/jpn/press/press051109_11_02.pdf and http//www.expo2005.or.jp/jp/ jpn/press/press051109_11_03.pdf

Itami, H. (1984). *Shin-keiei senryaku no ronri* [New logic of business management]. Tokyo, Japan: *Nikkei.*

Ito, K. (1994). *Gendai kaikei nyumon* [Introduction to modern accountings]. Tokyo, Japan: *Nikkei.*

Ito, K., & Kagaya, T. (2008). Kigyoukachi wo souzousuru intangible tougou [Intangible integration to create corporate value]. *Hitotubashi Business Review,* Winter 2008, 6.

KER (The Kagoshima Regional Economic Research Institute). (2008). NHK Taiga-Dorama "Atsu-Hime" Houei niyoru Kagoshima-ken eno Keizai-Koka [The economic effect of the broadcasting of the TV drama "Atsu-Hime" for Kagoshima Prefecture]. Retrieved from http//www.ker.co.jp/investigation/pdf/survey7.pdf

Kaplan, R. S., & Norton D. P. (2001). *The strategy-focused organization.* Boston, MA: Harvard Business School Publishing.

Morita, M. (2003). Hishijyou-zai no keizai-hyoka [Economic assessment of non-market goods]. *Best Value, 4,* 11.

Nakai, T. (2005) *Seisaku hyouka* [Policy assessment]. Kyoto, Japan: Minerva Shobo.

NILIM-MLIT (National Institute for Land and Infrastructure Management – Ministry of Land, Infrastructure, Transport and Tourism (Japan)). (2004). Gaibu-Keizai-Hyouka no Kaisetsu (An); Dai 2 Hen: Kaku-Shuhou no Kaisetsu [An exposition of external economy assessment (draft); Chapter 2, Expositions on various methods]. Retrieved from http://www.nilim.go.jp/lab/peg/siryou/gaibu/nihen.pdf

Ohara, S., et al. (2003). *P2M purojekuto & puroguramu manejimento hyoujun gaidobukku (jyoukan)* [P2M project & program management for enterprise innovation (vol. 1)]. Tokyo, Japan: PHP Institute.

Origo, I. (1957). *The merchant of Prato.* London, U.K.: Jonathan Cape.

Swiss, J. E. (1991). *Public management systems.* Upper Saddle River, NJ: Prentice Hall.

Ulrich, D., & Smallwood, N. (2003). *Why the bottom line isn't.* Hoboken, NJ: John Wiley.

Chapter 5

Project Organization and Project Management Competency

Chapter Overview

Chapter 5

Project Organization and Project Management Competency

Chapter Overview
Chapter 5 discusses the organization and the capability of its members responsible for program implementation.

The first subject is the organization required to implement a project or a program. The discussion here is mostly on project organizations, because program organizations are not different greatly from project organizations in terms of their organizational nature. Project organizations are one type of general management organization, and the requirements for such management organizations apply to project organizations as well. Section 1 describes the fundamental views of management organizations, then discusses project organization itself, including the topics of project managers, the project management office, and organization maturity. A major subject of the project management discussion is the *community of practice*, which leads to better accomplishment of projects by encouraging cooperation and intrinsic motivation among project organization members.

Section 2 discusses project managers' capability and its improvement. As discussed here, project managers include program managers, because their required capabilities are similar in breadth, though different in depth. A project is implemented with the organization's resources, which include members' individual capabilities. The project manager appropriately bundles resources and provides people with direction and energy. This capability does not merely require knowledge; project managers must possess the ability to take action. Section 2 deals with this capability, discussing (i) learning and proficiency, (ii) capabilities, including leadership, insight, and creativity, and (iii) an outline of the competency model.

1. Project Organization and the Community of Practice
1.1 Management Organization
1.1.1 Organization and Its Role
In general, the larger the scale of work, the bigger the working group has to be. The purpose of an organization is to mobilize a number of people and to concentrate their efforts on a large task. Where the work's scale is large, implementation becomes more complicated, and a larger and more complex organization is

required. This is true with private enterprises, the government, and other public entities.

In what way, then, would an organization's scale increase in accordance with the increase of the workload? When the workforce simply meant people's physical labor, the organization would grow ten times in size if the work grew ten times in scale. Now that the systematic division of labor (i.e., specialization) and installation of equipment (i.e., mechanization) are well developed, organizational efficiency is also subject to economies of scale. The history of industrial development is that of organizational efficiency development, which is closely related to advancement in productivity supported by mechanical power. This is why business administration studies emphasize organizational management along with strategic management.

The role of an organization is to manage the growing complexity of work and to enhance the efficiency of task implementation. The question is "In what ways can an organization be better structured?" A common response to complexity is a hierarchical structure. In general, a large task is composed of a large number of routine tasks and a small number of non-routine ones.

This leads to the following three important requirements in an organization:

- Systems to deal with many routine tasks and some non-routine tasks
- Precise and efficient implementation of routine tasks handled by specialized staff in the hierarchical organization
- Control by the commanding authority and the duty of obedience (i.e., establishment of a management system) to perform all functions

In addition to these are clarification of operational processes and systematic information transfer with programs for evaluation and remuneration for personnel.

1.1.2 Bureaucratic Organization

The basic form of organization that satisfies these requirements is a hierarchical structure of a bureaucratic organization as explained in organizational theory. Bureaucratic organization is traditional in governmental bodies, and has also been adopted by groups and entities in many fields, such as private enterprise, public enterprise, labor unions, and public corporations. A bureaucratic organization basically has the following structural and operational characteristics:

- A top-down command system, which is based on the organization's hierarchical structure
- Responsibility and authority that are allocated according to defined rules
- Lower-ranking members of the organization are independent of their superiors when working within the scope of their own responsibility.
- Task implementation that is instructed through, and recorded in, documents
- Organizational function that is achieved through cooperation among sections with specialized duties
- Members meeting selection criteria are assigned to specific tasks, positions, and pay grades according to their individual performance.

- Routine work is done within the authority allocated to lower-ranked members, so that higher-ranked members are not bothered by a mass of detailed routine jobs. Non-routine tasks beyond the scope of lower-level authority are handled by upper-level authority. If the scope of the upper-level authority is still insufficient, the tasks are then entrusted to yet higher authorities. In this way, higher-ranked members are able to concentrate their experience and capability on non-routine work.
- Non-routine work done by the highest level authority includes development and implementation of organizational strategy, as well as organizational reform programs.
- Due to specialization, individual expertise is enhanced, and each section of the organization can integrate specialist resources for its functioning.

Routine task processing and specialized duties based on the hierarchical division of labor are highly effective for a bureaucratic organization to optimize job implementation. At the same time, however, the hierarchy's features, such as fragmentation, rule-based operation, and document orientation, cause the following problems, which are called "dysfunction of bureaucracy":

- Hindrances to information circulation or damage to information quality, such as misinformation during circulation due to the multi-level hierarchy
- The principle of rule supremacy, which justifies evasion of responsibility, such as "we cannot do what is not in the rulebook," or irresponsible behavior, such as "nothing can be wrong as long as it is done as the rulebook says"
- Authoritarianism based on the power granted by a larger organization
- Excessive emphasis on rules and documents that leads to standardization around internal conventions, where, in turn, the organization becomes so observant of precedent that creativity and flexibility to change are sacrificed
- Sectionalism caused by hierarchical structural fragmentation, such as vertical segmentation of business operation, uncooperative and exclusive manners of duty implementation, and concealment of information

Today, the word *bureaucratic* is often used as a criticism of the rigidity brought about by the dysfunction of bureaucracy. However that may be, large-scale work is necessarily accompanied by a large volume of routine work. For a manufacturer, typical routine work may be fitting products with parts on the production line, but there are a huge number of other routine tasks, such as:

- Ordering and receiving parts that satisfy stipulated quality requirements, and ensuring their distribution to relevant worksites
- Testing products and recording the results according to designated procedures
- Checking test results, packing products in a standardized manner, and shipping them to customers
- Collecting receivables, settling purchases, and entering receipts and payments in the books, totaling them properly

Modern business organizations require routine work. The absence of routine work or deterioration of routine work systems immediately causes a flood of inferior goods. Although an organizations' internal accidents or failures are generally invisible to outsiders, they often come into the public eye in the form of frightening incidents, such as food contamination (Asahi, 2000), plant fires (Nikkei, 2003), nuclear plant criticality or other accidents (Asahi, 1999), leaks of personal information, collisions between fishing boat and military vessels (Ministry of Defense, 2009), and even missing pension accounts (Ministry of Health, Labor and Welfare, 2007). Organizational accidents or failures, even if not catastrophic, can be serious enough to result in grave damage to organizational performance. To ensure that routine work is done efficiently, maintaining a certain quality level, the baseline is the proper operation of the bureaucratic organization. A methodology to control and eliminate dysfunction in bureaucracy is an important challenge.

1.1.3 Teams and Flat Organizations

A small team or a flat-structured organization is more creative and efficient than a bureaucratic hierarchy. The driving force of creativity and efficiency in this approach is communication, sharing high quality information and encouragement of individual initiative. Teamwork in a flat organization may maximize individual capabilities and make best use of skills. It may also lead to individualized capability and behavior, where creative thoughts and behavioral patterns are valued. This is the opposite of bureaucratic organizations, where large-scale routine work is made efficient by impersonal uniformity, or specifically, standardization of work processes and homogenization of worker capabilities. Thanks to the recent progress in information network technology, distribution of high-quality information is dramatically extended to more recipients, to a broader range of organizational components, and over a greater coverage distance. A flat organization, along with small-team effects from advanced technologies, simplifies large multi-layered organizational hierarchies and minimizes the dysfunction in a bureaucracy.

1.1.4 Structural Solutions to Organizational Problems

Deterioration in a bureaucratic organization is a cause of increased failure and accidents. The consequence is an increased volume of non-routine work that managers have to deal with. Failures or accidents affect the relevant cost schedule and product quality. If this happens frequently, higher-level members of the organization are affected. They get pressed into non-routine, ad hoc tasks to solve problems, eventually becoming deprived of time to engage in important tasks, such as strategic planning, drastic reforms, and new market development. The impact of such a situation on the organization's competitiveness and long-term growth is far more serious than temporary losses or delayed deliveries. One underlying aspect of a well-managed organization is that its bureaucratic activity is sufficiently healthy for sound implementation of routine work.

Among discussions on how to fully take advantage of the efficiency of bureaucratic organizations while controlling dysfunction, five structural solutions were summarized by Numagami (2003, p. 27), as outlined in Exhibit 5.1.1.

Solution	Approach
(a) Improvement of Employees' Knowledge-based Capability	Provide workers with multifunctional training and educational programs to raise their capability levels, so that frequently occurring low-level non-routine tasks can be handled directly at the worksite to some extent.
(b) Creation of Assistant Staff	Provide leaders with assistants such as secretaries or deputies, who take over leaders' routine tasks (e.g., collection, analysis and communication of information, and preparation of documents) so that leaders can efficiently process non-routine tasks.
(c) Application of Information Technology	Fully use information technology to enhance individual and organizational proficiency with information processing, such as by sharing business management information, allowing for optimization of information communication, and automation of routine work processes, such as processing of accepting orders.
(d) Divisional Organization	Divide the hierarchical structure into two levels, assigning lower level divisions to daily operations, including non-routine task processing, while the upper level or headquarters is dedicated to strategic tasks. Divisions are autonomous business units that are granted the authority and resources to deal with daily operations.
(e) Creation of Horizontal Relations	When a non-routine task impacts widely on the organization, the flow of information in the organizational hierarchy suddenly expands upward and downward, paralyzing upper-level functions. This can be avoided by an organizational structure that facilitates direct exchange of necessary information among relevant sections on the same level. Examples of such organizational structures include project-based organizations and matrix organizations. In matrix organizations, business lines in charge of products or markets are positioned on the same footing with functional departments in charge of research, sales, or production.

Exhibit 5.1.1: Structural Solutions for Organizational Problems (Numagami, 2003, p. 27)

1.2 Project Organization

1.2.1 Requirements for Project Organization

A project is distinguished by its uniqueness. It is essentially a non-routine task and does not fit naturally in a hierarchy that places great importance on the efficiency of routine work processes. However, a project also involves many routine tasks in its detailed levels of work, especially in the downstream stages of the workflow. When a project is larger in scale, the volume of routine tasks reaches an extent that requires a processing capacity equal to that of an ordinary functional organization. On the other hand, in the project's upstream stages, such as conceptualization, planning, and designing, the weight of non-routine tasks far exceeds that of an operation-oriented organization. This means that project organizations must be steadfast and efficient in routine tasks, as well as in maintaining the team-based organization's characteristics, discussed in the previous section.

Another characteristic of a project, that is, the temporary nature caused by a fixed-term duration, imposes a few more organizational requirements:

- Human resources are used only during project execution, becoming unnecessary once it is completed.
- An organization or system needs to be created and made functional for the project to start.
- With no lead time allowed for on-the-job training, a project needs personnel who are ready to function immediately.

These are challenging requirements, particularly for the Japanese business community, where labor mobility is low for institutional and cultural reasons. In Japan it is difficult for a project manager to directly pick up and gather the best individuals, which is a typical American way to form a project organization. The usual way a Japanese enterprise recruits members is to seek its principal organization's cooperation or to exercise influence derived from organizational and personal relationships. The recruited members are not always prepared for their new tasks. Some are expected to improve themselves through information sharing and cooperative practices within team-based organizations. Even so, as a project-executing organization, the majority of its members need to be sufficiently skilled to perform their tasks successfully. One approach to ensure project success is to contract out project execution in whole or in part to a capable organization, or to use a matrix organization, where multiple projects share and develop human resources.

1.2.2 Forms of Project Organization
(1) Basic Forms

A manufacturer's business activity is a repetition of operations, such as production, sales, and so on. These activities are carried out by specialized functional departments, which are integrated into an overall organization. When the organization intends to execute a non-routine task as a project—organizational reform, for instance—it creates a temporary organization ("Project X" in Exhibit 5.1.2). Its members are engaged exclusively in Project X. In Exhibit 5.1.2, "Business Executive" means a person who has ultimate responsibility for running a business organization: specifically, a chief executive officer of a company, a chief officer of a division, or a general manager of a department.

In the construction and IT industries, where business means concurrent execution of multiple project activities, many firms take the form of an aggregation of multiple project-based organizations, as indicated in Exhibit 5.1.3.

These organizations are formed on the assumption that each project is staffed by personnel who are exclusively dedicated to its mission. In reality, however, applying this to all personnel can obviously cause considerable variance in their workload intensity as the project progresses, or can make it difficult to attract personnel who are efficient enough for tasks requiring high expertise. It is therefore a common practice in many areas that projects take the form of a matrix organization. In a matrix organization, each project has its own exclusive personnel for its unique tasks, while performing a number of expertise-oriented tasks through functional organizations in the relevant specialties. The functional organizations assign personnel for a specific period of time or a specific scope of work. As indicated in

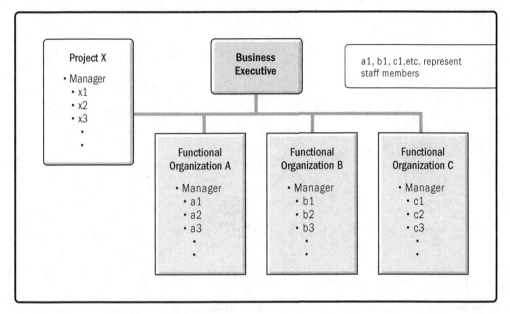

Exhibit 5.1.2: Project Organization in an Operational Business Organization (e.g., A Project for Organizational Reform)

Exhibit 5.1.4, in a matrix organization that executes multiple projects concurrently, it is not unusual that one member is in charge of multiple project tasks at a time, or one after another. The advantage of this is that expertise is enhanced and technical skills are accumulated. The disadvantage is that multiple projects handled this way are apt to influence each other.

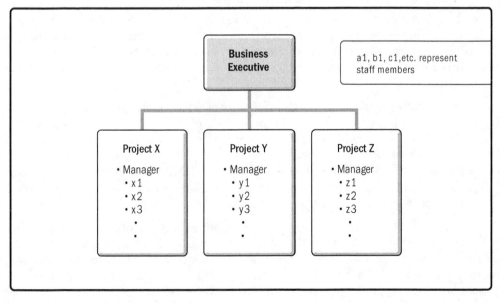

Exhibit 5.1.3: Projectized Organization (Projectized Firm)

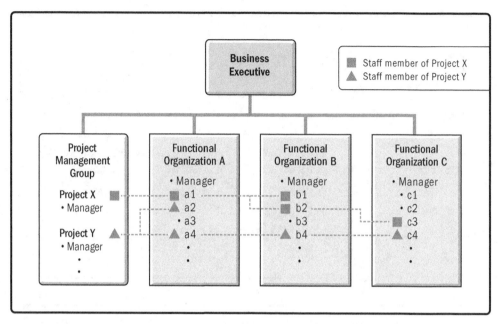

Exhibit 5.1.4: Matrix Organization (Multiple Projects)

The merits and demerits of these organizational forms relative to project execution are summarized in Exhibit 5.1.5. Functional organizations are better suited to routine tasks, but their workforce mobility and managers' authority are insufficient to implement a project unsupported by other organizations, because they usually do not have surplus personnel. Projects that can be handled within a functional organization are generally limited to those that don't have finance or workload problems. Examples would be small projects, or a project managed by a committee in which the cost and workforce requirements are covered by functional organizations. When a strategic program is implemented by this structure, sufficient care by top management is required for personnel and budget allocation.

Projectized organization is effective for integrated management of non-routine tasks. It may not be adaptable to some large-scale routine tasks, in which case such tasks should be contracted out or treated otherwise. Exclusive use of human resources by each project can reduce operating rates. This often rebounds on projects in the form of understaffing problems. Matrix organizations are adaptable to projects that deal with both unconventional non-routine tasks and routine tasks, though they are prone to being affected by functional organizations.

Aside from these, there are unique types of project organization. Some examples are Linux and Wikipedia, which are platforms built by innovative leaders to facilitate loosely bound participation. These are large-scale projects shared by voluntary participants beyond the boundary of the organization. This type of spontaneous project activity occurs also within individual firms as unorganized or informally organized activities for voluntary improvement, or unofficial advanced R&D, and

	Merits	Demerits
Functional Organization	• Highly efficient for routine tasks Workforce mobility and manager responsibilities are generally insufficient for executing a project within a functional organization. The types of projects are limited to either: (i) small ones, or (ii) projects that have fewer financial and workload restrictions, such as those planned by a committee and executed at each functional division's cost and initiative. Special care is needed for resource allocation for strategic programs.	
Projectized Organization	• Effective for integrated management of non-routine tasks • Information flow and command system are simple and clear. Task prioritization can be decided at an individual project's discretion.	• Not efficient for large-scale routine tasks • Difficult to secure human and material resources • Dedicated use of human resources diminishes the utilization rate of personnel. • Difficult to obtain/maintain professional and advanced disciplinary skills • Difficult to accumulate skills and experience and to share these with other projects
Matrix Organization	• Flexible with unconventional non-routine tasks, and efficient for routine tasks • Quality and efficiency can be achieved due to expertise. ▪ Expertise of functional organization (technology, maintenance, special skills) ▪ Expertise in project management ▪ Easy to secure human and physical resources • Flexibility in response to changes of business situation ▪ Multiple projects facilitate workload leveling, and information/experience are shared and accumulated. ▪ Maintain specialized functional organizations. ▪ Economies of scale with specialized human resources (accumulated experience, enhanced expertise and skills)	• Sensitive to influence of other projects' tasks through functional organizations • Information flow and command system tend to be complicated.

Exhibit 5.1.5: Merits and Demerits of Organizational Forms in Project Execution

the like. When these activities develop within the firm, they usually take one of the organizational forms listed in Exhibit 5.1.5.

(2) Organizational Structure and Assignment of Responsibility

To ensure optimization of its objectives and goal achievement, a project is divided into work packages defined by a WBS. The firm's internal or external organizations that are qualified for the work packages are selected to develop a project organization headed by a project manager. Work packages are basic units for planning the project and monitoring its progress; organizations assigned to work packages are basic units responsible for the progress. These organizations within the project need clearly defined responsibilities and interrelationships based on an OBS (organization breakdown structure) that corresponds to the WBS. When a large functional organization (e.g., an engineering department) is assigned to a work package, appointment of an appropriate person is a common practice to direct work package execution representing the segment's responsibility. This is on behalf of the department manager, who is also responsible for many other tasks.

In some project tasks, unlike routine tasks, it is not clear who is responsible for decisions. Possible reasons for this are as follows:

- Understanding of responsibility and authority for a task is not shared by managers and players at different levels.
- The scope of responsibilities is understood differently among organizations.
- One or more essential work packages are missing from the WBS.

An important preventive measure to take in early stages is to integrate individual tasks and work packages into a responsibility matrix, which clarifies responsibilities and encourages independent efforts to scrutinize the respective ranges of responsibility. The responsibility matrix does not merely indicate tasks and responsible persons. With persons' names on the vertical axis and individual tasks (work packages or their sub-tasks) on the horizontal axis, the matrix identifies who is responsible or authorized to execute, approve, be informed or consulted, and so forth (Cleland, 1994, p. 212; PMAJ, 2007, p. 288).

When discussing a program, *work packages* in the context above can also be regarded as *projects*.

1.2.3 Using Support from External Organizations
The previous section outlined the fundamentals for a project organization owned by a single entity. An owner of a program or a large-scale project, however, has to deal with another important issue—systematic use of external capabilities.

A project often requires resources and new technologies beyond its owner's means. In program or large-scale project implementation, it is in many cases difficult for an individual project organization to internally secure human resources (including skills), physical resources (including facility, equipment and raw materials), and financial resources, as well as to acquire information necessary for the program or project efforts. Further, in a program or a large-scale project implemented overseas, knowledge and experience of local situation and practices are crucial. The owner in such a case needs to build its program organization based on inter-corporate cooperation of various forms, including consortia, joint ventures (JV), special purpose companies (SPC), and so forth.

Clear-cut definition of these cooperative forms is difficult due to legal systems differing by country, and business customs differing from industry to industry. However, in relation to project implementation, a consortium can be roughly defined as a group whose member corporations act independently pursuant to a cooperative agreement among them, while a JV is an enterprise jointly organized by two or more corporations contributing capital and human resources. An SPC, although somewhat similar to a JV, is more a fundraising scheme than a framework for practical job cooperation. Dedicated to program/project implementation, these cooperative bodies are dismissed once their purposes have been fulfilled, which is very different from the operational joint businesses typically found in the manufacturing industry.

Corporations participating in a JV or an SPC inevitably share risks arising from their capital contribution or from the program/project implementation they cooperate in. The risk sharing occurs on the assumption that profit from the program/project would be distributed among the participants—and the profit distribution represents the program/project's capital cost. So, in order to minimize the cost of capital, it is important that a cooperative body consists of highly risk-tolerant participants. Basically, each participant corporation is to receive its portion of profit distribution in accordance with its share in capital contribution. Some participants may sell their shares to earn capital gains before the program/project closes.

How to compensate for lack of technologies and resources is an important issue also for a project owned by a single company. An important question is what the company should do with all the skills and resources when the project is over. Of the skills and resources required by a project, those that have the potential for continuous use may deserve major investment, but those for exclusive use in a specific project may better be outsourced in many cases. In projects involving technological development, "Not Invented Here" (NIH) syndrome often leads component technology development to be mistaken as the final goal. Investing precious human resources in this activity may result in weakening the competitiveness of the project outcome. Technological deficiencies could be handled more effectively through business partnerships or outsourcing.

Use of external resources is particularly important in industrial fields that face rapid changes in technologies and business environments, especially IT networks, new energy, and emerging market-related fields. Entrepreneurs with insufficient resource accumulation also need to become users of external resources. Consortia or business partnerships help in acquisition of sales channels, fundraising, risk mitigation, or risk transfer. A project organization as a whole must be formed from the viewpoint of total optimization—without corporate or divisional barriers and with access to external resources, such as job outsourcing, business partnerships, or technological introduction.

1.2.4 Project Team

A team is a group of people cooperating for the same purpose. A project team is a group of people working as the core members who promote the coordinated activities of the entire project organization. It must be noted that the term *project team* places an emphasis on proactive and cooperative efforts among the team members. In general, each segmental organization for routine operation is responsible for efficient implementation of tasks within a clearly defined scope, whether explicit or tacit, and is usually free of concern about what is happening in other segments or the entire organization. In a project, a negative situation or outcome from an individual task (e.g., a delay, quality failure, etc.) affects other tasks, possibly with serious effects on the entire project. Projects are also vulnerable to external influences. All of these are caused by the complexity and the uncertainty that are inherent to projects. To accomplish an objective on schedule within the allotted time and budget, organization members are required to cooperate in an effort to solve or prevent problems beforehand. Therefore, project participants must not forget that they are team members who share understanding and information about the overall project, who are creative enough to cooperate in finding solutions, and who do not limit their efforts within the boundary of their assigned jobs.

This is what a project team is. When a project is small in scale, it is not unusual that every person involved in the project is called a project team member. In a larger scale project, as shown in Exhibit 5.1.6, the project team is composed of the project's central figures, including those who are responsible for work packages with significant influence on project implementation. More specifically, the project team members include:

- Managers and personnel in charge of project implementation
- Managers and supervisors in charge of field administration
- Leaders and core engineers representing functional organizations in charge of deliverable systems management

This configuration is much the same as that of the responsibility matrix. The "Project Board" in Exhibit 5.1.6 is the project's highest decision-making body, comprising the project owner, the project director acting on the owner's behalf, and the representatives of users and key suppliers. The total number of project board members is usually less than 10. A large-scale project often has a multi-layered project team structure, where each task is entrusted to a subordinate organization. The subordinate organization regards the task as its own project, forming a secondary project team consisting of the subordinate organization and its suppliers.

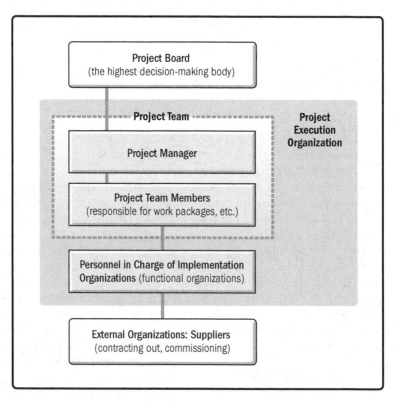

Exhibit 5.1.6: Project Team (large-scale project)

1.3 Project Manager

(1) Authority, Responsibility and Accountability

The project manager implements the project, exercising the authority granted by the project owner to lead the organization. The authority of a manager generally includes power over people (e.g., the right to command) and power over property (e.g., the right to determine expenditures). This authority is accompanied by obligations, such as responsibility to implement assigned duties and accountability related to implementation of the duty. Exhibit 5.1.7 summarizes the project manager's authority, responsibility, and accountability. Authority is usually granted in a top-down manner. But because projects deal with exceptional matters, in some cases managers acquire de facto authority based on trust from stakeholders. The project manager, including in the case of de facto authority, requires the ability to make trusted and reasonable decisions without specific instructions from superiors.

(2) Viewpoints of Matrix Organization Managers

Matrix organizations, which are frequently used to execute projects, are run by a combination of the functional organizations' activities and project management's efforts, both toward accomplishment of work packages. Although both efforts are directed to the same purpose, the project manager's main interest is the work package's overall plan and progress in quality, process, and cost, while the functional organization managers focus on the plan and execution of individual work processes that define who, where, and how, taking the operational capabilities of own organization into account (Cleland, 1994, p. 191).

Authority	• Legitimate power to order project members to perform or not to perform a specific action
	• Usually granted by the project owner or other superior with higher authority (authority through appointment)
	• In some projects the manager performs duties based on de-facto authority, not on appointment. This is often grounded in unique personal abilities that are broadly recognized by stakeholders (knowledge and skills, including organizing and coordinating abilities, etc.).
	• Though appointed, project managers should be competent enough to be recognized as having de facto authority.
	• Authority to represent an organization (a firm) in all project-related issues ranging from contracts with customers to internal and external negotiations
	• Project members need to report to the project manager on items related to contractual specifications, schedules and budget, while they should report on technical matters to their functional organization managers.
Responsibility	• Obligation to execute necessary tasks and achieve outcomes, without failures, consistent with the granted authority
	• Project managers are expected to have the ability to implement their responsibilities, and make trustworthy and reasonable decisions independently without specific instructions from superior authorities.
Accountability	• Able to explain the legitimacy of his/her actions
	• Charged with representing the project to the stakeholders and responding to stakeholder concerns
	• Project managers are required to provide relevant stakeholders with reports on the results of their activities and of the exercise of authority, as well as to provide convincing explanations for plans.

Exhibit 5.1.7: Authority, Responsibility and Accountability of Project Manager (Cleland, 1994, p. 219)

1.4 Project Management Office (PMO)

In a large-scale project or a program, highly advanced expertise and ample experience are required to plan the project schedule and budget, to monitor progress along the way, and to detect and solve problems arising in the course of project execution. Electronic information systems to support these efforts are highly sophisticated today, but applying such systems to the entire project organization is also a matter of expertise. It was already a common practice in the 1950s that U.S. government projects were staffed by a large number of experts in planning/management and customer relations. This is said to have been a result of the government procurement contract system. In Japan, there were many projects by the 1980s that had an organization in charge of both customer relations and support of in-house project efforts. This organization was formed under a project manager and staffed by experts in general affairs, financial affairs, planning/controlling, systems engineering, and information systems. Names of these organizations were various, but traditionally a preferred name was project office (PO).

Later, with the increase in project-based tasks, it became a vitally important challenge, particularly for projectized firms, to enhance project management ability across the company or division, without limiting it to each project. This led to a great increase in the number of firms with an independent organization with permanent staff specializing in project management support. The roles of such organizations have come to include (i) promoting project management, (ii) supporting project execution, (iii) preparing project management infrastructure, (iv) providing education and training, (v) providing instruction and consultation, (vi) accumulating information, and (vii) motivating organization members. The detailed roles of such organizations vary company by company, and so do their names: project office (PO), project management office (PMO), strategic project office (SPO), project management center of excellence (PMCoE), and the like. Of these, project management office (PMO) is used as a common way to identify organizations with similar roles.

An SPO is an organization that supports strategic decision-making and implementation at an executive or program manager level. A PMCoE is a staff organization with roles such as: (i) developing, coordinating and spreading project management tools and IT systems or methodologies that are commonly applicable to all project management efforts, (ii) standardizing project management processes, (iii) collecting success/failure cases and circulating them inside the firm, and (iv) benchmarking against other companies (PMAJ, 2007, p. 284; Kerzner, 2001, p. 1039; Rad & Levin, 2002, p. 59).

Assistance for managers in motivating organization members is an increasingly important role of the PMO, as the methods and skills used to motivate people become more important with the growing project size and complexity.

1.5 Organization Maturity

For corporations based on large projects mobilizing large human resources or on many smaller projects, a crucial requirement is project management proficiency—not of the project manager alone, but of the entire organization, including functional organization leaders, key engineers, and other personnel in charge. The promoter

Organization Maturity	Outline
Level 1: Haphazard	Projects are poorly understood across the organization and managed haphazardly. Whether a project succeeds or not depends on individual capabilities. Intensive labor is spent in "putting out fires." Corporate strategies and projects are not connected to each other, and a coherent program concept is essentially absent.
Level 2: Systematic	Prevention of problems is emphasized, with greater weight placed on planning efforts. Success or failure of a project depends on the capabilities of a team, not of individuals. A new project can be confusing if it has no similarity to any precedent. Strategies are developed top-down, and the program concept is understood.
Level 3: Scientific	Management is conducted in a scientific manner and provides systematically visualized data analysis, on which stakeholders and participants rely to take action. Previous project outcomes are reflected in strategy planning. Long-term plans for personnel skill development become possible at the program level or at the entire organization level. Progress is made in data accumulation and task standardization.
Level 4: Integrated	Multiple projects are executed in an orderly manner. Corporate vision spreads across the organization, enabling integrated management from corporate strategy down to projects. Divisional walls are removed, and fusion of knowledge and technologies is promoted. Program data is unified to provide a basis for portfolio management.
Level 5: Optimized	Linkage between corporate strategies and projects is firmly established to ensure effective management of strategic projects. Strategy development processes that actively embrace ideas from experienced individuals lead to a free and open corporate culture. Accomplishment of corporate strategies is measured through various indices.

Exhibit 5.1.8: A Model of Project Management Maturity Levels
(PMAJ, 2007, p. 296)

of such proficiency is the PMO. A business organization, whether or not it has a PMO in place, always needs to assess its project management proficiency and make necessary improvements. As projects are not recurring tasks, project management proficiency can hardly be evaluated accurately using "results-based" measures, such as product quality level and production lead time. What is necessary instead is to assess, for example, whether management-related processes are standardized and if they are observed properly. What to be evaluated, therefore, is the level of maturity of the organizational management framework. This maturity level can be graded in several ways, and Exhibit 5.1.8 shows an example that is described in P2M (PMAJ, 2007, p. 296).

1.6 The Community of Practice

For perfect execution of a project, all of its work packages and tasks are assigned, along with relevant authority and responsibility, to specific functional organizations or individuals in the project organization. However, when a project is a complex of intertwined tasks, or is planned for innovative value creation, stakeholders are required to put their heads together beyond the boundaries of organizational responsibilities and positions. The effects of such collaboration beyond the scope of official organizations were discussed in Senge's "learning organization" (1990, p. 9) and Wenger, McDermott, and Snyder's "community of practice" (2002, p. 4). P2M also offers a useful view of the community in a project. The following discussion focuses on the community of practice and its application to projects.

1.6.1 What Is The Community of Practice?

The word *community* means a group of people sharing the same residential locality. Members of a community are expected to participate in mutual aid and ritual activities that contribute to the community. There is no formal difference between the controlling and the controlled among members, and contributions are voluntary rather than mandatory. In times past, when living was almost impossible outside a community, members' contributions may not have always been voluntary, but at least they knew that their contributions were beneficial to their community, unlike land taxes and labor services that were imposed by the feudal lords.

Besides the local community, there are many kinds of community today, including schools, workplaces, hobby clubs, and the like. These communities benefit their participants, while the participants themselves provide benefits of retention and growth to their communities. A workplace is where labor is exchanged for wages and a school is where tuition is exchanged for knowledge and skills. Today's workplace or a school could not expect organizational improvement if its workers or teachers were not motivated to work to achieve more than their mere wages. Even civil servants, who engage strictly in legally defined duties, would become the target of public criticism if they were content to stay only inside the narrow scope of their prescribed tasks. Members of an organization are required not only to offer their respective labor hours, but to also serve their workplace through such voluntary efforts as acquiring necessary new knowledge, making improvements in their activities, and working in cooperation with each other. This requirement, although somewhat specific by its nature to organizations of knowledge-based, non-routine jobs, is now a trend in all kinds of organizations, including assembly plants and construction sites, because knowledge-based tasks are expanding into skill-based workplaces as well.

For a business organization to remain excellent or sustainable in these rapidly changing times, it is important to have a structure to encourage its members' voluntary contributions to the organization along with a formally organized administration system. A group of specialists who gather and act through such a structure is called a *community of practice* inside an organization.

A community of practice is an informal group who share the same interest in a subject area. Wenger et al. (2002) stated that "communities of practice are groups of people who share a concern, a set of problems, or a passion about a topic, and who deepen their knowledge and expertise in this area by interacting on an ongoing basis." Regardless of where they formally belong, the members of a community of practice jointly appreciate specialist knowledge and expertise in their area of common interest. Through exchanging information and ideas, and inspiring and supporting each other, they reach levels of knowledge and expertise that are unattainable by individual effort. Members of a community of practice, who share the same interest in the subject area, usually have different areas of specialization. For example, a community of practice for a large solar power plant could comprise a diverse group of specialists in solar cell physics, products development, materials engineering, production engineering, power conversion, power supply networks, local meteorology, and others. Members of a community of practice pool their practical knowledge and expertise to enhance knowledge of the subject area and improve the members' skills. In this respect, the nature of communities of practice differs from that of local communities, hobby clubs, or social circles.

Modern organizations are subject to an ever more sophisticated and complicated business environment that changes rapidly, and are compelled to increase the sophistication and specialization of their members' capabilities. A large-scale business operation requires proper organizational support. This support is typically provided by an organization with a hierarchical authority/responsibility system and functionally specialized groups (i.e., functional organizations) that are combined as described in section 1.1 of this chapter. However, such organizations are inevitably accompanied by the dysfunctions of bureaucracy. To enhance and sustain competitive advantage, the organization members' knowledge and expertise are crucial to be rallied and expanded, regardless of the organizational structure, along with the need to optimize the organizational structure itself to meet current business requirements. The concept of a community of practice must be spread within the organization, or within the group that includes affiliates and business partners.

1.6.2 Learning Organizations and the Role of the Community of Practice

According to Wenger et al. (2002, p. 42), communities of practice are formed for the creation, expansion, and exchange of knowledge, and the development of individual capabilities. A community of practice consists of voluntary participants with a passion for specific expertise or themes, which lasts as long as the members consider it helpful. They explain that communities of practice are different in this sense from similar groups, such as working groups in charge of specific tasks or processes, or project teams that implement tasks during a fixed time period.

The activities of specialty-based communities are familiar in technological fields. They are typified by workshops for new technologies (e.g., high-performance rechargeable batteries, new cancer diagnostic methods), a corporation's cross-organizational circle to learn new technologies (e.g., digital image processing), and campaigns for new design techniques (e.g., standardization of 3D CAD, use of QFD and TRIZ). These activities further extend from advanced research groups of science or engineering societies (e.g., studies on nuclear fusion experimental facilities, planetary exploration technologies) to nature conservation research groups, with membership ranging from researchers to non-academic citizens. Specialty-based communities of these kinds usually start as an active fellowship. But as its subject area starts to evolve toward a business orientation, competition and conflicts of interest arise among community members and, in many cases, activity shrinks accordingly. Senge advocated the concept of "learning organization" as the most important element of a competitive business organization (Senge, 1990, p. 9). A community of practice is comparable to a learning group of specialists without organizational boundaries. Its members voluntarily interact and collaborate with each other, exchanging and combining their tacit and explicit knowledge, in order to enhance their knowledge and explore new horizons.

Projectized firms have cross-organizational structures, such as matrix organizations and project teams, which compose the command and responsibility/authority structure of the formal organization to execute projects. However, value creation and improvement of the firm's capabilities are not really attainable without promoting a mutual learning cycle in the spirit of a "community of practice."

The significance of a "community of practice" in a program has two aspects. One is improvement of organizational capabilities. Communities of practice provide continuous and creative cycles of collective learning opportunity for each domain of engineering, and are open to specialists from different sections of the corporation, its affiliates, and business partners, without the boundaries of individual projects. The other is value creation or outcome improvement. Communities of practice facilitate better outcomes in each domain by providing organizations in charge of the project's work packages with opportunities for voluntary interaction and mutual learning, regardless of the relationships among the organizations. The following are examples of how the community of practice can benefit an organization:

- The community of practice, throughout the firm, can improve the organization's capabilities in its key component technologies and important processes through cross-sectional activities.
- For a program to create highly effective value, it is essential that experts from various fields be gathered during mission profiling. The community of practice gathers ideas from diverse perspectives that are needed at the concept stage.
- In project planning and design, different interfaces, including the user interface, are important. An interface is like a window of a house, the view through which can be quite different from the inside and from the outside. Interface design requires mutual learning activities participated in by all stakeholders, including organizations in charge and customers. The community of practice is a place where the mutual learning activities occur.
- Measures against risks identified during project execution must be optimized by broadly gathering wisdom, which the community of practice is particularly good at.

1.6.3 Building Communities of Practice

Many communities of practice arise spontaneously from participating volunteers' enthusiasm. In projects these communities are expected to play the role of a learning organization in which project members and other relevant specialists take part, in order to achieve project goals. Therefore, communities of practice are better built intentionally, rather than spontaneously, and managed actively. However, it is obvious that a community of practice created and run under the authority of a project manager would not be successful due to the nature of "community." For an effective community of practice, it is important that the project's principal organization accommodate a culture to sustain and develop the community and that the management and managing officers of the firm make organized and continuous efforts to promote and lead such activities.

Exhibit 5.1.9 illustrates relationships between a project organization and a community of practice in value creation during a project. The exhibit shows that the community of practice provides information exchange and learning to create information about the project's challenges. The knowledge created is applied to practical use in the formal organization, creating value for the project. Notice that it is new knowledge that the community creates. Value is created as a result of the project organization's formal process. As a matter of course, the formal project organization also solves problems by itself. Expectations for a community of practice are centered on problem solving that is beyond the capacity of individual formal organizations.

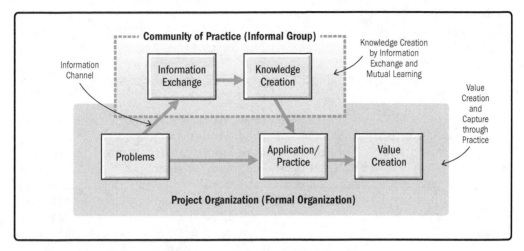

Exhibit 5.1.9: The Role of A Community of Practice

In a community of practice, professional information is exchanged between specialists irrespective of their position and experience. This type of activity can create knowledge that enables in-depth comprehension and solution of problems. To this end, a proper "space" must be prepared for a wide range of unrestricted information exchange and freely inspired knowledge creation. Also needed are information channels to absorb the formal organization's problems and return the created knowledge to it. It is important, therefore, that the program manager prepare a proper environment for a community of practice besides the formal project organization.

(1) Space for Information Exchange
Within a community, tacit knowledge is often shared, assisted by commonality of experience. However, tacit knowledge by itself is extremely difficult to communicate unless it is converted into explicit knowledge and communicated as information. Therefore, it is crucial that a space where people collaborate in the creation of new knowledge be set up so that information is exchanged in the form of explicit knowledge. Such a space requires (i) information infrastructure to distribute, exchange, and accumulate information in a variety of forms (written, printed, audio, visual, or electronic data); (ii) settings for members to interact directly, such as at meetings, conferences, and TV conference; (iii) standardization of descriptions and expressions (e.g., terminology, notation, use of industry standards, etc.) to ensure that information is understood accurately and uniformly among community members; and (iv) security of information. The information exchange can use the existing systems for the project or of the firm, but care should be taken when membership of the community of practice comprises participants from outside the formal project organization.

Note
The original Japanese word translated as *space* here, is *ba*, which implies the idea of a framework, ground, or space, real or virtual, for mutual interaction and co-existence.

---

(2) Space for Knowledge Creation

Knowledge is part of the information that an individual or a society acquires or creates within itself—in particular, the kind that carries objectivity and logical universality. And it supports individual or organizational problem solving, providing a basis for decision-making. Wisdom, perspective, and a sense of value are included in knowledge.

Managers should support space for the creation of knowledge, which is more than the mere exchange of information. This is where members of the community enjoy interacting and sharing to create new knowledge in an effort toward goal achievement. This effort is based on the members' insight into project tasks and is made through interactive processes that externalize tacit knowledge, making it explicit knowledge. Combinations of explicit knowledge create new knowledge for achieving objectives. The principle place for knowledge creation is dialogue and debates based on deep thinking by participants. There is neither a winner nor a loser in these debates, because the purpose is collaboration to create knowledge. An environment and an atmosphere that encourage free ideas and creative discussion, irrespective of positions and titles, are essential requirements for the venue. Requirements on the part of the participants include sincerity rooted in professional competency and in-depth expertise, along with a combination of fundamental knowledge to understand the context of discussion, professional ethics, and good faith (Nonaka & Takeuchi, 1995).

(3) The Information Channel

In general, primary members of a community of practice are also project organization members. This means that once established, the community of practice is naturally connected with the formal organization through such people, who function as information channels. However, if any of these people lack the ability to comprehend and communicate the issues in question or the knowledge created, the community's efforts can be ruined. The quality of the information channel requires careful attention.

2. Project Management Capability

2.1 Capabilities of Individuals

Having knowledge represents a kind of capability, and we use it when we judge, make a decision and put it into action. Decision-making is another capability, but it is quite different from that of mere knowledge. The capability to put decisions into action is yet again different. Which one of these capabilities do we mean when we say someone is a capable person? Exhibit 5.2.1 is an example of a systematized view of capability and typical methods for assessment (JMAM, 2007).

The exhibit assumes that people have five types of capabilities in the brain and other parts of the body, as indicated in the broken-lined box. These capabilities are realized through "behavior" by individuals, which leads to results ("performance"). All or any of these five capabilities (altogether, called "possessed capability") are often regarded as the capability of a person. But in reality, possessed capability produces value to society or business only when it is realized through behavior and performed. Individual capability should be evaluated together with behavior and performance.

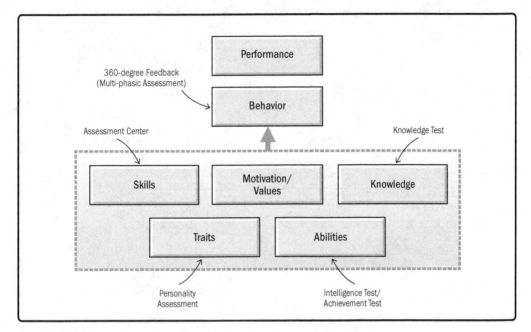

Exhibit 5.2.1: Capabilities of Individuals and Assessment

Source : JMA Management Center ed., 2007, Zukai-de-wakaru Bumon-no Shigoto: Jinzai Kaihatu-bu [Illustrated Works in Functional Divisions: Human Resource Development Division], Tokyo, Japan: JMA Management Center, p 24.

For example, the possessed capability of a baseball pitcher is very high if he throws a ball at a speed of 100 mph. However, he would not be considered capable unless he wins games; throwing fastballs is insufficient. He must be capable of applying various theories to generate actual results, using tactics against batters and runners. He is recognized as a capable pitcher only when he integrates these capabilities to win games. Similarly, a project manager must achieve an expected output and demonstrate performance repeatedly, to earn a high appraisal from stakeholders regarding his/her competency in task implementation. No matter how knowledgeable, professionals can never win excellent appraisals if their knowledge is not accompanied by behavior and results.

2.2 Learning and Proficiency
2.2.1 Learning through Experience
One's possessed capability is transformed through job implementation and other learning opportunities. This requires not only knowledge, but also the individual's competency as a whole, including attitude and skill in action. As illustrated in Exhibit 5.2.2, an individual takes action (behavior) to achieve performance. This experience is evaluated and interpreted according to his/her own belief, and reinforces the possessed capability through feedback. Behavior and performance here are not necessarily referred to in the context of the entire project, but have to do with important tasks, regardless of scale, such as a new customer sales promotion that takes a whole week, or troubleshooting that requires only

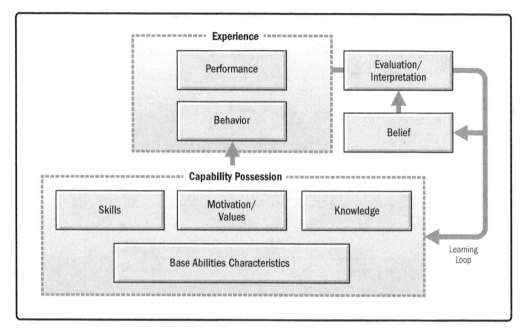

Exhibit 5.2.2: Learning from Experience

one day. These tasks may incur unexpected failures or bad results, which still provide lessons. While engineering textbooks and lectures that enhance knowledge and motivation are valuable, learning through practical experience in an actual environment is the most important and effective way to improve management competency.

2.2.2 Domains of Learning

The contents of learning can be roughly grouped into three domains: cognitive, psychomotor, and affective. The cognitive domain relates to linguistic information (i.e., knowledge in a narrow sense, like the description of facts) and intellectual skills (e.g., skills in problem solving, such as judging by statistical values). The psychomotor domain includes skills such as bicycle riding or engaging in crafts, and often involves tacit knowledge indescribable through words. The affective domain is related to behavioral attitudes and senses of values. Leadership and fairness, for instance, have much to do with this domain. In the cognitive domain, classroom learning is usually effective and its achievement is measurable by examinations. The affective domain, in contrast, cannot be satisfied by classroom learning alone, and is thought to require experience from which to learn.

Obviously, learning from experience in management involves the cognitive and affective domains. Cognitive domain learning consists of linguistic information and intellectual skills acquired through research, surveys, reports, and analyses. Affective domain learning includes successes and failures in behavioral processes. Performance as the behavioral result, and reactions to the behavior, are also part of affective domain learning (Tsutsumi, 2007, p. 39).

2.2.3 Experts

An expert is a person who has acquired special skills and knowledge in a specific field after receiving specialized training and gaining practical experience. There are two categories of expert. One is a *routine expert*, who has acquired excellent skill in swift and accurate handling of specific work through repetition. The routine expert is typified by the craftsman, cook, calligrapher, pianist, pilot, and athlete. The other is the *adaptive expert*, who skillfully implements different tasks, none of which has been done before. Examples of the adaptive expert are those who are specialized in the development of new products or new markets (Matsuo, 2006, p. 25).

Routine experts are found in diverse areas, ranging from hobby classes to *kabuki* actors and Olympic teams. In industrial circles, the recent trend of standardized mass production and the flood of electronics has caused a great decrease in demand for such experts. Those being displaced have been operators of general-purpose lathes and typists. Some of these types of experts have virtually disappeared. On the other hand, there are also efforts to keep up with the times, and the type of routine experts in demand is changing. Industrial designers and chemical product analysts, for example, are adding a variety of informational elements to their conventional manual procedures.

Adaptive experts are also found in various types of jobs, typically as project managers and system engineers.

(1) Expert Competency

Experts are distinguished by their specialized field, organized knowledge in their specialty, in-depth comprehension and swift problem solving, and excellent self-examination (Matsuo, 2006, p. 35). Experts in general are competent because of their accumulated experience and knowledge in their specialty, which does not mean they are possessed with universal competency. An excellent baseball player does not always make a good coach or a successful manager of a team, and neither would an excellent football player. This is because the necessary domain of experience and knowledge between a player and a manager is quite different. From experience, an expert understands and accumulates a huge volume of organized patterns of information, storing new responses as patterns. This accumulation helps the expert to gain deep insight into problems and their root causes, which facilitates quick, accurate action. In addition, with self-examination ability based on an objective view of his/her own behavior, an expert can grasp causes of failure correctly.

It is incorrect to say, "Even an expert can fail." It would be more accurate to say, "An expert is one who constantly engages in self-improvement efforts through repeated (minor) failures and subsequent corrections." A new effort for betterment is always required in a competitive environment. The limits of success cannot be attained by aiming at easy targets. An Olympic gymnast would never win by focusing his training only on performances that he could never fail to accomplish. He needs to attempt performance of maneuvers that he has yet to succeed at, analyzing and correcting causes of failure with a cool head. Repetition of this process leads to learning and builds competency. Failures, however, must be minor, as catastrophic failures could lead to career-ending injury. Similarly to the gymnast example, project and business activities always need to take some risks for the sake of business growth, by undertaking tasks that are beyond current capacity. Determining the seriousness of risk is an important capability of an expert.

Legitimate Peripheral Participation is an important concept that elucidates the essence of learning, explaining the learning process within an occupation. It analyzes the process through which an apprentice in a community grows to become an expert (Wenger & Lave, 1991). In Japan, the process to become an expert in the world of *noh* play (a traditional theatrical art), as well as martial arts, is explained as "observe tradition, break tradition, move away from tradition" which is the key to acquiring competency. Initially, an apprentice is required to faithfully imitate his master's style. Once he becomes proficient in his master's style, he seeks the way to "break" the style, modifying it to apply his own interpretation. When he eventually finds and establishes his own style ("move away from tradition"), beyond his master's limits, he has become a master-level expert. Even from such old saying we can surmise that people in many centuries ago understood that improvement ("breaking") and innovation ("moving away") were important for organizations (schools of art) to grow. They also knew that to become an expert, one needs original interpretation and creativity.

(2) Business Belief

What people learn from an experience differs, depending on the person. Some even learn nothing. With regard to learning from experience, Matsuo emphasized the importance of *business belief*. Belief is a kind of meta-knowledge (see note below), which functions in a top-down manner, giving direction to an individual's behavior, decisions, and point of view, or providing an interpretation for a new experience. Business belief is thought to act like a filter, affecting one's view of the environment or when dealing with new information (Matsuo, 2006, p. 125). Business beliefs such as *customer orientation* and *target achievement orientation* have been identified by surveys in several occupational categories. Skill or knowledge derived from such business beliefs act as a guideline for behaviors in business implementation, and such behaviors generate learning experiences. Belief grows strong through long-term repetition of learning from experience. Belief is based on the individual's values and the accumulation of judgments made from his/her knowledge and experience. A "good learner" is not one who adopts an experience immediately into his/her knowledge or belief, but one who does so after making a close and strict examination, including counter-arguments, in the light of his/her knowledge and experience. This ensures that new knowledge learned from experience causes no self-contradiction. Business belief can be learned from personal experience, and also from superiors or colleagues. Belief is reinforced by accumulating experiences of successful decision-making in business.

Note
Meta-knowledge is knowledge about knowledge. "The analysis on Chinese economy of this newspaper is always reliable" or "Seventy percent of the weather forecast is right for the next day" are statements of meta-knowledge. Meta-knowledge is knowledge that is generally applicable for a group of knowledge in specific domain. Intellectual techniques such as WBS, CPM, and PDCA are also a kind of meta-knowledge, because they can be used regardless of the application or field.

(3) Proficiency Level

Experts improve their knowledge and skill through experience after starting to work in their field. Matsuo (2006, p. 38) noted the Ten-Year Rule of Proficiency that is a result of many researchers' surveys of proficiency. This empirical rule states that it takes at least 10 years for anyone to achieve world-class performance in chess, music, sports, or any other field. Management is no exception, it requires at least 10 years of experience to reach a level of management that would be accepted anywhere. In any field, it is not merely the length of experience that raises the skill level. What really matters is passion, effort, and creative ideas to transform experience into competency, and when all these have been achieved, further results are due to talent. Habu (2005, p. 168), a grand champion of *shogi* (Japanese chess) said, "A talent is an ability to retain passion and continue efforts for a long span of time." Behind this statement, his basic ability as a first-class *shogi* player is uncontested.

Dreyfus and Dreyfus (1980) proposed a five-stage model of mental activity and Matsuo summarized the five levels of proficiency with profiles of each level, revising the Dreyfus model, as shown in Exhibit 5.2.3.

Returning to managers, novice managers tend to make haphazard judgments in reaction to the phenomena happening before their noses, when they are supposed to make appropriate decisions considering the overall situation. Advanced beginners who are slightly more experienced can grasp individual elements and analyze the overall situation partially, before making a reasoned judgment to the extent of their capacity. Competent managers, on the other hand, are able to find important characteristics in the situation, and make judgments based in their experience. They are also able to grasp the total situation by making an analytical review for each element. Proficient managers, based on their long experience, can organize key characteristics into patterns that permit swift and efficient judgment. Their approach provides them with a comprehensive or holistic view of the overall situation. Experts, with an even greater accumulation of experience, make decisions by intuition, employing combinations of knowledge from their huge stock of experience and solutions, rather than by reasoning based on theories.

		Cognitive Ability			
		Grasp of Individual Elements	Grasp of Distinctive Characteristics	Grasp of Total Situation	Decision Making
Proficiency Level	Novice	Situation Ignored	N/A	N/A	Haphazard
	Advanced Beginner	Situational	N/A	Partially Analytic	Reasoned
	Competent	Situational	Deliberate Selection	Analytic	Reasoned
	Proficient	Situational	Based on Experience	Holistic	Reasoned
	Expert	Situational	Based on Experience	Holistic	Intuitive

Exhibit 5.2.3: Five-Level Model of Manager Proficiency

Source: Matsuo, M., *Keiken karano Gakushu* [Learning from experience], Tokyo, Japan: Dobunkan Publication, 2006, p. 41, (with minor modifications).

2.3 Complex Capabilities

The capabilities of individuals, and their accomplishments, are analyzed in Exhibit 5.2.1. Projects involve people with various jobs and roles. The purpose of project management is to orient and motivate these people efficiently in the direction that the project requires. The management competency required for this purpose is a complex of knowledge, motivation, values, skills, and other capabilities. These capabilities are found in harmony within the manager. Among those capabilities, some distinctive elements are (i) leadership – the capability to put the organization into action, that is, to motivate people; (ii) insight – important in coping with complexity; and (iii) creativity – the force driving innovation. Each of these capabilities is also a complex of various other capabilities, some of which necessarily overlap.

2.3.1 Leadership: Putting People into Action
(1) The Role of Leadership
The role of leadership is to have a large number of people together sharing the purpose of enhancing the members' motivation and encouraging them to act efficiently. Unifying the will of the organization and representing it externally are also roles of leadership.

The relationship between leadership and management is an area of active discussion among scholars. Some say that management is included under leadership, while others insist that leadership is part of management. Kotter (1999, p. 52) summarized the argument applying a narrow sense to both sides. He explained that functions of management and leadership are identical in that both specify their respective tasks and achieve them through human networks. But while management copes with complexity through a hierarchical structure and has interest in things that are schedulable and measurable, leadership's interest is to promote the reform of the organization, harnessing new thought processes, awakening people's energy and giving direction to it. As a result, the practical approaches differ between the two, as compared in Exhibit 5.2.4.

(2) Source of Leadership Power
Leadership is the power to encourage people to action. Leadership power is based on three areas: (a) knowledge and judgment about the domain of activity, (b) skills

	Management (narrow sense)	Leadership (narrow sense)
Purpose	Cope with complexity	Promote reform
Viewpoint	Planning and control; Specially interested in the numerically measurable elements	Encourage people and the organization to draw out their potential and give it direction
Process	(a) Specify tasks (b) Structure human networks to complete the tasks (c) Carry out activities to achieve tasks	
Approach	Planning and budgeting Organizing and staffing Control and problem solving	Task definition (vision) Unification of effort among organization members Motivation and capability development

Exhibit 5.2.4: Management and Leadership (Kotter, 1999, p. 52)

for action, and (c) support from subordinates and, preferably, also from other stakeholders.

(a) Knowledge and Judgment

Knowledge about the scope of the activity and judgment includes:

- Confidence in the purpose or direction of the activity
- Expertise in domain subject matter
- Foresight, flexibility, judgment
- Skill at risk recognition

The leader's most important role is to give direction, entrusting details to subordinates. The leader may deal with technical details from time to time, but only to remind the organization of its direction. The leader must never be smothered in daily details, but must maintain focus on strategic decision-making.

Expertise includes knowledge, analysis, judgment, and decision-making in the specialty. Logical accuracy is required, but more important is *practical accuracy*, which can only be proven after the fact by results demonstrating the correctness of past judgments.

Foresight in business is, for example, the ability to sense latent market trends (of customers, products, competition, etc.) before they surface. The awareness of risk is somewhat the same. The ability to predict the complicated influences that daily trifles may have on an entire project, or to read subtle early signs of coming major problems, are particularly important in large and complex projects.

(b) Skills for Action

The action skills required of the leader are:

- Coordination and persuasion
- Negotiation
- Determination

The leader's action skills are not the kind required of those who act under his/her initiative. The leader does what the subordinates cannot do, breaking down walls confronting the project. This may include persuading higher-level staff or external stakeholders to cease opposing the project plan, getting a budget proposal passed, or providing guidance to overcome deadlocks when plans are agreed to in principle, even though some stakeholders remain strongly opposed to execution details.

This requires the leader's strong determination for project implementation, as well as the skill to coordinate and persuade stakeholders to execute it. Communication skills are very important and the leader must make sure that (i) he/she is providing clear direction (directionality), (ii) explanations are lucid and easy to understand (explicitness), (iii) reasons or causes are displayed logically (reasonableness), and (iv) his/her direction is consistent and free from unnecessary changes (consistency). To make these possible, the leader must understand the project thoroughly and have firmer conviction than anyone else.

Negotiation is the skill to represent a project's interests when building a consensus with stakeholders with different interests. Determination is to make difficult decisions, such as sacrificing an important element or putting heavy burdens on an individual or group in order to maintain a project's objectives. This calls for strong willpower, not mere technical capability, supported by awareness of purpose and a high sense of responsibility.

(c) Support from Subordinates/Stakeholders

Leaders cannot perform their duties without support from subordinates and colleagues or stakeholders, customers or business partners. People support leaders when they generate sympathy, motivation, and a sense of security in working together, inspired by:

- Proven success
- Human skills to motivate people
- Sense of responsibility, enthusiasm and cheerful liveliness, self-confidence
- Fair-mindedness
- Personal charm and charisma

People gravitate toward success. The higher is the probability of success, the higher become their motivation. Subordinates and stakeholders follow the leader's behavior, and so a leader with a successful record is highly desired, which wins stakeholder trust. The experience of success is highly important for a leader's own growth as well. Human skills are represented by the ability to make warm-hearted communication, which, along with fair-mindedness, heightens subordinates' motivation and creates an environment for actively working without unnecessary cares.

While ideally a leader should have all the traits discussed here, some aspects of knowledge, judgment, and skills for action could be done by someone else. Here it is important to note, however, that traits related to "support from subordinates and stakeholders" are indispensable for the leader, with no room for substitution—except "charisma." Charisma is not a prerequisite for the leader, since it is not something acquired through learning or effort, even though it is very desirable for a leader to possess it.

(3) Types of Leadership

The purpose of leadership is to spread the leader's achievement motivation throughout the organization, primarily by developing and increasing admirers and supporters to spread motivation through a variety of means of communication. How is this purpose served, or how is leadership performed? This varies depending on the leader's personal abilities and nature, organizational traits, the business environment, and the stakeholders' situation. Leadership can be classified into types, as summarized in Exhibit 5.2.5. Leadership by an excellent leader requires a complex combination of these types.

2.3.2 Insight: Coping with Complexity

The characteristic of "insight" is that it clears up complex problems and throws light on their essence rapidly. In projects, which are complex and typically constrained by a defined period of time, there are many cases where insight has a dramatic effect. Although a hierarchical approach is the usual way to cope with complexity,

Types	Outlines
Authoritarian Leadership	Makes command and control strongly, taking advantage of possessing authority, also using subordinates' fear, in some cases. Excessive domination with power is not useful for long-lasting leadership, though authority is necessary for leaders.
Exemplary Leadership	Does not command but sets an example by voluntarily undertaking difficult tasks. With steadfast achievement the leader wins trust from subordinates and customers.
Principle Leadership	Declares high-value targets that motivate members and prompts their voluntary action
Charismatic Leadership	"Charisma" originally meant a distinctive heaven-sent gift that attracted a group of loyal followers (e.g., Caesar, Napoleon, etc.). The modern notion includes business founders or leaders who are believed to have special talent. Some leaders try to display charisma by emphasizing their strength and greatness through theatrical effects, but such leadership is not likely to succeed.
Empowerment Leadership	Enhances subordinates' motivation and loyalty by delegating power to them and, where necessary, by supporting them with the leader's own authority
Motivational Leadership	Motivates subordinates through individual commendations (reinforcement in the sense of accomplishment), remuneration plans (pay raises, promotions, incentives, paid leave, etc.) and improvement of the work environment
Fostering Leadership	Fosters subordinates to share values in the course of the organization's growth. This can be a lengthy process, but it is necessary for a growing organization.

Exhibit 5.2.5: Types of Leadership

an excessive number of hierarchical elements could adversely affect accurate analysis of elemental correlations. This is also the case with conceptualization/design, systems architecting, and operation/utilization phases. These are situations where the insight of business managers or project managers is vital.

The ultimate problem at the initial stages of a complex project is to understand "to be," which is the essence of a project. This includes answering many questions of differing importance, such as:

- Which one of many potential goals should be emphasized?
- Where are major risks hiding?
- What is the key to schedule/cost optimization?

In the project execution phase, there are technical problems with complex, intertwined causes, or there are conflicts in interests involving stakeholders. Insight is an intuitive ability to identify the essence of problems in complicated situations.

Insight, however, refuses any analytical definition, probably because it is a comprehensive mental capacity to extract essentials, based on broad knowledge, experience, and belief. The following paragraphs discuss two possible traits of excellent leaders' insight, efficiency in thinking and modeling skill, together with the insight that develops in a team inspired by these traits.

(1) Efficiency in Thinking
Insight is an ability acquired through the application of knowledge from broad experience and proficiency in making judgments. Knowledge is not merely for accumulation. It must be extracted after accumulation, combined with other knowledge, and used. Insight is the unique ability to extract and use specific knowledge that has accumulated.

(a) Heuristics

Heuristics, a Greek word for "discovery," can be defined as wisdom to find a solution, not by logical thinking but from experience, knowing that "it will work" (see note below). Problems can be solved in several ways. In the schematic diagram in Exhibit 5.2.6, there are many alternative paths for moving from status A to status B. All these paths should be tried to find the best one. A novice would try any of the paths from a1 to a4, and then think what to do next. A manager who knows from long or similar experience that the paths marked by the thick-arrows would be the best to select would not hesitate to ignore other paths to make an efficient move from A to B. The retention of thought processes patterned in this way is an important part of an expert's competency, along with the retention of knowledge itself. Right and efficient judgment based on experience is required of managers.

(b) Conviction and Judgment Criterion

Another important factor that determines efficiency is the manager's judgment. If the manager is unable to judge, no conclusion is possible. Conviction in business practice is an aspect of the expert's competency that is a criteria for judgment. When judging, the question of whether to pursue an optimized outcome, or to settle on a satisfactory outcome level, makes a great difference in the efficiency of both thought and execution processes. Indiscriminate optimization of a complicated task consumes huge amounts of time and money, ending in failure for the overall optimization effort. The manager is required to know what the satisfactory level for optimization of crucial items is.

Note

Heuristics is a "rule of thumb," which does not necessarily guarantee logical validity. Depending on context, the word can represent negative meanings, such as "fixed ideas" or "layperson's judgment."

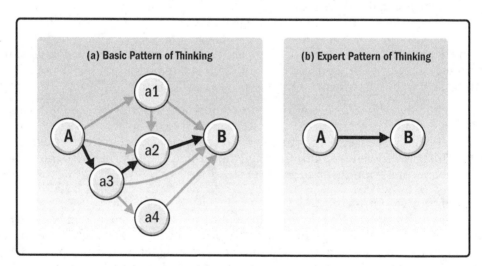

Exhibit 5.2.6: Efficiency of Thought Process

(2) Modeling Skill

Skill in modeling is the core of insight. It is the ability to identify the essence of a thing's entire complexity. It is an effort to transform the entirety into a simple model to study its essence. An expert manager creates a boldly simplified model through his/her intuition. Once the model is verified to meet his/her values and belief, the manager begins to elaborate his/her thoughts in sequence. In many cases this process is carried out within his/her own mind, hidden from the eyes of others. The "intuitive ideas" here are not the kind associated with illogical and irresponsible ideas. On the contrary, the manager makes assumptions that are logically plausible from the essentials that he/she perceives. The manager, at the same time, formulates several counter-assumptions to test the idea's validity in a logical manner. Assumptions that survive this process are then elaborated.

Three-dimensional views cannot be obtained with one eye closed. The important element in the modeling process is to examine the model from various points of view, making verification from multiple viewpoints to gain better understanding. *Viewpoints* here means perspectives, supposing standpoints of various parties involved in the process, including (i) one's own and that of others, (ii) the entire system design as viewed from a certain subsystem, (iii) the view from the users' points of view, or (iv) the view by competitors and other business associates, as well as (v) analysis of cases where certain premises turn out not to be valid.

(3) Team Insight

Projects are complex, and programs even more so. No matter how competent he/she may be, a project manager can fail to grasp a project's entirety, or his/her experience may be limited to only part of the whole. Expert managers make up for lack of insight into certain areas, or complement their verification, by making queries and gathering insight from subordinates, supporters, and experts among their customers and their communities of practice. Even if in the form of queries, this is virtually an interaction of views that constitute the team's insight. A similar interaction empowers teams' creativity and leadership. Two heads are better than one, and collaboration among experts is a very helpful and inspiring experience for other participants because it may lead to discovery of new values. In this regard, the project manager should note the importance of the art of questioning to draw out valuable ideas.

2.3.3 Creativity: A Driving Force for Reform

When aiming at new value creation, projects and programs engage in tasks with tremendously high originality and novelty. Practical execution of these tasks requires solution and avoidance of obstacles and constraints. These may be structural, theoretical, or technical (e.g., designs, components, resources, production techniques, complexity management). They also include those related to cost, funding, marketing (e.g., competition, market structure) or social/cultural/legislative systems. To cope with these obstacles and constraints, the project manager must exercise his/her creativity in order to enhance the organization's creativity.

(1) What is Creativity?

In ancient Greece, Pythagoras explained that the Earth was round. In the Age of Discovery, it was not only Christopher Columbus who thought that sailing to the west would lead Europeans to India. However, coming up with the idea and putting it into practice were totally different. An idea will never capture its own value until its truth is proven by final success after surviving difficulties. Creativity is not simply an idea or the ability to think of an idea. It is to think of something new, to put it into practice and to make it happen. A "creative person" is recognized only when successful in the whole process. There is no creativity without strong will and intense effort. Whether business person, researcher, artist, or other, creative deeds come from people with strong will who constantly endeavor.

(2) Ability to Realize Creativity

Exhibit 5.2.7 shows three elements of personal ability that generate creativity (Amabile, 1998). "Expertise" represents knowledge, experience and practical skills in the relevant specialty. In management, it means professional experience and knowledge in the particular industrial segment, knowledge in the job assigned (e.g., design, production techniques, sales), and skills in managing and leading an organization. "Will" means the ability to perceive new value in something and have the willpower to take practical actions and risks (like Columbus). "Creative Thinking" is the skill or intellect to think of something novel. Creativity is set to work when these three abilities are combined properly.

(3) Creative Thinking
(a) Logical Thinking

Capability of logical thinking is the basis of all intellectual work. Creativity is associated with unprecedented ideas or thinking unbounded by convention, and tends to emphasize inspirational ideas. However, logical thinking underlies creative thinking. Mind-boggling ideas may occur, but significant results can be obtained only from a thorough and logical quest for "to be."

General Electric (USA) is famous for its approach to business, in which it aims to maintain all of its business segments within the rank of the world's top two. The

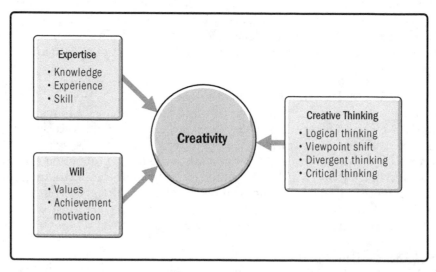

Exhibit 5.2.7: Creativity and Personal Ability

company's strategy, developed by Jack Welch, the former CEO, emphasized making effective investments in promising businesses, while selling or abandoning second class businesses. GE's strategy was introduced to Japan with its "Concentration in Core Competence" approach, creating a sensation. But no Japanese corporations were as successful as GE. GE's strategy was "novel" in that no other firms had thought of it or had carried it out thoroughly. Yet it was not an unusual inspiration at all. On the contrary, it was a standard that GE obtained through a serious pursuit of "to be" during the slow economic growth period of the 1980s. This is a good example of logical thinking that led to tremendous creativity.

Realization of creativity by logical thinking is not an exceptional event. It is seen everywhere. Examples include Toyota (Japan), which developed a production system that greatly reduced its inventory costs; Southwest Airlines (U.S.), which made a major success of its passenger convenience-oriented network of direct flights through regional airports; and Samsung Electronics (Korea), which made an intensive investment in the DRAM business. Realizing creativity through logical thinking requires steady (and sometimes daring) efforts at research into problems, and exhaustive execution of the research results. A successful result of logical thinking is so logical that it may be regarded as "commonplace," which, of course, is a failure of recognition.

Toyota has the *"Naze-naze Go-kai"* ("quintuple whys") method, used at all its worksites, both engineering and manufacturing. This is a logical approach to identify root causes of defects or failures through a five-level investigation process that pursues the causes of the causes. Persistent logical pursuit leads to extraordinary solutions.

(b) Viewpoint Shift

There are many cases where a strategy made a great success although it seemed unfeasible, illogical, and counter to commonsense. Frequent among management-related dilemmas are cases such as (i) a choice must be made between A and B when both are wanted; (ii) B needs to be achieved despite the fact that A, which is a prerequisite for B, cannot be achieved; or (iii) achievement of A is a prerequisite for achievement of B, while the achievement of B is a prerequisite for achievement of A. When facing such dilemmas, looking at events or premises from a different angle often leads to a way out.

When the price affordable to the Indian public for a car was around 100,000 rupees (approx. U.S. $2,000), the lowest price of cars in production was not below U.S. $8,000–10,000. By not merely cutting costs, but by switching to a perspective of building a car within reach of the Indian public, TaTa Motors decided to develop the Nano, targeting a price the market could bear.

Japan was significantly behind Korea and the U.S. in broadband network diffusion at the end of 2000. SoftBank (Japan) wanted to make a profit from the sale of ADSL modems and broadband services operated by its affiliate, Yahoo! JAPAN. However, subscriber growth showed little progress and, accordingly, the content service business was stagnant. Modems themselves were too expensive and there were insufficient services and content. Yahoo! JAPAN decided to abandon modem sales altogether and concentrated on a user expansion campaign, including free modem giveaways on the streets and substantial reductions in provider fees. Yahoo! JAPAN then built the world's easiest-to-use broadband environment, which cost its users $0.18 per 100 kbps as of March 2003, compared to $2.86 in the U.S and $0.28 in Korea. This gave the company a competitive edge and expansion of profits from the broadband service market.

(c) Divergent Thinking

When logical thinking reaches a deadlock, or when any known approach is not likely to succeed, or when something completely new must be worked out, divergent thinking has a role to play. The important thing here is to think of diverse variants, regardless of right or wrong. An organization that is most flexible to changes survives.

As part of creative thinking, divergent thinking is important because it is a thought process for seeking diversity. Various approaches have been proposed. The word *creativity* is often perceived to emphasize inspiration or illogical jumps, which do not match reality or commonsense. But no bright idea springs from nothing. Most ideas are prompted by some precedent or something heard from others. Proposed approaches for divergent thinking include (i) Analogy: obtaining ideas for solutions by analogical inference from successful examples, including those in other fields; (ii) Metaphor: making metaphorical explorations of purpose, such as "life is a journey"; (iii) Brainstorming: discussing freely in a small group ideas that seem capable of solving the problem; (iv) KJ Method: obtaining new ideas by organizing data cards according to their relationships; and (v) Checklist and Matrix: finding holes in logic and filling them in.

(d) Critical Thinking and the Art of Questioning

Critical thinking is used to examine the relevance and order of one's thought process. It must be conducted in a cool and critical manner—in other words, from an outsider or opponent's point of view. Criticism is not negation. Information, or a theory, that survives this critical verification can be promoted with confidence. No matter how brilliant and sophisticated the proposer may think the idea to be, logic or an idea can fail in its execution if one crucial element is missing or if one risk is overlooked.

An idea or thought must be thoroughly and critically examined by the proposer him/herself. It must then be assessed critically by the group or organization. The manager's approval in an organization can be regarded as official completion of organizational critical thinking. Because *creativity* means perfect execution of an idea, this type of critical thinking process is indispensable.

An element that underlies critical thinking is the art of posing questions or the ability to explore questions. Questions can be constructed to do many things, such as:

- Is this purpose right? Is there any other tacit purpose?
- Is the premise right? Is it insufficient or excessive?
- Is the cost overestimated or underestimated? Is there any less expensive or faster way?

This thought process is used to eliminate baseless ideas and impressions and to secure objective reasonableness. It is important that examination through critical thinking sufficiently cover the necessary scope. This should be ensured with the help of divergent thinking as well.

2.4 Competency Model

An expert manager's competency is evaluated as an aggregation of capabilities (Exhibit 5.2.1), through long accumulation of performance. Competency is the power formed by this aggregation. Expert knowledge alone does not constitute total power. If it were ever evaluated separately, it would just be an element of capabilities. On the other hand, performance is not always the result of personal competency alone. For example, a manager in a large organization has a chance to participate in a big project or get the strong support of the organization members' expertise. When business is improving, even a less competent manager may take part in contributing to profits, while a project assigned during a recession may be very likely to fail even if the manager is highly competent. The environment, and luck as well, are not to be ignored.

The terms *competency* and *capability* are similar in meaning, except that the latter connotes experience and performance. An emerging trend in capability evaluation is the use of the Competency Model, which analyzes personal competency from the viewpoint of behavioral traits instead of performance records.

In personnel administration and education, competency is defined as "basic characteristics of a person whose job performance is effective and excellent." If defined as "capabilities possessed by high performers," it would be difficult to make practical use of it in human resource training. It must be complemented by another term, "high performer's behavioral patterns," which is a representation of how high possessed capabilities are realized as behavior (Lucia & Lepsinger, 1999, p. 6).

In the today's severe competitive business environment, the value of knowledge is wasted unless it is linked to behavior. Without behavior, there would be no failure; without failure, there would be no learning, and accordingly, no growth in capabilities. The traditional method of personal ability evaluation that emphasizes educational background or practical experience is obviously inadequate, because its deviation from actual performance has grown too large. On the other hand, excessive emphasis on performance does not necessarily lead to success either. The Competency Model takes a moderate stance between these two, evaluating personal behavioral characteristics that lead to business outcomes (PMAJ, 2007, p. 39). As an example of the Competency Model, Exhibit 5.2.8 shows P2M's taxonomy of competency evaluation criteria which comprise ten patterns of thinking and behavior.

PMI's (2002) *Project Manager Competency Development Framework* described project management knowledge competency, project manager performance competency, and personal competency for each management process described in the *PMBOK® Guide,* as well as performance criteria and assessment guidelines. Rad and Levin (2002, p. 59) provided a table that summarizes the responsibilities, knowledge, and competencies required for six positions in project management (e.g., project manager, deputy project manager, PMO staff, etc.). The summary is made for each of the processes, starting from project planning to scope definition, cost management, and quality control. The detailed table provides another guide in designing a competency model for an organization.

	Compound Capability Pattern	Criteria
I	Overall thinking pattern	Mission pursuit Able to discover problems, address them, and develop a process to create solutions
II	Strategic thinking pattern	Strategic key perception Able to find strategic elements, prioritize orders, and adopt measures to get around obstacles
III	Integrated thinking pattern	Value pursuit Able to adapt, maintain value, and apply alternatives
IV	Leadership pattern	Leadership for innovation Able to address changes, make decisions, and improve the present situation
V	Deliberate behavior pattern	Management in planning Able to make plans for goals and resources, form organizations, and frame rules
VI	Actual behavior pattern	Management in execution Able to understand contracts, take systems into consideration, and give directions
VII	Adjusting behavior pattern	Management in coordination Able to forecast progress, address obstacles, and solve problems
VIII	Human relationship pattern	Human communication Able to maintain teams, to motivate their members, and provide opportunities
IX	Result pursuit pattern	Attitude to achievement Mind and energy focusing on results, ability to feel empathy, a sense of responsibility, and ability to persuade other organizations; ability to consider value and feedback results
X	Lifestyle	Attitude of self-control Self-disciplined, able to observe best practices and good behavior, take responsibility, and have a constructive attitude

Exhibit 5.2.8: Competency Evaluation Criteria

Source: PMAJ, *Shinsa-hantei-youso Bunrui-taikei* [Capability Based Professional Certification Guidelines (CPC Guidelines)], 2004, p. 29.

References

Amabile, T. M. (1998). How to kill creativity. *Harvard Business Review*, 76(5) 76–87.

Asahi (1999; Newspaper, Tokyo), *Criticality accident suspected at nuclear fuel plant*, Sept. 30, p. 1.

Asahi (2000; Newspaper, Tokyo), *200 people get sick from Snow Brand's processed milk*, Jun. 30, p. 39.

Cleland, D. I. (1994). *Project management, strategic design and implementation* (2nd ed.), New York, NY; McGraw Hill.

Dreyfus, S. E., & Dreyfus H. L. A five-stage model of the mental activities involved in directed skill acquisition. Retrieved from http://www.dtic.mil/cgi-bin/GetTRDoc?AD=ADA084551&Location=U2&doc=GetTRDoc.pdf

Habu, Y. (2005). *Ketsudanryoku* [Decisiveness]. Tokyo, Japan: Kadokawa Shoten Publishing.

JMAM (JMA Management Center). (2007). *Zukai de wakaru bumon no shigoto: Jinzaikaihatsu bu* [Illustrated explanation of how divisions work: Human resource development division]. Tokyo, Japan: JMAM.

Kerzner, H. (2001). *Project management: A systems approach to planning, scheduling and controlling* (7th ed.). Hoboken, NJ: John Wiley and Sons.

Kotter, J. P. (1999). *What leaders really do.* Boston, MA: Harvard Business Review Book.

Lucia, A. D., & Lepsinger, R. (1999). *The Art and Science of Competency Models: Pinpointing Critical Success Factors in Organizations,* San Francisco, CA: Pfeiffer.

Matsuo, M. (2006). Keiken *karano gakushū* [Learning from experience]. Tokyo, Japan: Dobunkan.

Ministry of Defense. (2009). Reports on the collision between escort vessel Atago and fishing boat Seitokumaru. Retrieved from http://www.mod.go.jp/j/approach/hyouka/chousa/atago/090522b.htmlandhttp://www.mod.go.jp/j/press/news/2009/05/22b.html

Ministry of Health, Labour and Welfare. (2007). Explanatory material on the "Pension Account Issue", Jul. 4, 2007. Retrieved from http://www4.sia.go.jp/top/kaikaku/kiroku/shiryo3-1.pdf

Nikkei (2003a; Newspaper, Tokyo), *Tank fire kills 4 workers (at Exxon Mobile fuel-storage facility in Nagoya),* Aug. 30, p. 43.

Nikkei (2003b; Newspaper, Tokyo), *15 injured in a blast at Nippon Steel's Nagoya plant"* Sept. 4, p. 1.

Numagami, T. (2003). *Soshiki-senryaku no kangaekata* [Perspectives of organizational strategy]. Tokyo, Japan: Chikumashobo.

PMAJ (Project Management Association of Japan). (2007). *New edition P2M project & program management standard guidebook.* Tokyo, Japan: JMAM (JMA Management Center).

PMI. (2002). *Project manager competency development framework.* Newtown Square, PA: PMI.

Rad, F. P., & Levin, G. (2002). *The advanced project management office.* Boca Raton, FL: St. Lucie Press.

Senge, P. M. (1990). *The fifth discipline: The art and practice of the learning organization.* New York, NY: Currency and Doubleday.

Tsutsumi, U. (2007). *Hajimete no kyouiku-kouka sokutei* [The basics of education effect evaluation]. Tokyo, Japan: JUSE Press.

Wenger, E., & Lave, J. (1991). *Situated learning: Legitimate peripheral participation.* Oxford, U.K.: Cambridge University Press.

Wenger, E., McDermott, R. A., & Snyder, W. (2002). *Cultivating communities of practice: A guide to managing knowledge.* Boston, MA: Harvard Business School Press.